Relational Research and Organisation Studies

This volume lays out a variety of ways of engaging in research projects focused on exploring the everyday relational practices of organizing and leading. The main focus is elaborate examples from the authors' own research to further the understanding of how it is possible to carry out relational constructionist research inquiries. The book presents a series of examples ranging from conversations with top managers, relational action learning processes in management groups, polyphonic inquiries for project management teams, transformative roleplaying in organizations, analysation of organizational dialoguing, and polyphonic future-forming ways of writing up research.

Relational Research and Organisation Studies does not only present and discuss guidelines for practice at an onto-epistemological level but also presents and discusses concrete cases of research projects building on relational constructionist ideas. Furthermore, excerpts of data are presented and analysed in order to explain the co-constructed processes of the inquiries in more detail.

Relational Research and Organisation Studies invites the reader into the process of planning and carrying out relational constructionist research inquiries. Based on the authors' own experiences, it inspires readers to develop their own relational inquiries within the field of organizing.

Charlotte Øland Madsen is associate professor in the Department of Business and Management at Aalborg University, Denmark.

Mette Vinther Larsen is associate professor in the Department of Business and Management at Aalborg University, Denmark.

Lone Hersted is assistant professor in the Department of Learning and Philosophy at Aalborg University, Denmark.

Jørgen Gulddahl Rasmussen is professor in the Department of Business and Management at Aalborg University, Denmark.

Routledge Studies in Management, Organizations and Society

This series presents innovative work grounded in new realities, addressing issues crucial to an understanding of the contemporary world. This is the world of organised societies, where boundaries between formal and informal, public and private, local and global organizations have been displaced or have vanished, along with other nineteenth-century dichotomies and oppositions. Management, apart from becoming a specialized profession for a growing number of people, is an everyday activity for most members of modern societies.

Similarly, at the level of enquiry, culture and technology, and literature and economics, can no longer be conceived as isolated intellectual fields; conventional canons and established mainstreams are contested. **Management, Organizations and Society** addresses these contemporary dynamics of transformation in a manner that transcends disciplinary boundaries, with books that will appeal to researchers, students, and practitioners alike.

Recent titles in this series include:

The Work of Communication
Relational Perspectives on Working and Organizing in Contemporary Capitalism
Tim Khun, Karen Ashcraft, and François Cooren

Socially Responsible Capitalism and Management
Henri Savall, Michel Péron, Véronique Zardet, and Marc Bonnet

Counterproductive Work Behaviors
Understanding the Dark Side of Personalities in Organizational Life
Aaron Cohen

Relational Research and Organisation Studies
Charlotte Øland Madsen, Mette Vinther Larsen, Lone Hersted, and Jørgen Gulddahl Rasmussen

For a full list of titles in this series, please visit www.routledge.com

Relational Research and Organisation Studies

Charlotte Øland Madsen, Mette Vinther Larsen, Lone Hersted, and Jørgen Gulddahl Rasmussen

NEW YORK AND LONDON

First published 2018
by Routledge
711 Third Avenue, New York, NY 10017

and by Routledge
2 Park Square, Milton Park, Abingdon, Oxon, OX14 4RN

Routledge is an imprint of the Taylor & Francis Group, an informa business

© 2018 Taylor & Francis

The right of Charlotte Øland Madsen, Mette Vinther Larsen, Lone Hersted & Jørgen Gulddahl Rasmussen to be identified as authors of this work has been asserted by them in accordance with sections 77 and 78 of the Copyright, Designs and Patents Act 1988.

All rights reserved. No part of this book may be reprinted or reproduced or utilised in any form or by any electronic, mechanical, or other means, now known or hereafter invented, including photocopying and recording, or in any information storage or retrieval system, without permission in writing from the publishers.

Trademark notice: Product or corporate names may be trademarks or registered trademarks, and are used only for identification and explanation without intent to infringe.

Library of Congress Cataloguing-in-Publication Data
A catalog record for this book has been requested

ISBN: 9780815394150 (hbk)
ISBN: 9780429507557(ebk)

Typeset in Sabon
by Apex CoVantage, LLC

Contents

Figures and Tables vii
Foreword viii
ANN L. CUNLIFFE

1 Studying Organising through Relational and Social
   Constructionist Inquiries: Introduction and Concepts 1
   CHARLOTTE ØLAND MADSEN, JØRGEN GULDDAHL RASMUSSEN,
   METTE VINTHER LARSEN, AND LONE HERSTED

2 Using Adjusted Responses to Engage in Research
   Conversations with Organisational Members 15
   METTE VINTHER LARSEN

3 Exploring Unadjusted Gestures and Responses in Research
   Conversations with Organisational Members 40
   METTE VINTHER LARSEN

4 Engaging in Relational Action Learning Processes: A Way to
   Make Sense of Everyday Relational Management Practices 64
   METTE VINTHER LARSEN AND JØRGEN GULDDAHL RASMUSSEN

5 Polyphonic Inquiry for Team Development, Learning,
   and Knowledge Production 85
   LONE HERSTED AND CHARLOTTE ØLAND MADSEN

6 Doing Relational Research through Roleplaying 117
   LONE HERSTED

7 Analysing Organising as Dialogical Practices 142
   CHARLOTTE ØLAND MADSEN

8 Working with Data Is a Polyphonic and Future-Forming
  Endeavour   160
  METTE VINTHER LARSEN

Contributors   191
Index   193

Figures and Tables

Figures

4.1	The Introduction Letter	72
5.1	The Spatial Setup of the Dialogue Process	92
5.2	A Typical Dialogic Session	93
6.1	The Setup of the Roleplaying Session	126
6.2	Phases in the Inquiry of Reflexive Roleplaying	127
8.1	Relational Constructionist Worldview	166
8.2	Reflective Exercise	173
8.3	Reflexive Exercise	173

Tables

1.1	Relational Research Practices	10
7.1	In-situ Dialoguing	143

Foreword

Relational Research and Organisation Studies

In today's academic climate of research metrics and increasing pressure to publish in 'top-ranked' journals that have a narrow view of what 'good' (i.e., positivist) research is, it's refreshing to come across a book that offers an alternative. As a counter to what seems to be a descent into reductionism and abstraction, the four authors focus on how to study the lived experience of leaders and managers from a co-constructed relational perspective. Essentially, what this means is collaborating with organizational members to inquire into their practices and facilitate change. It draws on the experience of each author in carrying out this form of inquiry in a variety of contexts and dealing with a range of issues: the strategic processes in a consulting company, paying suppliers in China, brand development, the implementation of an IT system, role change and team development in an NGO, and creating better relationships in a care centre for adolescents.

Based on what they call an onto-epistemological social constructionism, they explore the various ways in which organizing, leading, managing, and identities occur in the in-situ dialogical practices between organizational members. But what does this mean? Social constructionism is often perceived as being about language, leading to a focus on the role of language, the words, metaphors, stories, characters, etc. that construct culture, leadership, strategy, etc. Yes, the form of social constructionism the authors espouse in this book is about language – but not just language – it's about what I would call 'lived language', i.e., dialogue and meaning-making in its speaking. This form of social constructionism means being reflexive about our own practices as well as encouraging organizational members to be reflexive about theirs; recognizing that we are co-authoring 'realities' and knowledge; that we need to engage in before-the-fact (Shotter, 2016) thinking and acting, i.e., being sensitive to the present; pausing to address our feelings of uncertainty or discomfort; and experiencing writing (or storying) as a continuation of the process of exploration.

This is therefore not a book on methodology and methods in the usual sense. The reason for this is that the authors view research not from a self-interested academic perspective, but as a form of polyphonic inquiry in which knowledge is co-constructed between academics and organizational members. So the authors challenge us to think about what we see as 'data', 'analysis', and 'theory', and what the outcome or the product of our inquiry is – academic, practical, or both. A striking example of this is given in Chapter 5, where Lone Hersted and Charlotte Madsen show how their four academic research questions were reformulated by the research participants to provide a more inside-out perspective relevant to their concerns. In this way, the book offers resources for doing relational inquiry while engaging with the complexities that organizational members face. We learn how we can make meaning collaboratively while being sensitive to our relationship with others and the world around us. The various chapters examine how we might do so one-on-one with individuals or as a group in the form of action-learning seminars and reflecting teams (Chapters 4 and 5). The reader is taken through practical examples, case studies, and excerpts of conversations as a means of offering ways of engaging with participants in this form of inquiry and of showing how it unfolds, not as principles or techniques, because these would be counter to the philosophical underpinning of their approach, but as practical resources such as unadjusted gestures (Chapter 3), adjusted responses (Chapter 2), questions that help surface different stakeholder positions (Chapter 5), and roleplaying (Chapter 6). And, what is crucial is that we are shown *how* these resources work, how to pay attention to small nuances.

The authors also explore the implications for being a researcher as a co-inquirer and co-constructor. Instead of a detached observer, the researcher becomes a 'conversation partner', 'disturber', 'facilitator', 'reflexive inquirer', and 'future former'. And we are shown what this means.

Written in an accessible way, the authors offer examples from their own experience of engaging in this form of inquiry. Rather than a practical 'how-to' book in the popular literature sense, the approach and resources offered are firmly grounded ontologically, epistemologically, and theoretically in social constructionism, hermeneutics, pragmatism, and systems thinking (Chapter 1).

As Mette Vinther Larsen states in the final chapter, the authors' purpose is to invite you to reflect upon and develop your own practices as a relational researcher and to recognize that there are 'multiple stories to tell', 'multiple ways of taking part', and 'multiple possibilities for moving on'. This form of inquiry is about learning in practice and is therefore of value to leaders, managers, professionals, and consultants, as well as researchers.

Ann L. Cunliffe
Professor of Organization Studies
Fundação Getulio Vargas-EAESP, Sao Paulo, Brazil
November 2017

1 Studying Organising through Relational and Social Constructionist Inquiries

Introduction and Concepts

Charlotte Øland Madsen, Jørgen Gulddahl Rasmussen, Mette Vinther Larsen, and Lone Hersted

Introduction

Relational Research and Organisation Studies is a book on how research methods can be developed and used when the main objective is to collaborate with practitioners to study organisations, cooperation, groups of people, etc. from constructionist perspectives. Thus, it also becomes a book on inquiries for collaboration between organisational members and researchers, exploring relational and social dimensions together. In this first chapter, important terms and concepts of relational research are outlined and some of the bodies of thought that have inspired us are presented.

As Kenneth Gergen (1985: 266) wrote, 'Social constructionist inquiry is principally concerned with explicating the processes by which people come to describe, explain, or otherwise account for the world (including themselves) in which they live'. Neither the relational and social constructionist philosophy as such nor the method, or as we prefer to call it in this book 'inquiry' (Gergen, 1985; McNamee & Hosking, 2012), used to study relational and social dimensions includes a specific definition. Instead, it can be seen as a broad philosophy that has some common points as well as variations in concept and approach. These variations are constantly forming due to the multiple bodies of thought which make up relational and social theory and inquiry and are accentuated by the degree of freedom each group of researchers has. This freedom allows researchers constructing inquiries to adapt to the specific processes they are studying in the organisations with which they are collaborating.

To explore from a relational and social constructionist perspective is to co-construct inquiries with the participants in a way that is relevant and interesting for all participants. Such an exploration also contributes to the ongoing, and never-ending, development of inquiries. Thus, relational and social constructionist research can be seen as a living field, meaning that while some of the terms and words we use today are more common than others, this might be different tomorrow.

The authors of this book have spent a number of years using and developing techniques of co-constructed inquiries. As researchers, we strive to apply ongoing reflexivity to important, central themes and processes to ensure the strength of such inquiries. At the same time, we also explore weaknesses to improve our research efforts. Areas for improvement are related to both very specific and concrete 'technical' bits and pieces of inquiry approaches as well as to more profound ontological and paradigmatic questions on how approaches could interact.

However, first and foremost, we want to underscore the one thread that runs through each chapter and is the steering principle that structures this book: the importance of dialogue, language, and conversation. For us, there could be no relational and social construction research without conversation between different partners. The theme of this book is, therefore, to describe how we engage in constructing inquiries from 'with-in' local organisational practices, as co-constructors with the aim of studying 'before-the-fact processes of becoming' (Shotter, 2016).

This book shows possible ways of constructing inquiries and transforming the sometimes-difficult concepts in social constructionism and relational philosophies into research practices. It is our experience that many students wish to construct relational inquiries, yet they often lack inspiration on how to apply these ideas in practice. With this book, we invite you into our practices of co-constructing relational inquiries.

The ideas of relational and social constructionism are well known to some readers of this book. To others, they open up something new and unfamiliar. This chapter presents some important terms and concepts to assist readers in the construction of meaning within this methodological field, especially readers who have not worked methodically with a relational perspective before. At the same time, we would also like to invite readers more experienced in the relational world into an ongoing conversation on methodological activities.

Inspiration for the Relational and Social Dimensions of Organising

The paradigm related to the inquiries presented is called relational constructionism (McNamee & Hosking, 2012: 1) and social constructionism (Gergen, 1985; 2009) and grows from the philosophy of subjectivism from Immanuel Kant in the eighteenth century, hermeneutics (Gadamar), phenomenology (Schütz), pragmatism (Dewey, James, and Pierce), symbolic interactionism (Mead), system thinking (Bateson), and social constructivism (Berger and Luckmann).

The book *The Social Construction of Reality*, published by Berger and Luckmann in 1966, spurred new interest in the idea that the social world must be studied and understood as social constructions. This also includes all kinds of organisations: firms, public institutions, and third-sector organisations. Socially constructed institutions, such as organisations, are made by people, but at the same time seen as realities by people in their everyday lives. Thus, organisations can be seen dialectically as having been constructed by people while, at the same time, they are seen as socially constructed realties that play an important role in forming people and their actions.

The contribution from Berger and Luckmann (1966) is usually called *social constructivism*, but to reach the foundation of this book it is necessary to take a step further into *social constructionism* (Gergen, 1994; 2001; 2009). Thus, from this point of view, processes of organising are constructed relationally (Gergen & Thatchenkery, 2004), including the ongoing activities of everyday life, and the more formal decision-making processes can be studied. This includes how strategies, organisational culture, and management practices are formed.

Gergen (Gergen, 1994; Yang & Gergen, 2012: 132) views social constructionism as 'ontologically mute', by which he means that it is not possible to make any assumptions about 'real world' phenomena because these phenomena only are real as they are constructed via language-based interaction (Bakhtin, 1981; Vološinov, 1929/1973). In relational constructionism, it is the in-situ and ongoing processes of social construction that we seek to study. Inspired by Ludwig Wittgenstein (1953), it relates to his seminal work on a changed conception of language. Language in its use is, from this perspective, no longer seen as a way of mirroring or of making a map of phenomena 'out' in the world. Language becomes instead a set of ways of co-constructing the world. Since then, this way of understanding language has been heavily used and discussed, but undoubtedly most intensely in the 1990s (Alvesson & Kärreman, 2000a). What the book has taken away from the many debates is close to Wittgenstein's way of conceptualising language, which is through the expression of language games (Wittgenstein, 1953).

Understanding language use in this way was a precondition for the development of the term 'linguistic turn' (Alvesson & Kärreman, 2000a) in the social sciences and organisation studies. It has spurred an increased interest in studying language use and has underscored the significance of relations and social construction in organisational life (Corradi et al., 2010; Denis et al., 2012; Gergen & Thatchenkery, 2004; Golshorkhi et al., 2010). Further inspiration on the importance of language use can be found in research on organisational discourse (Alvesson & Kärreman, 2000b; Fairhurst & Putnam, 2004).

A relational constructionist perspective supports inquiries into how dialogue between people is actionable and constitutes what we perceive as knowledge and reality (Cunliffe, 2003; Gergen, 2009; McNamee, 2015; McNamee & Hosking, 2012). Following this tradition, the inquiries presented in this book aim to study organising as language-based 'living, responsive relational activities' (Shotter, 2005: 114).

All the chapters in the book are connected to these lines of relational and social constructionist philosophies. Thus, we draw upon the work of a number of researchers who, over the last three decades, together with Kenneth Gergen, have constructed the field (Cunliffe & Eriksen, 2011; Gergen et al., 2004; McNamee & Hosking, 2012; Ospina & Uhl-Bien, 2012; Shotter & Cunliffe, 2002). This process of constructing the field has been done through a combination of inquiries into practice as well as theoretical and philosophical analyses.

Organising in Flux and Becoming

The first steps of organisational research inspired by social constructivism (Berger & Luckmann, 1966) led to the replacement of the noun 'organisation' by the verb 'organizing' – a concept first introduced by Karl Weick (1979). The replacement of words represents an important ontological shift in organisational research from studying organisations and organisational life as static entities and phenomena to studying processes of organising.

This shift has played an important role in developing relational constructionist research into the field of organising. However, from a social constructionist perspective, research is not about portraying THE socially constructed worldview and taken-for-granted assumptions of the organisation members, departments, or workgroups. It is about studying the local, everyday, relationally responsive dialogic practices of groups of organisation members (Chia, 1996; Cunliffe, 2011; Shotter, 2005), which includes finding variations in these practices and noting how they interact and co-construct locally produced moments of organising and how these moments are influenced by past, present, and future constructions of reality (Larsen & Madsen, 2016; Larsen & Willert, 2017; Shotter, 2005).

The focus on 'flux' and constant change was inspired by pragmatism as it was developed from the late nineteenth to the early twentieth century, especially in the US, where researchers such as John Dewey (1916) and William James (1909) viewed the world as being in constant flux and change. From this perspective, it becomes impossible to find, and uninteresting to search for, fixed understandings and established truths. The idea of pragmatism is instead directed toward finding, in the moment, plausible meanings about the local world to make it possible to act upon.

The themes in pragmatism are important for how this book works with relational and social constructionism. Pragmatism was further developed by Tim Ingold (2008; 2012), who reinstated the term 'becoming'. Becoming underscores the constant change at play in processes of organising and takes an interest in understanding flux. From a 'being' perspective, an organisation is rather steady and stable; it is in a state of equilibrium or the management tries to bring it into equilibrium. From this perspective, it is assumed that an organisation, as much as possible, follows a rather linear, planned development and is only momentarily brought into imbalance. A becoming perspective interprets processes of organising, as well as the world, as constantly under development and only occasionally in a state that only seems to represent a balance. Rather, an organisation develops, to a large extent, in uncoordinated movements and actions shaped by the interactions between the different local groups and individuals both inside and outside the organisation (Larsen, 2014).

The importance of studying organising as processes of dialogue, flux, and becoming is further highlighted by the social and relational constructionist onto-/epistemology that people are bound to co-construct (Cunliffe, 2002a; Gergen, 2010; Larsen & Rasmussen, 2015; Shotter & Billig, 1998). People co-construct through words, actions, gestures, preferences, music, food, how they dress, what they acknowledge, etc. In relational and social constructionism, every action is based on interpretation, and such interpretations are constructed through collaboration and conversation between human beings. This means that everybody is always involved in not only relations that shape the actions he or she is occupied with but suggestions that those actions shape the person and the ways he or she co-constructs and interprets the world. This includes mundane daily activities like answering the phone or setting up a meeting as well more formal activities such as confirming a new strategy or a new organisational plan.

Becoming a Relational Researcher

How can these ongoing processes of organising, flux, becoming, and co-construction be studied? In the following paragraphs, we will turn our attention to unfolding the role of the researcher in relational constructionist research, while in the following chapters of the book, we use examples from our own practices to show how we co-construct our own roles in shared organisational inquiries as 'disturbers', 'facilitators', and 'co-constructors' immersed in the flow of the dynamic world we study (Shotter, 2016).

By following a relational constructionist onto-/epistemology, the role of the researcher changes from one engaged in classic qualitative and social constructivist research (Cunliffe, 2011). The role shifts from constructing a subject position as 'The Researcher' (Hosking & Pluut, 2010; Shotter, 2016), often described as being able to put brackets around ourselves and our activities in the field, to a position as co-constructor of the inquiry by acknowledging that we play an equal part in the meaning construction processes during our inquiries.

Constructing inquiries based on the ideas of relational constructionism means co-constructing the inquiry by immersing ourselves, together with the participants, into the constructionist flow of meaning creation during the unfolding research processes. As Shotter (2009: 3) describes, we join the organisational members for a walk in 'somewhat foggy surroundings'. By inquiring into the process with the participants, we encourage the organisational members to find their own way in the sometimes bewildering landscape of new circumstances in which they find themselves. It is important to join them on a shared journey and walk down unfolding and multiple pathways through shared dialogic explorations.

The aim of our inquiries is not to find or show the appropriate path to follow, but rather to keep exploring the emerging possible ways to move on (Shotter, 2009). This role as a researcher has been described as 'before-the-fact' ways of exploring different 'landscapes of possibilities' (Shotter, 2016: 60). Through constructing inquiries in this way, softer subject positions as researchers can be made, while at the same time, researchers can acknowledge that they too are co-constructors of the inquiry.

By acknowledging that all participants occupy different subject positions, and perceiving this as a strength in the inquiry process, researchers as co-constructors can be invited into the joint processes of constructing new possible pathways with the organisation members. In this process, we jointly explore new paths and possibilities of 'what is imaginatively available to us' in our 'inner landscape of possibilities', and this can be further explored in dialogic processes with others who occupy different subject positions (Shotter, 2016: 67). This book offers different examples of inquiries focusing on co-constructed dialogic processes, both in conversations with single organisation members and in groups.

There are also examples of how inquiries can include a study of important organisational documents and texts produced during the inquiry by the participants. Such texts can be read by both members of the organisation and the researchers conducting the inquiry to form a basis for further dialogic exploration. The shared dialogue on important documents following these readings provides new opportunities for shared meaning construction, more than the initial reading of the documents. This underlines the inquiry process as co-researching between all participants.

Practical activities and artefacts can also play an important role in studying processes of organising (Shotter, 1996). Attention can be paid to production activities, development activities, or other activities concerning employees, in addition to artefacts belonging to such activities. When activities and artefacts are included in a study, the dialogical process between participants and co-researchers on possible interpretations of these activities is important.

This type of flexibility regarding the choice of techniques and practical ways of constructing a relational inquiry does not mean that all choices are equally useful. The choice of techniques is important because it should support a relational process between the participants in handling what may appear to be important in the moment during joint processes (McNamee, 2014).

The Relational Research Process

When conducting relational inquiries, it is important to acknowledge and constantly reflect on our subject position as researchers. Engaging in social constructionist research is a form of social action and can bring about change from a 'future-forming perspective' (Gergen, 2015: 9; McNamee & Hosking, 2012). Gergen advocates a form of 'research in which knowledge is acquired through the complex and creative process of constructing a successful practice. [...] When such knowledge is shared, it becomes a resource for others' (Gergen, 2015: 11). Thus, when undertaking research projects, we aim to further ideas of co-construction, multiple perspectives, and constructive ways to move forward for all participants in our inquiries.

To achieve this, it is useful during the entire process of inquiry from moment to moment to apply a form of meta-awareness or reflective pragmatism (Gergen, 2015), constantly reflecting on how the approaches and co-constructed dialogues might bring new generative ways to move forward (McNamee, 2014). When conducting relational inquiries, it is important to participate in each conversation as living process from within (Shotter, 2006) and to participate in the inquiry by engaging as an equal communicative partner. It is a process of co-generating knowledge while exploring within the process itself.

When studying language construction as processes of organising, it is important to develop research inquiries involving the participants in processes of relational reflexivity (Cunliffe, 2002b; 2004), which calls for all members of the inquiry (including the researcher) to have the ability and will to listen with an open mind, aiming to be responsive and to participate in the conversations with those who are active in organising – and thereby to become part of the organising processes. Active listening and participation are requirements in the construction process and a way to understand aspects in organising (Larsen & Rasmussen, 2015).

When researchers engage in an inquiry from a constructionist perspective on language, dialogue, and meaning construction, it is important to invite all partners into these processes. Dialogue in this form defines equal yet different tasks for all participants. The understanding of dialogue as ongoing construction of organising processes and the concept of organisational members as co-constructers, thus making them co-researchers in an inquiry, do not exclude or include specific techniques for conducting the inquiry, but it does define certain principles in an inquiry (McNamee & Hosking, 2012). Firstly, in every organising process, different meanings are constructed within the many different relations of the local groups. Secondly, meanings are permanently under construction and are never completely fixed.

When studying organising, the idea of language as constructing the social world means seeing and using language as it sounds in organising and as an ongoing process of many voices. There are different voices that relationally and polyphonically construct several meanings in the local groups in organising processes (Larsen & Rasmussen, 2015). Some voices may be louder than others, and it is not necessarily those loud voices that alone are interesting and important when researching organising. An important feature of a relational approach includes listening to the softer voices (Cunliffe, 2002b).

Truth

In relational constructionist onto-/epistemology there is no truth out there to be found (Shotter, 2016). Truth is based on an ontology of relational processes and, in the form of emergent constructions, is continuously reshaped and reconstructed. As researchers we can only invite other participants into reflexive dialogues, hereby constructing processes of shared reflection and reflexivity by acknowledging that our existence is always in becoming and that we as individuals only are able to exist 'in responsive, living relations to each other – [this] will change the focus of our inquiries radically [...] there is no single meaning to be found in the world, but a vast multitude of contesting meanings' (Shotter, 2016: 65–66).

When constructing inquiries, researchers often ask how they can participate in these processes in ways that can inspire curiosity and reflexivity, thereby encouraging different ways of knowledge sharing and forms of dialogue in the organisation. By co-constructing different ways of interacting, listening, and dialogue in the inquiry, it is possible to invite the participants into 'relational responsiveness' by making space for variation, dissensus, complexity, and multiplicity (McNamee & Hosking, 2012: xiv). All participants in an inquiry have different backgrounds and worldviews. Thus, the researcher's aim is 'moving out of an idealized world and into the indeterminate world of responsive living beings, where "truth" only can be seen as an ongoing accomplishment in local time/space' (Shotter, 2016: 65). It is, therefore, important to be aware that, in the process, all participants are responsible and must reflect on the 'truths' being constructed. This calls for a relational responsibility by constructing power with all the participants in the inquiry, not simply power over, or only with some of the participants, by continuously inviting the research participants into reflexive dialogue and communal reflection. Constant reflection and questioning such as *'Am I listening to the voices of all the participants? Are we constructing the best possible way for the participants to move forward after the inquiry?'* are important components in an inquiry.

Problem Solving

The idea that 'truth' can be found and guide the right path to follow and act in an organisation is questioned in the previous paragraph. This means that the role of the researcher changes from constructing an identity as a problem solver and alters the researcher's purpose when conducting research. This is a process described as constructing 'emerging research identities' and engaging in 'participatory ways of knowing' (Cunliffe & Shotter, 2006; Hosking & Pluut, 2010: 69–70).

In relational research, the aim of an inquiry is not to show the research participants how to move forward. Instead, the researcher invites organisational members on a shared journey to explore current taken-for-granted ways of constructing organisational life. Thus, we as researchers engage in joint exploration in their quest to develop new understandings of their organisational life as well as encourage shared processes of finding new 'possible pathways' and 'ways to go on' (Shotter, 2016) and develop shared responsibility for making desirable changes (Hosking & Pluut, 2010).

Ethics

Listening to all voices in the research process was mentioned previously, but should also be highlighted from an ethical standpoint. When planning and conducting inquiries, one must always be attentive to power relations, both between researchers and organisational members and also among organisational members. Researchers should also avoid silencing any voices or indirectly and without common acceptance steering the conversation in certain directions (Cunliffe, 2002b). Remember to listen, to pause, and to be curious during the conversations and the entire inquiry.

To construct meaning in a relation between equal partners means not only giving participants a voice, but also giving them a say in constructing the theme of the conversation and the direction of the entire inquiry. This is of utmost importance in the conversations that go on directly between the practitioners and the researchers initiating the inquiry. Ideally, each conversation should build to ensure that everyone has a voice that is listened to in open and flexible ways. Therefore, prior to the beginning of the study, only a broad framework can be defined, and the concrete activities of the entire inquiry should be flexible. The researcher must be willing to change the entire setup, depending on the directions the inquiry takes.

Writing up Research

How can we, then, analyse and write up research if 'truth' is at best an ongoing accomplishment in local time/space? This idea changes the researcher's role completely when analysing and writing up social constructionist research. When writing up research it is extremely important to cast a reflexive gaze on our taken-for-granted research practices and how we construct the 'after-the-inquiry process'. This calls for reflexivity and 'ongoing dialoguing' in acknowledging the different social worlds and culturally embodied and embedded views and assumptions of others (McNamee & Hosking, 2012; Hosking & Pluut, 2010) while at the same time writing for a scientific community (Gergen, 1999). The process of writing can stimulate new dialogues within the field of study and among practitioners. A text is always in relation to those reading it and creates new meaning for the readers according to their subject position. It will mean different things to other researchers, members of the inquiry, and other practitioners.

It is important to realise that 'The Text' is not a final stop, but rather it becomes part of the ongoing process of 'turning back' to the inquiry by stimulating reflexive dialogues and re-constructing the inquiry. These processes of the inquiry are important to include in the processes of writing up research because they can be some of the most informative ways to express to the reader an open, self-reflecting (Cunliffe, 2002b), and critical presentation of how the inquiry techniques have been used in practice, how they play together and in some cases against each other in an inquiry, and how the entire methodology of the inquiry was formed. These influences guide researchers in our ongoing quest to improve our research practices by reflecting on the points stated in Table 1.1.

Table 1.1 Relational Research Practices

Ontology & epistemology	*Relational constructionism*
The relational researcher	Embraces the role as co-constructor. A co-constructor is interested in subject-to-subject processes and is always a co-constructor of these processes. As co-constructors of the inquiry, everyone occupies different subject positions. This viewpoint aims to narrow the gap between the researcher and the local practitioners.
What we aim to study	In the relational process with local practitioners, what we come to see as important and relevant depends on the joint exploration of everyday organisational life. Aiming to study before-the-fact processes of becoming, we invite relational sharing of ideas on past, present, and future themes relevant for both practitioners and researchers.
The research process	A never-ending process of radical reflexivity and 'ongoing dialoguing'. By adopting soft self-other relations, we acknowledge the embodied and embedded views and assumptions of others. By constantly questioning our own research practices before, during, and after the inquiries, we are able to uncover our own taken-for-granted practices and develop our inquiries and understandings in dialogue with others.
Truth	By adopting the onto-/epistemology of relational constructionism, we acknowledge that researchers and local practitioners construct truth through the dialogic process as an ongoing accomplishment in time/space. Truth is always in a fluctuating process of becoming.
Problem solving	We do not see ourselves as problem solvers. We see ourselves as partakers in dialogic processes, always inviting local practitioners to jointly explore indeterminate situations and possible new pathways in the inquiry process.

Ontology & epistemology	Relational constructionism
Ethics	By embracing relational responsibility in our inquiries, soft self-other relations, and joint processes of co-construction, we aim to ensure that all voices are heard. By engaging in ongoing dialogic reflexivity before, during, and after the inquiries, we question our own role in positioning some socially constructed worldviews over others and what this might mean for the local practitioners during the inquiry and after.
Writing up research	When writing up research, the text is not a final stop as it becomes a part of the ongoing reflexive process of 'turning back' to the inquiry. A text is always in relation to those reading it and creates new meaning for the readers according to their subject position. It will mean different things to other researchers, members of the inquiry, and other practitioners. Our aim is to stimulate further dialogue and reflexivity.

(Sources: Cunliffe, 2011; Hosking & Pluut, 2010; McNamee & Hosking, 2012; Shotter, 2016)

Developing Relational Research Practices

As outlined previously, philosophies and principles indirectly require the initiating researchers to have a number of important competencies when conducting a study on organising from a relational constructionist perspective (McNamee & Hosking, 2012). In the following chapters, we invite you into our inquiry practices and hope to inspire the development of competencies in conducting relational inquiries.

In addition to these competencies, we outline practical ideas on such things as how to arrange meetings or time schedules and, very importantly, how to constantly bring meaning construction forward. We aim to answer important questions like 'What is and what should be expected of the participants from the organisation, and the researchers?' and 'How can the practical knowledge and experiences the participants have gained through the inquiry be best used to construct reflection and reflexivity, thus creating new and useful knowledge concerning practice and the everyday activities within the organisation?'

Furthermore, it is important to take into consideration the fact that relational and social constructionist inquiries have never been and indeed never will become a finished and fixed concept. New contributions will always appear and well-proven contributions might be forgotten or integrated into new contributions. Thus, this book contains a number of inquiries that were developed by practitioners and by one or several of the authors of chapters in this book. Each chapter elaborates on how relational and social constructionist philosophy can be used in specific concrete inquiries.

Therefore, the specific inquiries constructed and described in the following chapters should serve as inspiration and not as cookbook recipes for future studies. Inquiries must be developed and re-developed during the research process. Inspiration for this constant development can come from both the actual situation and from other previous or ongoing studies.

The preconditions described in this chapter for inquiries into relational and social constructionism are important criteria that are developed and applied in each of the following chapters. However, the reader must bear in mind that each new inquiry requires a construction of its own specific approach by combining new techniques with well-established ones. The chapters in this book aim to inspire your process by presenting specific, co-constructed inquiries into the field of organising, leading, and development.

References

Alvesson, M. & Kärreman, D. (2000a) Taking the Linguistic Turn in Organizational Research. Challenges, Responses, Consequences. *The Journal of Applied Behavioral Science*, 36, 136–158.

Alvesson, M. & Kärreman, D. (2000b) Varieties of Discourse: On the Study of Organizations Through Discourse Analysis. *Human Relations*, 53(9), 1125–1149.

Bakhtin, M. M. (1981) *The Dialogic Imagination. Four Essays by M. M. Bakhtin.* Holtquist, M. (ed.). Austin, University of Texas Press.

Berger, P. & Luckmann, T. (1966) *The Social Construction of Knowledge: A Treatise in the Sociology of Knowledge.* Garden City, NY, Doubleday.

Chia, R. (1996) The Problem of Reflexivity in Organizational Research: Towards a Postmodern Science of Organization. *Organization*, 3(1), 51–59.

Corradi, G., Gheradi, S. & Verzalloni, L. (2010) Through the Practice Lens: Where Is the Bandwagon of Practice-Based Studies Heading? *Management Learning*, 41, 265–283.

Cunliffe, A. L. (2002a) Reflexive Dialogical Practice in Management Learning. *Management Learning*, 33 (1), 35–61.

Cunliffe, A. L. (2002b) Social Poetics as Management Inquiry—A Dialogical Approach. *Journal of Management Inquiry*, 11(2), 128–146.

Cunliffe, A. L. (2003) Reflexive Inquiry in Organizational Research: Questions and Possibilities. *Human Relations*, 56 (8), 983–1003.

Cunliffe, A. L. (2004) On Becoming a Critically Reflexive Practitioner. *Journal of Management Education*, 28 (4), 407–426.

Cunliffe, A. L. (2011) Crafting Qualitative Research: Morgan and Smircich 30 Years On. *Organizational Research Methods*, 14 (4), 647–673.

Cunliffe, A. L. & Eriksen, M. (2011) Relational Leadership. *Human Relations*, 64 (11), 1425–1449.

Cunliffe, A. L., & Shotter, J. (2006). Wittgenstein, Bakhtin, management and the dialogical. In: Hosking D. M & McNamee S. (Eds.), *The Social Construction of Organization*. Malmö, Sweden: Liber & Copenhagen Business School Press, pp. 226–241.

Denis, J., Langley, A. & Sergi, V. (2012) Leadership in the Plural. *The Academy of Management Annals*, 6, 211–283.

Dewey, J. (1916) *Democracy and Education: An Introduction to the Philosophy of Education.* New York, The Macmillan Company.

Fairhurst, G. & Putnam, L. (2004) Organizations as Discursive Constructions. *Communication Theory,* 14, 5–26.

Gergen, K. J. (1985) The Social Constructionist Movement in Modern Psychology. *American Psychologist,* 40, 266–275.

Gergen, K. J. (1994) *Realities and Relationships. Soundings in Social Construction.* Cambridge, MA, Harvard University Press.

Gergen, K. J. (1999). *An Invitation to Social Construction.* London: Sage.

Gergen, K. J. (2001) *Social Construction in Context.* London, Sage Publications.

Gergen, K. J. (2009) *Relational Being: Beyond the Individual and Community.* Oxford, Oxford University Press.

Gergen, K. J. (2010) Co-Constitution, Causality and Confluence Organizing in a World Without Entities. In: Hernes, T. & Maitlis, S. (eds.) *Process, Sensemaking, and Organizing.* Oxford, Oxford University Press, 55–69.

Gergen, K. J. (2015). From Mirroring to World-Making: Research as Future Forming. Winner of the 2014 Essay Competition, Independent Social Research Foundation, London, UK. *Journal for the Theory of Social Behaviour,* 45 (3), 287–310.

Gergen, K. J., Gergen, M. M. & Barrett, F. J. (2004). Dialogue: Life and Death of the Organization. In: Grant, D., Hardy, C., Oswick, C., Phillips, N. & Putnam, L. (eds.) *The Sage Handbook of Organizational Discourse.* Thousand Oaks, CA, Sage, 39-60.

Gergen, K. J. & Thatchenkery, T. (2004) Organization Science as Social Construction Postmodern Potentials. *The Journal of Applied Behavioral Science,* 40 (2), 228–249.

Golshorki, D., Rouleau, L., Seidel, D. & Vaara, E. (2010) *Cambridge Handbook of Strategy in Practice.* Cambridge, Cambridge University.

Hosking, D. M. & Pluut, B. (2010) (Re)constructing Reflexivity: A Relational Constructionist Approach. *The Qualitative Report,* 15 (1), 59–75.

Ingold, T. (2008) *Lines. A Brief Story.* Oxon, Routledge.

Ingold, T. (2012) Toward an Ecology of Materials. *The Annual Review of Anthropology,* 41, 427–442.

James, W. (1909) *A Pluralistic Universe.* New York, Longmans, Green and Co.

Larsen, M. V. (2014) *Strategising Through Organising—the Significance of Relational Sensemaking.* Chagrin Falls, OH, Taos Institute Publications.

Larsen, M. V. & Madsen, C. Ø. (2016) Exploring How Social Poetics Can Be Used to Understand Processes of Management Learning. *Management Learning,* 47 (5), 1–17.

Larsen, M. V. & Rasmussen, J. G. (2015) *Relational Perspectives on Leading.* Houndsmills, Basingstoke, Palgrave Macmillan.

Larsen, M. V. & Willert, S. (2017) Using Management Inquiry to Co- Construct Other Memories About the Future. *Journal of Management Inquiry.* [Online publication, March 17].

McNamee, S. (2014) Research as Relational Practice. In: Simon, G. & Chard, A. (eds.) *Systemic Inquiry: Innovations in Reflexive Practice Research.* Farnhill, UK, Everything Is Connected Press, pp. 74–94.

McNamee, S. (2015) Radical Presence: Alternatives to the Therapeutic State. *The European Journal of Psychotherapy and Counselling,* 17 (4), 373–383.

McNamee, S. & Hosking, D. M. (2012) *Research and Social Change—a Relational Constructionist Approach.* New York, Routledge.

Ospina, S. & Uhl-Bien, M. (2012) *Advancing Relational Leadership Research. A dialog between Perspectives*. Charlotte, NC, Information Age Publishing.

Shotter, J. (1996) Now I Can Go On: Wittgenstein and Our Embodied Embeddedness in the 'Hurly-Burly' of Life. *Human Studies*, 19 (4), 385–407.

Shotter, J. (2005) 'Inside the Moment of Managing': Wittgenstein and the Everyday Dynamics of Our Expressive-Responsive Activities. *Organisation Studies*, 26 (1), 113–135.

Shotter, J. (2006). Understanding Process From Within: An Argument for 'Withness'-Thinking. *Organization Studies*, 27 (4), 585–604.

Shotter, J. (2009) *Movements of Feeling and Moments of Judgement: Towards an Ontological Social Constructionism*. Paper presented at the Constructing Worlds conference, Taos Institute and MacMann Berg, 20th–23rd August, Denmark, [Online, July 17].

Shotter, J. (2016) Undisciplining Social Science: Wittgenstein and the Art of Creating Situated Practices of Social Inquiry. *Journal for the Theory of Social Behavior*, 46 (1), 60–83.

Shotter, J. & Billig, M. (1998) A Bakhtinian Psychology: From Out of the Heads of Individuals and into the Dialogues Between Them. In: Mayerfeld Bell, M. & Gardiner, M. (eds.) *Bakhtin and the Human Sciences: No Last Words*. London, Sage Publications, pp. 13–29.

Shotter, J. & Cunliffe, A. L. (2002) Managers as Practical Authors: Everyday Conversations for Action. In: Holman, D. & Thorpe, R. (eds.) *Management and Language: The manager as Practical Author*. London, Sage, pp. 15–37.

Vološinov, V. (1929/1973) *Marxism and the Philosophy of Language*. New York, Seminar Press.

Weick, K. (1979) *The Social Psychology of Organizing*. Reading, MA, McGraw-Hill.

Wittgenstein, L. (1953) *Philosophical Investigations*. Oxford, Blackwell.

Yang, L. & Gergen, K. J. (2012) Social Construction and its Development: Liping Yang Interviews Kenneth Gergen. *Psychological Studies*, 57 (2), 126–133.

2 Using Adjusted Responses to Engage in Research Conversations with Organisational Members

Mette Vinther Larsen

Introduction

The following two chapters will explore conversations between two persons: a researcher or student and, in this case, a leader. There is nothing in the practice that requires these conversations to be between a researcher and a leader; they can take place just as easily between a researcher, student, consultant, and a middle manager, employee, board member, etc. What characterises these conversations is that they often take place between two persons who do not, under normal circumstances, spend time together. The purpose of these conversations is to explore current and, from the leader's perspective, relevant organisational challenges with someone who is not personally involved in the challenge, as well as reflectively explore multiple perspectives on an organisational challenge.

In some cases, the leader and researcher have met each other only minutes prior to the conversation. Often, they do not know what motivates or frustrates one another or where the conversation will take them, and may not meet again afterwards. It is, in many ways, a peculiar conversation that can unfold; perhaps because of the unfamiliarity between the two persons, the conversation can often be quite beneficial and constructive to both the researcher and the organisational member with whom he or she converses.

How beneficial and constructive a conversation between the researcher and the organisational member is depends on the manner in which they communicate and whether or not the member sees the researcher as resourceful conversation partner: someone who is interested in understanding the organisational life to which he or she belongs. The following chapter is structured as a mixture of theoretical introductions to the guiding philosophy behind the practice and concrete inspiration points based on research meant to inspire the reader to develop his or her own practice.

What Does It Mean to Be Understood as a Resourceful Conversation Partner?

To be understood as a resourceful conversation partner means here to engage in conversations that are characterised by openness to, curiosity towards, and appreciation of the local understandings that emerge as people communicate about what is valued, disliked, and striven towards here and now (McNamee & Hosking, 2012). A researcher most likely has no organisation-anchored interest in any of the situations discussed during the research conversation. Nevertheless, a researcher takes part in this conversation because he or she is interested in reflectively exploring how organisational life and practices unfold and are understood from the local perspective with which the organisational member is acquainted (McNamee & Hosking, 2012).

To engage in the research conversations presented in this and the following chapter means to take part in a joint wayfaring process where neither researcher nor organisational member knows initially where the conversation will take them. The purpose of these research conversations is to initiate a shared inquiry process where researcher and organisational member together explore a given organisational challenge that presently concerns the member. The conversation revolves around pursuing questions to which there is no answer at the outset. However, both the researcher and organisational member believe that by reflectively exploring them, they become capable of understanding and dealing with them in multiple ways.

As the researcher and the organisational member converse, they rely on a practice but do not follow a detailed agenda or script (Shotter, 2010). Prior to the conversation, the researcher considers the purpose of the conversation, though these thoughts and intentions are only preliminary. As the conversation unfolds, the researcher and the organisational member draw on ways of communicating that they also use in their everyday conversations (Shotter, 2010). The research agenda behind the processes presented here is embedded in a wish to jointly construct the relevant practices, questions, and intentions as the researcher and organisational member begin to converse.

The following example is an excerpt from a research conversation held between the author and the CEO of a medium-sized Danish consultancy company. Christian, who spent the first fifty minutes of the conversation explaining the strategic process the company recently experienced, showed many of the analyses the company had made to achieve its present accomplishments. Although he is pleased with the outcome, there is, nevertheless, a sense that something is missing; Christian's body language and intonations do not express excitement, and the following conversation ensues:

Christian (C): 'We dedicate some time to celebrate the successes, enjoy the success after so many years filled with crap; it's nice to have some good ratings and make money at the same time, enjoy the respect you gain from your employees. It gives you great credit when you succeed with something. Trust and confidence: you have to remember to enjoy that once in a while.'

Mette (M): 'For sure, you have to. I have this sense, and please do not hesitate to argue with me here. I have this sense that still, this is not enough?' (fifty-two minutes)

C: 'Yes. I want it, the development, I want it. I want it. It's the entrepreneur inside of me going YES, hell, I want this too. Now I've succeeded with this then it must be possible to succeed with the other things. There has to be some way we can make it work, it might be difficult, but it has to be possible.'
M: 'Yes'?
C: 'Yes, and this is also why I refer to the strategy as something, bigger, fatter, wider . . . I see it as a challenge, that's also the exciting part of leading, to drive something, to create something, to develop something.'
M: 'And it seems like the projects you have on your desk right now, sure they're alright, but it's not enough, you need something else, something bigger?'
C: 'Yes, YES.'
M: 'Give me a proper challenge, something I can work with?'
C: 'Yes . . . and some of the frustration you're experiencing, these are the first steps that I have to take to get there . . .'
(Research conversation 3 with Christian)

What I want to illustrate is that the questions had not been prepared beforehand; they emerged from within the conversation. The intention of the conversation – that Christian needed to be challenged in his everyday practice – was a joint construction that arose as Christian and I conversed. Even though such conversations often revolve around understanding organisational life from a local perspective, in this case Christian's perspective, focus is not on his individual cognitive or internal processes. The focus is on the 'processes of relating' (McNamee & Hosking, 2012: 36).

The invitations presented did not stem from premeditated thoughts; they emerged from the way we jointly communicated, our consideration for each other and our attention to our verbal and nonverbal communication (Cunliffe, 2003; Gergen, 2010; Lugo et al., 2014; McNamee, 2000, 2015). As presented in Chapter 1, co-research is understood in this book as co-authoring, and as Christian and I communicated, we co-authored (Cunliffe, 2001; Shotter & Cunliffe, 2002). In this specific case, we are relationally and responsively co-authoring a more perceptible understanding of the frustration Christian was experiencing at the moment. Neither Christian and nor I spoke in neutral, objective, or indifferent terms; we spoke in emotional-volitional terms that were filled with ideas concerning what next would happen (Shotter, 2008; Vološinov, 1986). Conversations previously held, sense already made, books read, texts written, and previous actions shaped the there-and-then constructions Christian and I jointly made. The responses Christian and I generated were in no way neutral or objective; they were responsive invitations to explore a sense that emerged as we communicated.

As I am not part of the organisational everyday that Christian lives in, we are jointly able to engage in a reflective co-authoring process that embraces the unfamiliarity between us; we are able to question and explore what we both take for granted, and make room for new understanding of how it will be meaningful to move forward. We jointly construct an understanding of Christian's desire to be strategically challenged.

Language Is Ontological

Unquestionably, as presented in the first chapter, communication holds a very significant position within a relational constructionist perspective on how '[t]he ways we relate with one another, the questions we ask, and the words we use create the worlds in which we live' (McNamee & Hosking, 2012: 75). Language is reality constituting (Gergen & Thatchenkery, 2004). As Christian and I talked together, the words we used reflected local, taken-for-granted assumptions about reality. Simultaneously, we co-construct this same local reality, but in a slightly different way; the way we here and now communicated and acted in the moment was unique and once-occurring (McNamee & Hosking, 2012).

Cunliffe (2002b) suggests perceiving language as ontology to underline the generative and constructive aspect language and communication play in the everyday becoming of organisational life. People do not talk about organisational life but talk as they lead an organisational life, and in doing so re-construct, de-construct, or change it (Cunliffe, 2002b).

The conversations in which a researcher engages with a leader or an employee can, due to the researcher's non-organisational anchoring at the outset, be thought of as free and imaginary talk about dreams and ideas. Conversely, language is generative, and once the dreams and ideas are formed into words and possible actions carried out mentally, the ideas and dreams suddenly seem within reach, approachable, and possible.

While this duality of language is a strength of these conversations, it can also become its fallacy. For example, a researcher must be respectful, sensitive, and humble to the local, common-sense understandings and actions being explored jointly. Simultaneously, a researcher has to use his or her non-organisational anchoring to, when needed, question the very same local, taken-for-granted, and common-sense understandings and actions. Based on this duality, the researcher should invite the member to engage in co-constructing in ways that both the researcher and organisational member here and now believe will enable them to progress in meaningful ways (Cunliffe, 2002b; McNamee & Hosking, 2012; Ripamonti et al., 2016).

Organisational Life: It Is a Mesh

This chapter draws on an understanding of organising as meshwork, which enables organisational members to acknowledge the complexity and confluent aspects of life (Gergen, 2010; Ingold, 2008). Imagine how it would look like if every act carried out in an organisation is like a ball of yarn tossed onto the floor at once from different places. Every time a new encounter takes place or members communicate and act, a new ball of yarn enters the meshwork. Some balls of yarn cross one another, some become tangled in knots, while others never approach each other. The yarn may break, or run out or bump into one another and change direction. This meshwork of lines or actions is what makes up organisational life (Willert & Larsen, 2015; Ingold, 2010; 2008).

The meshwork never settles down or stabilises; it is a conflux and continues to evolve in multiple directions based on how people act and communicate in the local here and now they take part in (Gergen, 2010; Willert & Larsen, 2015). This also means that there will be multiple polyphonic, local understandings and practices co-existing within the meshwork, because people take part in a different 'inter-act' (Hosking, 2010) or see things from a specific local 'somewhere' (McNamee & Hosking, 2012). No one is capable of gaining a momentary overview of the entire meshwork, the multiple different local understandings and practices, nor is anyone able to predict what the meshwork will become. Everyone is immersed in the practices taking place locally in their local here-and-now encounter. Boje (1995) refers to Tamara-land as a metaphor for signifying the fluctuating, meshed, and once-occurring local aspects of organisational life, where it is impossible to get a complete sense of the multiple activities taking place and sense being made.

Regarding understanding language ontologically, the researcher and the organisational member do not discuss organisational life; they co-construct it here and now as they talk in the present (Cunliffe, 2002b; Gergen & Thatchenkery, 2004; Vološinov, 1986). McNamee & Hosking (2012) argue that now-ness and the present are all there is. People can only live their lives in the here and now in the unique inter-act they take part in at the current moment. The past and the future are constructions people retain or alter in the present as they talk, act and generate relational meaning; there is no steady and given past that determines how the present will unfold, nor is there any causal connection between the present and the future (Mead, 1934). It is peoples' joined processes of relating the here and now that shapes how both the past and the future influence their relational construction of meaning (Kornberger, 2013; Mead, 1934; Willert & Larsen, 2015).

This does not mean that the past or the future does not influence how and what meaning the researcher and the organisational member jointly construct in the present (Mead, 1934; McNamee, 2012; Shotter, 1990). Previously carried out actions may be situated in the past, but they affect how the researcher and organisational member construct meaning together in the present (Mead; 1934; McNamee, 2000). Thus, the meaning they create in the present alters their understanding of previously carried out actions. This signifies that when a researcher engages in a research conversation as a resourceful conversation partner, he or she partakes in co-constructing knowledge from within a given local 'somewhere' that not only makes the local 'somewhere' understandable but simultaneously alters it.

Here-and-Now Relational Construction of Adjusted Responses

The ontological understanding of language and the significance of here-and-now relational construction of meaning discussed previously in this chapter are due in large part to Mead's work. Mead (1934; 1974) argues that the construction of meaning is a joint process. Although Mead is not a relational constructionist but a symbolic interactionist who believes in the existence of independent selves, he still attributes relational processes as where multiple selves, social norms, and meaning are being constructed, re-constructed, and altered (Mead, 1934; 1974). According to Mead (1974: 81), '[Meaning emerges] in the triadic relation of a gesture of one individual, a response to that gesture by the second individual, and completion of the given social act by the gesture of the first individual.'

As the construction of meaning belongs to the present, no one can construct meaning on his or her own. It is out of our adjusted gestures that shared meaning emerges (Cunliffe, 2001; Mead, 1974; McNamee & Hosking, 2012). As one conversation partner gestures, he or she relies on shared and generalised symbols and understandings. When another conversation partner responds based on similarly shared and generalised symbols and understandings, the response is adjusted. An adjusted response is a response where the expectations and understanding correlate between the two conversation partners (Mead, 1974).

The following excerpt is from another research conversation with Christian. It illustrates how Christian and I use gestures and adjusted responses to jointly construct meaning. Preceding the insight, Christian has told me how the management team in his organisation tended to work only with a long-term and static understanding of strategy that he found unconstructive.

Christian (C): 'Couldn't we work with two strategic horizons? One that is called in two years and one that is called the next three months? It's kind of like sailing a submarine: once in a while you have to surface to make sure we're still on the right course with what we're doing. So, we discuss it a bit back and forth; how can we do this without shattering our long-term perspective and without missing out on all the opportunities and still pay attention to the short-term?'

Mette (M): 'It revolves around dissolving the distinction between long- and short-term perspectives and exploring how they can enrich one another . . . integrating them. To acknowledge this can be difficult because often we see them as two distinct processes.'

C: 'Yes, I think that's a really great point. Because it is always extremely difficult. We make these amazing strategic plans, a lot of thick pages, and we really work hard to make people see the benefits, but they just don't see them.'

M: 'No, people often think they have to get into a specific strategic mode like you enter a certain room where you're supposed to think strategically.'

C: 'Yes, and then when you come out, you have a completely different take on things . . . and it's interesting because a lot of what we decide are just incorporated. Strategically, we've decided to increase our sales and . . . people are assigned a sales course, but is that strategic to them – no . . . Sometimes people expect that the strategy will revolutionise everything.'

M: 'Yes, yes they sure do.'

C: 'Rally one's troops and tomorrow you'll have a completely different regime.' (smiles)

M: 'It is about realising that it happens incrementally and as a part of our everyday practice . . . do things a little different . . . just think about that [the change] . . . and you only realise it retrospectively.'

C: 'Exactly!'

(Research conversation 1, Christian)

As Christian and I discussed strategy, it was relatively easy for us to reach a shared understanding of how strategic processes should unfold, and the responses Christian and I each gave were adjusted accordingly. The intonation of words, non-verbal communication, and reactions illustrated how we both intuitively drew on tacit and existing knowledge about strategic processes. Based on adjusted responses such as, 'Yes, and I think that's a really great point,' 'Yes, yes, I know!' and 'Exactly,' Christian and I supported each other in co-constructing meaning.

When I here and now think back at this conversation with Christian, I recall the pleasant atmosphere and the lively conversation; there were scarcely any pauses between gestures and responses. Throughout the conversations, we, based on adjusted responses, co-authored an understanding of working with two strategic horizons, which became meaningful; it provided us with a here-and-now sense of certainty about the benefits of how it would be best to work strategically.

With the adjusted responses provided, Christian and I jointly reconstructed and further strengthened our respective understanding of existing norms, meaning structures, expectations, and ideas taken for granted as common sense (Mead, 1974). We allowed each other to quite rapidly rely on what we already knew and took to be true, including how the challenge Christian was facing could be dealt with in a certain way (McNamee, 2015).

A Need for Reflex and Reflective Actions

The complexity of life is incomprehensible. To be able to deal with this complexity people coordinate their actions. Through adjusted responses, people co-construct shared and local rituals, norms, meaning structures, and assumptions that are taken for granted. They come to shape how people communicate and what they believe is meaningful (McNamee, 2016; Shotter, 2008; Willert & Larsen, 2015).

Mead (1974) uses the term 'generalised other' (p. 154ff) to describe how society's multiple local groups function. The attitude of the generalised other represents locally accepted ways of acting and making sense of life that people in their local group can rely on in everyday practice (Mead, 1974). These attitudes are embodied, tacit, and shared; they enable people in a local group to function together, construct meaning, and make qualified guesses about what to expect next. They are also realised as people gesture in adjusted ways and give others an embodied sense of what it means to be a 'person of the world' (Gergen, 2014; McNamee & Hosking, 2012). The generalised other therefore helps people reduce complexity, construct meaning, and generate their way around the meshwork. As organisational members construct meaning, they prioritise one understanding and leave out many other possible understandings.

In everyday life, the embodied sense of what it means to be a person of the world leads to what Shotter terms as 'action guiding assumptions' and 'action guiding anticipations' (2006; 2008). They support people as they spontaneously and intuitively solve problems in ways that, within a given local interaction, are accepted and meaningful (Shotter, 2008). Action guiding anticipations and advisories represent shared and tacit assumptions, norms, meaning structures, standards, and assumptions that are rarely questioned locally (Cunliffe, 2002b; Shotter, 2008; 2010; Shotter & Billig, 1998). It therefore makes sense for a researcher to explore these assumptions together with organisational members through adjusted gestures, inasmuch as it allows the researcher and organisational member to generate knowledge about what it means to be 'a person of the world' in a given local 'somewhere.'

Even though Christian and I live our lives in different local inter-acts, we are here and now able to generate adjusted responses. By curiously exploring action guiding assumptions and anticipations constructed in earlier conversations and re-constructing them, knowledge about how strategizing unfolds in this local 'somewhere' emerges (McNamee & Hosking, 2012). Simultaneously, action guiding assumptions and anticipations are prefigurative; they indicate the appropriate here-and-now anticipations about strategizing (Gergen, 2010; Mead, 1934; Shotter, 2008).

Shotter's explanation of action guiding anticipations and advisories resembles what Cunliffe terms 'reflex' and 'reflective' actions (Cunliffe, 2002a; Shotter, 2008; 2010). Reflex actions are what Christian and I use in the previous excerpt when we for example smile or spontaneously utter words like 'exactly': situations where we instantaneously, in the moment, draw intuitively on our tacit knowledge and hold on to existing ways of making sense of a situation (Cunliffe, 2002a).

Reflective responses are responses that locally are understood as analytic, logical, and objective ways of acting and making sense out of a situation, event, or experience (Cunliffe, 2002a). They are 'a systematic thought process concerned with simplifying experience by searching for patterns, logic and order' (Cunliffe, 2002a: 38). Words such as 'incrementally' and 'retrospectively' emphasise existing understandings about strategy; they come to function as a 'rubber-stamp' to the understanding Christian and I co-constructed. As Christian replies with the word 'exactly,' our shared meaning construction becomes adjusted.

Reflex and reflective actions are pivotal to conversation partners as they, during conversations, enable people to create order out of a meshed world. They also enabled Christian and me to construct shared meaning about ourselves and the strategy work with which Christian is involved (Cunliffe, 2002a). A central part of gesturing in adjusted ways is to be curious about people's local reflex and reflective responses. As conversation partners communicate and explore organisational life, they help each other reflectively move understandings forward and re-construct them in more tangible ways (McNamee & Hosking, 2012).

This is where unfamiliarity can become a strength; when conversation partners do not take the same things for granted and live in different local 'somewheres,' reflex gestures are not uniform. If Christian and I want to construct here-and-now meaning and gesture in adjusted ways, we need to be curious and sensitive to the moment and relational processes. Being reflective and gesturing in adjusted ways supports this process.

How Can This Perspective Help a Researcher to Become a Resourceful Conversation Partner?

The perspective on conversations and organisational life thus presented is meant to be an inspiration for you on how you can engage in conversations with organisational members as a resourceful conversation partner. Furthermore, respect and be sensitive to the local reality that during the conversation is being co-constructed. It is about acknowledging that any understanding of organisational life emerges through here-and-now relational constructions of meaning, a process where researcher and organisational member both gesture and respond in adjusted ways; the second a researcher enters the door, he or she takes an active part in the relational co-construction processes.

It also revolves around embracing the unfamiliarity the researcher brings to the conversation. The researcher comes from another local inter-act than the organisational member, which means that the researcher sees the world from a different 'somewhere' than does the organisational member. The researcher's language and actions are filled with other emotional-volitional terms. The researcher also embodies different action guiding assumptions and advisories as he or she gestures and responds to other local assumptions, meaningful structures, and norms that are articulated. This happens instantaneously and can be used as a strength.

It can become a strength as the organisational member is in the same situation as the researcher; he or she sees the world from a 'somewhere' that differs from the researcher. The researcher and organisational member can use these differences as a resource as they communicate and engage in co-constructing the organisational life they are jointly exploring. It is a process where both the researcher and organisational member, incrementally and through their gestures and responses, are attentive and sensitive towards each other. It revolves around using adjusted responses to make room for reflective conversations by paying attention to both parties, as well as paying attention to the various understandings, perspectives, aspects, details, and dilemmas that emerge as the researcher and organisational member gesture and respond. The purpose of gesturing in adjusted ways is to enable local understandings to emerge and allow them to shape how the researcher and organisational member understand each other and to move forward in more tangible ways (Cunliffe, 2002b).

Using Adjusted Responses to Engage in Conversations with Organisational Members

The following suggestions are not intended to be understood as tools or strict methods a researcher should follow if he or she wants to use adjusted responses in the conversations with organisational members. They are meant as invitations where a researcher, together with an involved organisational member, constructs his or her own adjusted responses and practice. Engaging in such conversations is a craft and not a set of mechanisms. The researcher and organisational member jointly constitute the tool they jointly have to master (Cunliffe, 2002b). Adjusted responses are about relating processes and being sensitive to what is being generated and what emerges as communication unfolds.

1) Prepare to come to a conversation unprepared
2) Be curious and explore processes from within
3) Let the conversation take its origin in what presently matters, then co-construct a here-and-now sensible story
4) Acknowledge that it is possible to co-construct a story and not THE story
5) Count to ten and sometimes more
6) Move understandings forward but let them remain open

Prepare to Come to a Conversation Unprepared

Over the years, I have come to appreciate that conversations with organisational members are not something that one can plan from home. What one, as a researcher, can do instead is to prepare oneself to come to the meeting unprepared. The researcher has most likely chosen the field, topic, or issue to be explored. The researcher has probably also been involved in the choice of institution or organisation. Furthermore, prior to the visit, the researcher has been in contact with someone from the chosen organisation who has agreed on the research topic, whom the researcher should communicate with, and how long the collaboration will last. The researcher has most likely also read articles about the organisation, looked at its website, read annual reports, visited social media, etc. prior to his or her visit.

Having said that, maybe the best thing a researcher can do to prepare for the conversation is to let go of the illusion of being in control of the conversation. Instead, the researcher could focus on engaging in a symmetrical co-authoring conversation with the organisational member by being sensitive to what emerges as the conversation unfolds (McNamee & Hosking, 2012). It revolves around being what McNamee refers to as 'radically present' during the conversation and jointly figuring out how and about what it would be meaningful to converse (McNamee, 2016). The concept 'radically present' is explained further in the following chapter.

It is important to highlight that it is not a question of coming unprepared, but rather a realisation that if a researcher wants to engage in an explorative conversation, then it is impossible to plan the conversation in advance. To exemplify I will share a little story. Some years ago, a colleague and I were involved in a research project where we would spend several hours in a car driving to and from the companies that participated in the research project. Initially, when my colleague and I left the university and drove to various organisations to engage in conversations with leaders, we used the drive to discuss what WE believed were relevant topics and questions we should discuss. However, in the process, we soon realised that this preparation was counterproductive; it was impossible to plan what the right questions were or what the focus should be in the pending conversation. In order to ask the right questions, the organisational members and the researchers had to be in conversation with each other.

The more my colleague and I discussed and agreed upon what interesting topics to explore and discuss in the upcoming conversations, the more we re-constructed and further strengthened our own reflex responses and existing meaning structures about what we took for granted. In that process, my colleague and I forgot that the reason we wanted to talk with the organisation's leader was that we wanted to explore how organisational life and practice unfold more reflectively while understanding an organisation from another local perspective than ours.

As time went by, my colleague and I began to use the time in the car to talk about how we could prepare ourselves to come to the conversation unprepared. This did not mean that my colleague and I stopped talking as we drove to and from each organisation; we still talked and generated local knowledge and meaning about what WE believed would be interesting to explore and discuss with the leaders. My colleague and I knew that the knowledge generated in that process was meaningful to us as we sat in the car. However, we knew that we had to co-author different understandings together with the leaders as the research conversation began.

A researcher has to prepare himself or herself to enter the door of an organisation and engage in a joint conversation. The relating processes between the researcher and organisational member are where they jointly decide what they believe is meaningful and relevant to discuss and explore.

The following excerpt illustrates how coming unprepared for a conversation can be very good preparation. In the excerpt, I speak with Paul, the manager of a smaller regional hospital, and he tells me about some of his organisational challenges. His difficulties revolve around engaging in strategic dialogues with the region's General Health Board. In the excerpt, Paul shares an incident that illustrates some of the challenges he is facing. Subsequently, Paul and I begin exploring how Paul can deal with the challenges:

Paul (P): 'We had a General Health Board meeting last week and the Regional Health Director and I had a fierce debate which really wasn't pretty. He called me afterwards and left an apology on my answering machine asking me to call him back. And here I am so old and bull-headed that I have not contacted him (sighs). And we are both of us well aware that something has to be done. That is why my big challenge is how we get to bury the hatchet.'

Mette (M): 'It is difficult because before you get to bury the hatchet someone has to have the courage to act in ways you have not acted before.'

P: 'Exactly . . . and personally, I find it really difficult to pick up the phone and call him because what should we talk about?'

M: 'What would be sensible to talk about, what would you like to talk to him about?'

P: 'Why . . . uh, I cannot understand why he does not like this hospital.'

M: 'Could you imagine yourself asking him that question?'

P: 'I think that if we were to sit down in front of each other, we would be able to have a good conversation at the time. How things would go from there, I don't know.'

(Research conversation 1, Paul)

Paul and I had met each other one time before this conversation. I had no idea that the conversation we would engage in would revolve around this organisational challenge. Furthermore, and significant within this perspective, I did not have to know about this challenge in advance in order to engage with him as a resourceful conversation partner. Paul and I jointly co-authored in situ what we found relevant to talk about, and we explored how it would be meaningful to move forward. This incident and the reflections it led to emerged as Paul and I talked together and generated gestures and adjusted responses.

This narrative was not the first time Paul had shared this incident with someone, and it was not the first time I had heard about collaboration difficulties between managers and General Health Boards. Both of our experiences and prior relational engagements shaped how we gestured and responded. However, it was a unique moment Paul and I experienced as we discussed his challenging situation. Furthermore, it was that specific here-and-now moment that mattered as Paul and I explored how to make sense of what had happened, and how Paul could move on in a meaningful way.

What was pivotal to engage in this conversation with Paul was not a detailed, initial plan, but an in-situ interest in the conversation and being attentive to one another. Additionally, we both had to be willing to use the different gestures that emerged as invitations in the conversation. These invitations constructed adjusted responses that invited both of us to be reflective and re-work our existing memories of the past and anticipations about a desirable future, as well as generate new ways to move forward that we, at that given point, found meaningful.

As Paul and I communicated, we curiously explored how he could move forward with his challenge with the Regional Health Director in ways that aligned with his existing action-guiding anticipations and assumptions. We then jointly imagined how a conversation between Paul and the Regional Health Director could unfold, what questions Paul could ask, and how to raise those questions. The purpose of this exploration was not for Paul to have the exact same conversation with the Regional Health Director in the future, but to use the conversation as a space to engage in reflective and curious conversations about the challenges the hospital was facing that would enable him to move forward.

Be Curious and Explore Processes from within

Regarding the value of being curious and explorative, a significant reason why a researcher engages in conversations with organisational members is to know how the organisational meshwork is being constructed and lived in inter-acts that are local and different from his or hers. In that process, it is useful to be curious and leave behind any assumptions that the researcher knows a priori what is at stake.

A researcher is 'not-knowing' when it comes to knowledge about what it means to be a person of the world in a specific local inter-act (Anderson & Goolishian, 1997). If the researcher wants to be able to co-author knowledge about this, he or she must avoid engaging in reflex re-constructions of what the researcher takes for granted. Instead, the researcher should jointly and reflectively explore how the meshwork is understood and generated from the organisational member's 'somewhere' and how the organisational member can deal with the balls of yarn coming from other parts of the meshwork.

Co-constructing an understanding from 'within' the experience can support this move (Cunliffe, 2002b). Co-constructing knowledge from within revolves around being curious and never assuming what a given organisational challenge is centred around. The following excerpt is from another conversation with Paul. Observe how Paul and I engage in an explorative conversation about the meshed challenges he is experiencing by having too few tenured medicals at the hospital where he is a manager.

Paul (P): 'Yes, and there's also something political in this that hasn't been dealt with yet. We're running two emergency rooms and at some point, the politicians have to realise that it can't continue. Many doctors are retiring soon and we cannot find replacements and we cannot run a hospital based on substitutes.'

Mette (M): 'Is it a possibility for you to bring this up?'

P: 'Yes, and I have tried to a few times and it hasn't always been well received. It has been met with criticism. Either you can give them a festive speech or ignore matters. It's my experience that some really liked that I spoke my mind and others gave me a slap on the wrist and that's fair enough. It's part of my strategy to tell it like it is, and I don't think it comes as a surprise to anyone, they just don't think it's appropriate to talk about. There are some really strong opinions about this hospital (fetches a newspaper article and shows it to me). Based on the presentation I gave, she [a local politician] sent the Regional Health Director sixteen questions regarding the daily management of this hospital.'

M: 'Where was she heading with this?'

P: 'I think that she believes that the politicians should be more involved in the everyday management of the hospitals than they already are. When I'm with the Regional Executive Committee, they tell me that they expect that I bring down the number of medical beds because that's the political agenda. Then I present how I plan to do so in the best possible way, and then they tell me I closed down too many medical beds here.'

M: 'But that's the room to manoeuvre you have at your disposal?'

P: 'We're getting paid to run this hospital, and we're responsible for making these decisions.'

M: 'Are they closing you down?'

P: 'No, we're not closing.'

M: 'Well, what are you going to do with the tenured doctors and the substitutes?'

P: 'That is exactly the crux of the matter.'

(Research conversation 2, Paul)

Based on the curiosity and 'not-knowing' character of the gestures and adjusted responses Paul and I generated, we co-constructed how the current meshwork is understood and generated meaning from Paul's 'somewhere.' This co-construction emerged as Paul and I explored how he deals with the lack of tenured doctors and the reactions from local and regional politicians from 'within' concrete processes. Likewise, as the organisational challenge was discussed, Paul and I jointly articulated and re-constructed what, within this local inter-act, is being taken for granted and understood as common, though in more reflective and contextual ways.

Paul responded quickly and intuitively and referenced the strategy and presentation of the region's General Health Board. Paul was well aware of this challenge and, as he and I explored it through adjusted responses, we re-constructed this knowledge reflectively. What is assumed in each of our local 'somewhere' meshes with and shapes the gestures and adjusted responses we jointly co-constructed, allowing a unique meaning to emerge.

Initially, I argued that to become a resourceful conversation partner, a researcher must be very respectful, sensitive, and humble towards life within the local inter-act of interest. If the researcher wants to understand life in a local part of a meshwork, he or she must understand the processes from within that local part and be curious towards what is taken for granted and take part in re-constructing it as he or she here-and-now co-constructs adjusted responses.

As a researcher explores the processes from within, it is commonplace not to question what is already assumed, which is sensible. Before a researcher can question what is taken for granted, he or she must use adjusted responses and take part in co-constructing the taken-for-granted together with the person who lives within the local part of the meshwork. Paul and I must co-construct from within a sense of what is meaningful in the local 'somewhere' he lives in if we are to use our respective 'somewhere' as a strength to co-author other meaningful ways of dealing with the organisational challenge which occupies Paul.

Let the Conversation Take Its Origin in What Presently Matters, Then Co-Construct a Sensible Story in the Here and Now

A researcher often engages in conversations with the same organisational member several times during a research project. When a researcher has met with an organisational member multiple times, his or her life and organisational challenges have often changed, often quite intensely, since the last conversation. What may have concerned him or her previously is no longer as important; old concerns have been resolved and new ones have come to the fore. Each time this happens a researcher has to smile; it is a reminder of how people live their lives in a long line of unique now-nesses.

Though the researcher may have met the organisational member before, each conversation is a unique encounter where they meet each other for the first time. In that process, the researcher and the organisational member draw on previous co-constructed conversations, but they must meet each other in the relational present to start the conversation about what matters here and now and take part in co-constructing the present sensible story. This often requires the researcher and organisational member to jointly co-author past experiences and desirable futures differently as they gesture and respond adjusted to each other.

To enable this, the organisational member and the researcher must, as discussed in the previous point, jointly re-construct what was initially presumed. The researcher and the organisational member have to, through curious exploration, co-construct a present sense of how processes are understood and dealt with from within the local 'somewhere' in the meshwork. Based on that knowledge, they can begin to question and use their respective 'somewheres' as a strength to co-author other meaningful ways to understand and deal with the organisational challenge.

In the following excerpt, I am talking with Laura, who is head of the Department of Regional Development in one of the Danish Regions. Prior to the excerpt, Laura and I had co-constructed, based on an exploration of her current challenges from within her organisation, a sense of how life is, what is taken for granted, and what is understood as common sense in the local 'somewhere' where Laura lives.

During the conversation, Laura and I discuss how she often says yes to extra assignments because it energises her even though she is aware that it also taxes her energy. Nevertheless, Laura sometimes feels that she is taken advantage of, which demotivates her. Earlier in the conversation, Laura explained that she was asked to take over the responsibility of a department for a year when a colleague was on maternity leave. Under those circumstances, no one encouraged her to think about or care for herself; looking back on it now, it frustrates her. In the excerpt, Laura and I return to the situation and jointly question her reflex and intuitive understanding of the challenge.

Mette (M): 'I'm thinking of the situation where you were asked to manage a department while your colleague was on maternity leave. What would you have needed that someone had told you?'

Laura (L): 'Well, I think I would have needed for someone to tell me to remember to take care of myself and not always only care about or act according to the well-being of the organisation. Someone could have said – and one of my personal acquaintances did say – that I shouldn't let myself be taken advantage of.'

M: 'Did you feel taken advantage of in this situation?'

L: 'I don't know. It was a mixture between being taken advantage of, and at the same time thinking, they must really trust me to let me handle this I know that when the Regional Director asked me to do this, it was because he didn't know what else to do. But, yes, he did use me and I know without a shadow of a doubt that I would have done the same if I had been in his situation.'

M: 'What if we put in a third alternative? You're very propelled by what's in the organisation's interest more than what's in your own, right?'

L: 'Yes.'

M: 'If we view this from that perspective, and for a moment don't think about you being taken advantage of, and think that you did what was in the best interest of the organisation, what would your response be then?'

L: 'Then I think I would reply that it was the best possible solution because you couldn't hire a temporary employee to manage a department and really there was no other solution. The fact of the matter is that everybody was quite content with the outcome. The employees were happy, the board of managers were happy, and the politicians were happy; they had all been allowed to perform their tasks as they found most beneficial and they were a bit concerned that this would change once the manager returned. It was a good solution for the organisation.'

(Research conversation 1, Laura)

As Laura and I gestured, we engaged in a reflective co-authoring process where we explored and questioned the reflex meaning constructed earlier. The future Laura and I co-constructed as desirable during the conversation was one where Laura took an active part in developing the Region and solving managerial challenges that required attention. However, the memory of feeling like she had been used still frustrated Laura; it made it difficult for her to move forward in a meaningful way.

Previous conversations with Laura had not proved this organisational challenge to be relevant, though it became relevant during this conversation. We therefore began the conversation in what mattered in the moment, and jointly co-constructed a new story. Laura and I began to embrace how people live in multiple, once-occurring local and unique inter-acts, where the meaning people construct here and now is what matters.

Due to my unfamiliarity with what in Laura's local 'somewhere' is taken for granted, it became possible for Laura and me to question the spontaneous action guiding assumptions and reflex actions initially being articulated. We could engage in a reflective exploration of how existing meaning structures and embodied action guiding assumptions could change, and jointly we questioned the existing memory of the past by co-constructing a different meaning. It then became possible, due to Laura's engagement in the development of the Region and the energy she gets from contributing to extra assignments, to replace the feeling of being taken advantage of and reconstruct what was taken for granted in reflective ways that allowed Laura to move forward in other and more meaningful ways.

Acknowledge That It Is Possible to Co-construct a Story and Not THE Story

To take part in jointly constructing a meaningful understanding of processes is, as mentioned in the beginning of the chapter, also a question of reducing complexity in one way at the expense of others. It is a question of engaging in one local reality construction and not others from a 'somewhere' in the meshwork. As a researcher engages in a conversation with an organisational member, he or she unavoidably takes part in shaping how the ball of yarn continues it, ay, meshes with other balls of yarn and makes new entanglements.

The following excerpt is from another conversation with Laura. She and I further explore how she feels trapped between being energised from taking on extra assignments and knowing that it taxes her energy, which ultimately can be a health risk if she continues at the same pace.

Laura (L): 'Well, I would have to say that I get a high from doing several exciting assignments for a period of time and making them all work. I think when I look back, I lived off an adrenalin rush for a year or so where everything was on full blast, but afterwards, I felt it. I didn't talk to anyone about it at the time, and I was completely exhausted afterwards, which tells me that it is not good for me to work at that pace for a whole year. Exhaustion is a stress reaction, and I am well aware of its dangers.'

Mette (M): 'Yes.'

L: 'And that has made me think that no one will come and give me a gold medal if I get a stroke because I worked too much or too hard. There is only one person who can look after me and that's me.'

M: 'Yes, and in relation to other people, you're absolutely certain that they need others to get by. You're caught in a paradox where it makes a lot of sense to do all of this because problems are solved.'

L: 'Yes.'

M: 'And things are moving in the right direction, but at the same time, achievements are coming a bit at the expense of you and your personal energy, and then you collapse.'

L: 'Yes, yes.'

M: 'And if you ask me, I don't think it can be an either/or because if you begin turning down assignments, then the joy you feel about your work will vanish, but if you keep at it at the same pace, then it will have some undesirable consequences for you. So how can you come up with a compromise that isn't an either/or? That would be extremely interesting for you to explore.'

L: 'Yes, and maybe that's my big challenge.'

(Research conversation 2, Laura)

As we explored how to untangle the meshed lines in which Laura has caught herself, we reduced its complexity by first identifying the crux of the paradox. We then considered how Laura could deal with the paradox in different ways, allowing her to still do what energises her without critically taxing her energy.

In a reflective conversation about how Laura could deal with this organisational challenge, we constructed the paradox by different and more tangible means that manifested other meaningful ways to move forward. In this process of minimising risk, Laura and I jointly co-constructed a way that enabled Laura to disentangle herself by engaging in the paradoxical processes differently.

There are several ways both Laura and I could also have gestured and responded to reduce the complexity differently. We could have dwelt on the health issues Laura feared, explored why Laura's superiors did not protect her from taking on extra assignments, co-constructed a different understanding, or supported another facet of the meshwork. The reduced complexity, spoken gestures, and responses were only partially conscious choices. They emerged incrementally as we communicated in ways in which Laura and I in our gestures and responses were attentive and sensitive to each other and the differences in what we each took for granted. Based on these differences, a meaningful way forward was co-authored and supported. The way the story was co-authored is also a question of relational reflexivity. I am an organisational researcher and not, for example, a psychological or medical researcher; exploring psychological or medical aspects of Laura's paradox would not be ethical. The conversation, therefore, revolved around organisational areas where the knowledge shared within my local 'somewhere' can mesh with knowledge shared in Laura's local 'somewhere.'

Count to Ten and Sometimes More

As a researcher, it is pivotal to appreciate the virtues of listening, silence, and allowing time to work its wonders. People especially need time when a researcher and an organisational member begin to question things taken for granted and invite each other to respond in different ways than their reflex responses. It is a question about 'listening with,' when a researcher must remain curious and open to what will come (McNamee & Hosking, 2012: 78). A process is allowed which provides space for reflection and time for the organisational member to respond (McNamee & Hosking, 2012).

I rehearse it each time I as a researcher engage in conversations with organisational members; even the simple task of counting to ten slowly is relaxing and can help. When the researcher reaches the count of ten and nothing has been said, it is then a question of being sensitive to what takes place and relationally and tacitly deciding if it is time for either one of us to say something or begin counting to ten again.

The following excerpt is from a third conversation with Christian. Previous to the excerpt and during other conversations, Christian and I explored how Christian enjoys and thrives on challenges that are complex and sometimes almost impossible to solve. In the concrete situation presented as follows, Christian explained that management had just succeeded in turning the company around in a big way, and everything was operating smoothly. However, based on Christian's non-verbal communication and the intonation in his voice, the sense that these changes had not sufficiently challenged him emerges. In the following excerpt, Christian and I talk about what energises him and how he could make room for more exploration in his organisational practice, who could challenge him inside the management team, and what he needs from his superiors relating to being a leader.

Notice how Christian and I gesture and respond in ways that make it clear that existing, reflex, and embodied action guiding assumptions, advisories, and what is normally taken for granted fall short as we make room to be more reflective and generate and co-author something new:

Mette (M):	'You need to get out of your comfort zone.'
Christian (C):	'But I like it in there.' (Laughter)
C:	'Yes, and now I've spent a lot of years working on this turnaround where I wasn't in any comfort zone, but now I am. Is this what great leaders do?'
M:	'It depends on what you want to do as a leader, but as I see you, you want to leave behind comfort, and then you do the more challenging things, I guess. There's new realisation in going places you haven't been before. As I see you, you seek that, and I don't think you'll get there if you stay where you are right now.'
C:	'Mmm.'
M:	'That is also the reason why I am challenging you here.'
C:	'Mmm.'
M:	'What does it take for you to get to where you have fun?'
C:	'That's also where I feel that spark, where there's really something exciting going on. (fifteen seconds silence) I guess that James and that Charlie (employees in the organisation). I could use some of that, he [James] thinks big sometimes.'
M:	'Yes, maybe this is the place to start?'
C:	'Mmm. Yes, yes. (five seconds pause) I'm going into my mode. This is exciting. How can I move forward from here? Yes, mmm. How do I put this into action and do something? This is what drives me, to initiate something that leads to something else. It takes a bit of practice. How can I let go of everything else? I think I have to practice letting go.'
M:	'And find out who you want to let go of things with, who would you like to practice with? To get to that you need someone else to go with you.'
C:	'Yes.' (eight seconds pause) 'I'll try to work on that, Mette!' (Laughter)

(Research conversation 3, Christian)

As shown, there were multiple pauses in this excerpt, more hesitation; the conversation does not run as smoothly as the previous excerpts. This is not a sign, however, that the conversation was unproductive or that no meaning was co-constructed. This excerpt was chosen to illustrate what can happen when an organisational member and a researcher jointly use the researcher's non-organisational anchoring and different action guiding assumptions, advisories, meaning structures, norms, and taken-for-granted assumptions as resources: resources to co-author a new and different advantageous future.

Though it might seem unorthodox to establish silence, as well as count to ten or more multiple times during a conversation, the decision to make room for such silence is a joint process between the researcher and the organisational member. This decision is often made tacitly and in the moment; it is not something that can be forced or decided in advance. It emerges out of the conversation, making it reflective and enabling the researcher and organisational member to embrace the conversation as a free space where they can engage in imaginative talk about a possible future. As this future is discussed and visualised, multiple ways of shaping the meshwork will emerge. In such a process, both the researcher and organisational member must acknowledge that if existing action-guiding anticipations and assumptions are to be reworked, pauses and silences are necessary.

Move Understandings Forward but Let Them Remain Open

One of the benefits of being a researcher and engaging in conversations with organisational members is the room for exploration without the necessity of making a decision. Research conversations are based on a shared interest in the topic, processes, challenges, paradoxes, etc. being explored. Different understandings which enrich each other are allowed to connect. Most commonplace conversations within organisational settings cannot be characterised in this way. In the following excerpt, Christian and I embrace the absence of a decision; we move forward and jointly construct new meaning. At no point do we discuss or settle on what Christian's next action should be; we keep the issues open for future explorations and meaningful constructions.

As in the previous excerpt, the following one depicts a free, imaginative, and creative discussion about what a desirable future might look like. There are also pauses here, and the communication is more abrupt as Christian and I jointly gesture and respond in curious and explorative ways. In this excerpt, Christian and I explore how we can make the abstract idea about a think tank more concrete.

Christian (C): 'Yes, and how the hell are we going to make Christian's think tank?'
Mette (M): 'Yes, who should be in it and who can help you build it?'
C: 'Yes, I have to find someone to help me build it.'
M: 'Yes, and it's no good if it's all based on your ideas, then we're back to square one.'

C: (ten seconds pause) 'Yes, I don't have a clue on how to do this.'
M: No, and if you did, it would be too easy. Then it wouldn't be a challenge and it has to be a challenge.' (Laughter)
C: 'Yes, I know, Mette. I realise that, but it's just – ohhh can we not do this? This is too bloody difficult.'
M: 'Of course you cannot do it.'
C: 'I know, but it's just my first intuition. This really sounds like hard work. Can't we just call someone and have him do it? Ohhh.' (Laughter)
M: 'I don't think it would make sense to you then. It has to be a challenge.'
C: 'I agree, and this is what motivates me. I want it to be challenging.'
M: 'And you cannot keep working on these challenges alone.'
C: (five seconds pause) 'No, I can't and it isn't what I want either.'
M: 'Maybe the road to get there is to think about who can ask you necessary questions?'
C: 'There is this Charlie guy (employee). I can use him. He would be able to go into this with an open mind. He would be able to ask questions where I would be "checkmate". Maybe, maybe not, but I could try. He dares to challenge me, and he isn't afraid to speak his mind. I wonder if he knows anyone else. At least it's a place to start. I wonder where I can find such a forum? It's not a professional forum, it's such a peculiar one.'

(Research conversation 3, Christian)

To embrace the value of the non-organisational anchoring means respecting that if parts of the free and imaginative talk have come to life within different local 'somewheres', then they have to be talked and acted into existence jointly by those who live in those local inter-acts. In that process, the researcher must acknowledge that what he or she and the organisational member here and now find meaningful and desirable will be co-authored differently and lead to different practices in future heres and nows.

There is no reason for Christian and me to reach a solution or decision about how the think tank should be realised. The future of the think tank will be constructed jointly in the subsequent encounters in which Christian and others from his or other local 'somewheres' engage. It will be based on the gestures and adjusted responses that they co-author. Christian and I, therefore, gesture and respond in ways that open up future co-authoring with others with an organisational anchoring. Christian could also continue the conversation with other organisational members if he wanted to further develop the idea of a think tank. The idea could develop into something else, or never be touched upon again.

There is nothing extraordinary about this way of conversing with organisational members. People live in one unique here-and-now encounter after another, and with each encounter, a new meaning is co-constructed. What may be extraordinary is that I here embrace it as a practice in research conversations with organisational members. To understand this as a research practice does not alter that we all live in brief and fleeting moments; the best any researcher can do is to engage in these moments with organisational members and attempt to co-construct new and meaningful ways to move forward. Further, researchers should allow future encounters to decide how meaningful conversations can remain meaningful by being co-authored differently.

Using Adjusted Responses to Engage in Conversations with Organisational Members

In this chapter, I have presented one take on how a researcher can engage in conversations with organisational members by using adjusted responses to work towards becoming a resourceful conversation partner. Along with this, I have theoretically positioned these practices and offered glimpses into my practice. It is now a question of how one might apply these practices in future conversations. This is a reasonable question because I have not left you with any specific method or set of tools to guarantee perfect execution.

The strength of all of this is that you master parts of this already. You have a lifelong experience with engaging in conversations in your everyday practice. The way forward is to rely on such experiences and work towards personalizing a practice with relevant organisational members and engage them in conversation. In addition, one must accept that gesturing in adjusted ways is a handicraft that is continually developed. Only by being sensitive and attentive to the communication in each encounter with the organisational member can the researcher, together with the organisational member, figure out if it is time to count to ten or say something, support the reconstruction of what is being taken for granted or question it, or explore new ways of moving forward. Lastly, one must accept that occasionally, despite good intentions and hard work, some conversations go haywire, even for seasoned researchers.

All conversations are characterised by both adjusted and unadjusted responses. Looking at the excerpts presented in this chapter, it is clear that the majority strive towards co-constructing adjusted responses, minimising complexity and figuring out how to move forward in what are considered meaningful conversations where the researcher and organisational member, jointly and from within a local 'somewhere,' re-construct existing norms, meaning structures, and what they take for granted. One must allow each other to rely on known and existing action-guiding advisories and anticipations; conversations like these are necessary, for they help the organisational member and researcher to reduce complexity, as well as enable them to understand the challenges they are facing and decide how to deal with them rapidly (McNamee, 2015).

The strength of these conversations is that they are very constructive. Communication based primarily on adjusted responses is beneficial because it creates space for reflective conversations where a researcher and organisational member can co-construct an organisational challenge in more tangible and significant ways; this allows for new, meaningful paths forward to emerge.

The following chapter builds on the ideas presented in this chapter and explores how to jointly pause the immediate reflex and reflective relational construction of meaning by also using unadjusted responses in conversations, as well as making room for reflexivity and co-authoring new meanings and possible ways to move forward.

References

Anderson, H. & Goolishian, H. (1997) The Client Is the Expert: A Not-Knowing Approach to Therapy. In McNamee, S. & Gergen, K. J. (eds.) *Therapy as Social Construction*, London, Sage, pp. 25–39.

Boje, D. M. (1995) Stories of Storytelling Organization: A Postmodern Analysis of Disney as Tamara-land, *Academy of Management Journal*, 38 (4), 997–1035.

Cunliffe, A. L. (2001) Managers as Practical Authors: Reconstructing Our Understanding of Management Practice. *Journal of Management Studies*, 38 (3), 35–371.

Cunliffe, A. L. (2002a) Reflexive Dialogical Practice in Management Learning. *Management Learning*, 33 (1), 35–61.

Cunliffe, A. L. (2002b) Social Poetics as Management Inquiry—a Dialogical Approach. *Journal of Management Inquiry*, 11 (2), 128–146.

Cunliffe, A. L. (2003) Reflexive Inquiry in Organizational Research: Questions and Possibilities. *Human Relations*, 56 (8), 983–1003.

Gergen, K. J. (2009) *Relational Being: Beyond the Individual and Community*. Oxford, Oxford University Press.

Gergen, K. J. (2010) Co-Constitution, Causality and Confluence Organizing in a World Without Entities Draft. In: Hernes, T. & Maitlis, S. (eds.) *Process, Sensemaking, and Organizing*, Oxford, Oxford University Press, pp. 55–69.

Gergen, K. J. (2014) From Mirroring to World-Making: Research as Future Forming. *Journal for the Theory of Social Behaviour*, 45 (3), 1–24.

Gergen, K. & Thatchenkery, T. (2004) Organization Science as Social Construction Postmodern Potentials. *The Journal of Applied Behavioral Science*, 40 (2), 228–249.

Hosking, D. (2010) Moving Relationality: Meditations on a Relational Approach to Management. In: Bryman, A. et al. (eds.) *SAGE Handbook of Leadership*. Thousand Oaks, CA, SAGE Publications.

Ingold, T. (2008) *Lines. A Brief Story*. Oxon, Routledge.

Ingold, T. (2010) Footprints Through the Weather-World: Walking, Breathing, Knowing. *Journal of the Royal Anthropological Institute*, 16 (1), 113–135.

Kornberger, M. (2013) Disciplining the Future: On Studying the Politics of Strategy. *Scandinavian Journal of Management*, 29(1), 104–107.

Lugo, N., Celis, R. & McNamee, S. (2014) Emergence and Evolution of Social Constructionist Ideas: A Conversation with Sheila McNamee. *University Psychology* 13(1), 381–390.

McNamee, S. (2000) The Social Poetics of relationally engaged research. In Deissler, K. & McNamee, S. (eds.) *Phil und Sophie auf der couch: Die sozialepoesietherapeutischergesprache* [Philosophy in therapy: The social poetics of therapeutic conversations] Heidelberg, Carl-Auer_SystemeVerlag, pp. 146–156.

McNamee, S. (2012) From Social Construction to Relational Construction: Practices From the Edge, *Psychological Studies*, 57(2), 150–156.

McNamee, S. (2015) Radical Presence: Alternatives to the Therapeutic State. *The European Journal of Psychotherapy and Counselling*, 17(4), 373–383.

McNamee, S. (2016) The Ethics of Relational Process: John Shotter's Radical Presence. In: Corcoran, T. & Cromby, J. (eds.) *Joint Action: Essays in Honour of John Shotter*, Oxon, Routledge, pp. 89–101.

McNamee, S. & Hosking, D. M. (2012) *Research and Social Change—a Relational Constructionist Approach*. New York, Routledge.

Mead, G. H. (1934) *The Philosophy of the Present*. London, The Open Court Company Publishers.

Mead, G. H. (1974) *Mind, Self and Society From the Standpoint of a Social Behaviorist*. Chicago, Chicago University Press.

Ripamonti, S., Galuppo, L., Gorli, M., Scaratti, G. & Cunliffe, A. (2016) Pushing Action Research Toward Reflexive Practice. *Journal of Management Inquiry*, 25(1), 55–68.

Shotter, J. (1990) The Social Construction of Remembering and Forgetting. In: Middleton, D. & Edwards, D. (eds.) *Collective Remembering*. London, Sage, pp. 120–138.

Shotter, J. (2006) Understanding Process From Within: An Argument for 'Withness'-Thinking. *Organization Studies*, 27 (4), 585–604.

Shotter, J. (2008) Dialogism and Polyphony in Organizing Theorizing in Organization Studies: Action Guiding Anticipations and Continuous Creation of Novelty. *Organization Studies*, 4 (29), 501–524.

Shotter, J. (2010) Situated Dialogic Action Research Disclosing 'Beginnings' for Innovative Change in Organizations. *Organizational Research Methods*, 13 (2), 268–285.

Shotter, J. & Billig, M. (1998) A Bakhtinian Psychology: From Out of the Heads of Individuals and into the Dialogues Between Them. In: Bell, M. & Gardner, M.E. (eds.) *Bakhtin and the Human Sciences: No Last Words*, London, Sage, pp. 13–29.

Shotter, J. & Cunliffe, A. L. (2002) Managers as Practical Authors: Everyday Conversations for Action. In: Holman, D. & Thorpe, R. (eds.) *Management and Language: The Manager as Practical Author*, London, Sage, pp. 15–37.

Vološinov, V. (1986) *Marxism and the Philosophy of Language*. Harvard, Harvard University Press.

Willert, S. & Larsen, M. (2015) Leaders' Use of Maps, Guiding Images and Momentary Meaningful Actions. In: Larsen, M. V. & Rasmussen, J. G. (eds.) *Relational Perspectives on Leading*. London, Palgrave Macmillan, pp. 129–152.

3 Exploring Unadjusted Gestures and Responses in Research Conversations with Organisational Members

Mette Vinther Larsen

Introduction

Similar to the previous chapter, the following chapter revolves around what it means to engage in research conversations from a relational constructionism perspective as a resourceful conversation partner. There is nothing in the method that necessitates that these conversations have to be between a researcher and a leader. As mentioned in the last chapter, such conversations also take place between researchers, students, and consultants and middle managers, employees, board members, etc.

What characterises these conversations is that they often take place between people who do not usually spend time together. The purpose of these conversations is to explore current and, from the leader's perspective, relevant organisational challenges with someone who is not personally involved in the organisational challenge, but who is prepared to reflexively explore multiple perspectives of an organisational challenge. To use unadjusted responses in conversations is to engage in a 'prospective and unfinalized dialogical form of talk' (Shotter, 2010: 275). In that process, the researcher and organisational member jointly seek to construct answers to organisational problems in other ways or, as Shotter states, 'We can achieve jointly what we cannot achieve apart' (2010: 275).

In the previous chapter, I presented and argued that using adjusted responses in research conversations is pivotal if a researcher without an organisational anchoring desires to take part in co-constructing knowledge about how organisational life unfolds. This chapter follows up on this point and introduces what is meant by the phrase 'unadjusted responses', theoretically and practically. As you read this chapter, consider previous research conversations you already have taken part in and reflect upon how to invite organisational members into exploring unadjusted responses.

A significant assumption in a relational constructionism perspective revolves around the understanding that in organisational life, or in parts of it, a researcher must contribute in a respectful, sensitive, and humble way. Gesturing in adjusted ways can support this; it is a way of conversing that ensures the local taken-for-granted understandings and actions that a researcher and organisational member jointly explore are acknowledged. If the term 'adjusted responses' is unfamiliar, please refer to Chapter 2. Using unadjusted responses in conversations with organisational members adds an extra dimension to research conversations. Gesturing and responding in unadjusted ways means to momentarily pause the immediate and instantaneous relational construction of meaning that using adjusted responses enables conversation partners. Unadjusted responses in conversations invite the researcher and organisational member to explore the consequences of how life is being lived within a local 'somewhere' and how people's actions and communication contribute to constructing this local life. Thus, gesturing in unadjusted ways explores if life could and maybe how it should be lived differently and what that would demand of the organisational members.

Making Room for Unadjusted Responses in Research Conversations

The following excerpt is from a research conversation between the author and an organisational member which exemplifies how unadjusted responses are used jointly to explore different ways of understanding organisational life. The example illustrates how the organisational member participates in co-constructing the organisational problem that concerns him. It also illustrates certain reactions a researcher can be met with as unadjusted responses are introduced. The excerpt stems from a conversation with Paul, the manager of a relatively small regional hospital. In the conversation, he explains how difficult it is for him to engage in strategic dialogues with the region's General Health Board. Paul does not trust what the board says owing to the fact that in the past it has redacted strategic decisions it has made regarding the regional hospital or, as it had in this case, taken the credit for a local production increase rather than credit Paul and the staff.

Paul is upset about this. In the conversation, Paul and I have primarily used adjusted responses to co-construct knowledge about how the situation is understood from Paul's local 'somewhere.' This knowledge is necessary for Paul and me to co-construct; it is only by building up knowledge of the dilemma from within the local 'somewhere' Paul lives in that we are able to explore and generate knowledge about other ways Paul can communicate with the regional General Health Board in the future. Paul has a meeting with the regional General Health Board the following week and wishes the dialogue during the meeting to be more constructive than it had previously been. We therefore begin to gesture in unadjusted ways and use my non-organisational anchoring as a resource that allows us to explore different ways Paul can understand and deal with the dilemma.

Mette (M): 'What if you tried to look at it from their [the regional General Health Board's] perspective?'
Paul (P): 'I don't know.' (Whistles) 'It [the problem] has something to do with how you think. Some people care for others and some only take care of themselves.'

M: 'Could looking at it from their perspective help you next week when you have to take part in the meeting? Could you say to yourself, "I might have handled this differently if I were in their shoes, but since we are here how can I work constructively from here on out, so we can get closer to having a strategic dialogue"?"' (Paul coughs slightly) 'It is not that I do not understand you, I do.'
P: 'It pisses me off!'
M: 'It might be completely incomprehensible and against reasonable thinking, but that does not help you in your everyday practice.'
P: 'No, that's right.'
M: 'There is a risk that these meetings turn out to become a play where you all act in certain ways during the meeting, use certain language, draw on certain discourses and realise that you already knew before the meeting how it would play out. Someone has to break it, change the game and invite all of you to play different parts and play differently. I mean, what is the worst that could happen at this point?'
P: 'Well, nothing terrible, and things cannot get any worse than they already are.'

(Research conversation 1, Paul)

Notice how the questioning of reflex responses regarding Paul's relationship with the regional General Health Board is not taken lightly. When a researcher introduces unadjusted responses, he or she will likely be met with humming, whistling, shifting anxiously in the chair, or even searching for the nearest exit. Despite these fleeting and – I promise – bypassing moments of discomfort, the use of unadjusted responses enables conversation partners to realise the part they also play in the mesh in which they have entangled themselves in and want to escape. Through unadjusted gestures and responses, Paul and I jointly decided to continue exploring how he also contributes to the dilemma, though it was a difficult and uncomfortable moment.

How Unadjusted Responses Can Pause the Immediate and Joined Construction of Meaning

The ideas behind unadjusted responses are inspired by Mead's understanding of how meaning is constructed relationally between people as they communicate and present each other with gestures and responses (1934; 1974). Mead argues that every gesture can be understood not only as a response but as an invitation that calls for an adjusted response if people are to construct new meaning (1974). In the previous excerpt, I do not respond with an adjusted response to Paul's gesture, as it would have re-constructed existing knowledge and meaning. Instead, I offer an unadjusted response that momentarily gives pause to the ongoing meaning construction. Paul and I invite each other into a reflexive exploration of what reality we are co-constructing as we communicate the way we do.

It is significant to underscore that every conversation consists of both adjusted and unadjusted ways of gesturing. Adjusted responses are often used more frequently than unadjusted responses, though how and when it is sensible to shift between them are choices the researcher and organisational member must make as they converse. It is a matter of being sensitive towards one another, respecting local knowledge and being curious about what is co-constructed as the conversation unfolds.

The inspiration to work with unadjusted responses emerges from reading Mead's philosophy on time (1934). Mead argues that people live in the present and that all of their memories about the past and their anticipation towards the future are constructed between people in the concrete present in which they are involved (1934). Mead's theory is similar to such relational constructionists as McNamee and Hosking (2012), Gergen (2010), and Shotter and Billig (1998), who argue that 'now-ness' is all there is. People live their lives in one unique encounter after the next and the meaning they construct here and now determines how organisational life unfolds and takes shape within the given local 'somewhere'. Gesturing in unadjusted ways 'reminds' researchers and organisational members alike about the multiple omnipresent possibilities to co-construct organisational life.

What the presented thoughts and 'unadjusted responses' show is an acceptance of the ontological aspect of language. What many researchers have noticed as they explore organisational life is that it consists of multiple local 'somewheres' where people think and act differently. Despite or because of this, organisational life continues, deadlines are met, and agreements upheld.

Accepting these multiple and polyphonic understandings and practices can enrich organisational life in the different local 'somewheres' as well as generate new possibilities for solving some of the organisational problems that emerge between conversation partners. This requires researchers and organisational members to leave behind the assumption that there is one best way to deal with an organisational challenge in which they have become entangled; instead, they should be reflexive and curiously engage in co-constructing multiple best ways of dealing with the organisational challenge. This practice relies on exploring alternatives and uncertainty, for 'while certainty . . . logically sounds appealing to us, it is precisely the stance that closes us to alternative views' (McNamee, 2012: 155).

To gesture in unadjusted ways, researchers and organisational members must leave behind certainty to make room for alternative views. This is, as argued previously and in the previous chapter, extremely difficult for people who coexist in a local 'somewhere'. Like Paul, people embody local knowledge that gives them an idea of what it means to be a competent member of an organisation (Cunliffe & Shotter, 2006). By relying on their shared generalised other and complying with their embodied action guiding assumptions, an organisational member can re-construct his or her local knowledge of what it means to be a person of the world in the local 'somewhere' where they live.

Nevertheless, organisational life consists of multiple local 'somewheres' that coexist in our everyday practice (Cunliffe & Shotter, 2006: 124). People are often unaware of how their everyday actions and conversations lead to local re-constructions of what they already take for granted within the local inter-act (Shotter, 2010). In the previous excerpt, Paul begins to whistle and replies with 'I don't know' as the unadjusted response is presented. This is not because he does not want to take part in exploring the dilemma he faces. It is merely not common sense to gesture and respond like this in the local 'somewhere' where he lives. To become reflexive, Paul and I must enable each other to see how our way of talking and acting are simply local and only represent a limited number of ways to move forward (Cunliffe, 2002b).

To explore unadjusted responses in conversations with organisational members is a joint move by the researcher and the organisational member to move away from questioning whether a certain action was 'right' or 'wrong'. It instead becomes a joint exploration of what local realities are being generated as a result of the actions that are being carried out within the local 'somewhere' where the organisational members live, and how these actions relate to others carried out within other local 'somewheres' in the meshwork (Shotter, 2010). It is, therefore, an invitation for both the organisational member and the researcher to look at a given case or problem differently (Shotter, 2010), and from afresh explore alternatives to how the organisational dilemma has emerged and how it can be dealt with (Cunliffe, 2002a).

In order to be a resourceful conversation partner, a researcher must pay attention to the understandings, perspectives, details, and aspects of an assumed dilemma and allow these elements to shape an unadjusted response. In the previous excerpt, Paul and I both respect what is taken for granted within Paul's local 'somewhere.' 'It might be completely incomprehensible and against reasonable thinking.' Simultaneously we question it: 'but that does not help you in your everyday practice.' It is not a question of forcing Paul to believe what is taken for granted within my local 'somewhere'; it is a process of using our respective differences as a resource that enables us to construct new meanings and move forward in ways we both find meaningful.

Gesturing and Responding in Unadjusted Ways Supports Reflexivity

The previous chapter introduced reflective responses as a method of gesturing in adjusted ways that allow a researcher and organisational member to minimize complexity and construct locally reliable meanings through channels of communication. Cunliffe presents the term 'reflexivity' as a third way of communicating and acting (2002). Reflexivity in conversations is an invitation to complexify thinking, explore dilemmas or doubts, and co-construct other solutions and understandings (Cunliffe, 2002a). To engage in reflexive conversations is to acknowledge and embrace the ontological understanding of language (Cunliffe, 2002a). Language is, as presented in the previous chapter, generative and reality constituting (Cunliffe, 2002a; Gergen & Thatchenkery, 2004; McNamee & Hosking, 2012).

As a researcher engages in a conversation with an organisational member, they do not talk about the member's organisational life. On the contrary, they jointly construct, de-construct, or change the very organisational life they are attempting to understand as they converse and construct meaning (Cunliffe, 2002b).

Embracing how researchers continually take part in co-constructing organisational life can provoke anxiety, though researchers and organisational members are not solely responsible for constructed meanings or the actions those constructions lead to; life is far too complex and meshed to formulate such simple connections. Meaning emerges and actions are initiated frequently and, for the most part, occur in spontaneous embodied and instantaneous ways without people being aware of it (Shotter, 2010; Mead, 1974).

The significance of language's ontology is that it often makes sense – at least once in a while – to be reflexive about it. Furthermore, the organisational lives researchers and organisational members co-construct during research conversations support the realities organisational members desire. For a researcher to be reflexive in conversations with organisational members means to work actively with their respective abilities to shape and co-construct the reality around them in multiple ways (Cunliffe, 2002a). Gesturing in unadjusted ways can support this reflexivity.

By engaging in reflexive conversations, the researcher and organisational member can assist one another to see how their own ways of talking and acting are guided by embodied, local, action-guiding anticipations and assumptions (Cunliffe, 2002a). Local knowledge within one 'somewhere' cannot account for meanings, action-guiding assumptions, anticipations, and what is assumed in other local 'somewheres.' This is where the researcher's non-organisational anchoring can be a resource. Different ways to act and understand a given organisational challenge do not have to be problematic; being curious and responsive to several possible actions and ways of understanding a given organisational challenge can enable 'infinite possibilities' to emerge (Cunliffe, 2002b; Cunliffe & Shotter, 2006; McNamee, 2016). Gesturing in unadjusted ways allows for the immediate co-construction of meaning to momentarily pause and encourage new understandings to incrementally emerge.

Having taken part in several of these conversations, I have to come to know that it can sometimes require persistence from both the researcher and the organisational member to pause the instantaneous reflex construction of meaning. Since the researcher is interested in exploring the organisational member's local 'somewhere,' it is primarily what the organisational member takes for granted that invites the parties to be reflexive. The invitations that allow the researcher and the organisational member to be reflexive should, therefore, be articulated by the researcher.

This is not due to the organisational member's aversion to taking initiative; it is difficult for the member to be reflexive about his or her life and the meaning constructed within the local 'somewhere' he or she upholds daily (Shotter, 2010; 1996). Language and actions are embedded in local somewheres, and to engage in reflexive conversation and gestures in unadjusted ways is not solely a matter of speaking differently; to explore one's life reflexively is a matter of acting differently, a question of relating and orienting in unique ways (Cunliffe, 2002b; Shotter, 2008). It is a question of living life differently.

Using Unadjusted Gestures and Responses Is a Joint Process That Enables People to Become Radically Present

To live differently is a question of being both sensitive and what McNamee refers to as 'radically present' in a conversation (2016). To be radically present is when the researcher and organisational member aim to recalibrate their perspectives and to understand differences and diversities as resources for creativity, novelty, and social transformation (McNamee, 2016). It is a matter of engaging in conversations that broaden one's perspective and allow both researcher and organisational member to question what they take for granted by paying attention to the new meanings that are unfolding as they converse (McNamee, 2015a). In the conversation with Paul, he and I jointly questioned if the way he acts supports generating strategic dialogues with the regional General Health Board, or if there were other possible ways he could act. It is a joint move towards being sensitive to and having respect for the different ways people live or, as McNamee states, 'I'm not saying agreement is bad, but it is definitely not my go-to place. We need to coordinate multiplicity and move forward from there' (2015b: n.p.).

By gripping too tightly to what is taken for granted within Paul's local reality, as we conversed Paul and I risked alienating ourselves from other local realities that, like Paul's, make up part of the organisational meshwork. These are local realities that Paul has to cooperate with as he attends to his everyday organisational tasks, as well as cooperate with the regional General Health Board. What they take for granted is just as meaningful as Paul's own assumptions (McNamee, 2016).

If Paul and the regional General Health Board want to solve their problems together, they must depend on each other and their ability to construct meaning together. They must gesture in unadjusted ways, pause their immediate co-construction of meaning, and be curious about one another and what each party takes for granted. Based on their differences, Paul and members of the General Health Board can begin to explore how they can communicate and initiate actions differently in order to move forward in ways that support a strategic dialogue between them. This requires the movement to become a shared and meaningful purpose for all persons involved in the conversation.

McNamee (2000) and Cunliffe (2002b) use the term 'social poetics' as a way people jointly can take a radical and reflexive stance to their everyday language as well as explore how they through their here-and-now gestures, responses, words, and intonations talk and act local realities into existence (Cunliffe, 2002b; McNamee, 2000). Social poetics is a practical understanding that allows people to work towards arresting moments. This is similar to pausing the immediate construction of meaning based on adjusted responses and inviting each other – through unadjusted responses – to see new connections or experience things differently (Cunliffe, 2002b).

When a researcher wants to attempt social poetics, his or her non-organisational anchoring can be a resource. Social poetic conversations are a space for free and imaginary talk about dreams and desires (McNamee, 2000). In our conversation, Paul and I jointly explore the hypothetical question, 'What is the worst that could happen at this point?' The intention was not that Paul implement this practice together with the board members, but rather, in a playful forum, give him room to explore and improvise different ways to move on and engage in conversation with them in the upcoming General Health Board meeting.

Social poetics revolves around being able to 'give wing to the imaginative . . . to engage in improvisation' (McNamee, 2000: 146). It denotes engagement in a conversation where the researcher and organisational member jointly explore the unknown, make room for creativity, play with future possibilities, embrace the generative aspect of language, and use different metaphors to question what is taken for granted (Cunliffe, 2002b).

To use social poetics during a research conversation and explore unadjusted responses revolves around allowing the researcher and the organisational member to explore the future by articulating how that future might appear. They experiment and play with talking a different future into being. Despite the conversation's function as a free space for imaginary talk, engaging in social poetics destabilises what is taken for granted within a local 'somewhere'; it invites the researcher and organisational member to consider how they relate to their surroundings and their life circumstances. They must be reflexive about whether the current lifestyle is generative for the future they here and now believe is desirable (Cunliffe, 2002a). To engage in these conversations and explore unadjusted ways of gesturing and responding demands persistence and focus from both researcher and organisational member. However, it is worth it, as each conversation makes room for new understanding and meaning to emerge and thereby expand what the organisational member can envision for the future.

Glimpses into How Unadjusted Gestures and Responses Can Be Used to Engage in Research Conversations with Organisational Members

The perspective presented here cannot be understood as a method but a joint process and practice where both researcher and organisational member discern when unadjusted gestures and responses should emerge and be explored. The subsequent glimpses regarding the use of unadjusted gestures and responses in research conversations with organisational members are only meant to illustrate the process. To generate unadjusted gestures and responses that give pause to immediate construction of meaning and leave room for reflexivity is a joint action.

Unadjusted responses are invitations to explore the possible ways organisational members can talk and act a local 'somewhere' into being. Neither the researcher nor the organisational member knows where such exploration will lead. These conversations are characterised by curiosity and a shared interest in generating desirable local 'somewheres.' The meanings that emerge as the researcher and organisational member communicate are stories that within this unique encounter contribute to the further becoming of the local 'somewhere' in the meshwork.

When considering the use of unadjusted responses in conversations with organisational members, it is important to remember that conversations cannot be built on unadjusted responses alone. Every conversation must embody elements of both adjusted and unadjusted responses, though conversations often contain more the former than the latter. As previously mentioned, for a researcher to become a resourceful conversation partner, he or she must respect, value, and listen to what is being assumed within the local 'somewhere' that is being explored. Simultaneously, conversation partners must be able to question the taken-for-granted to make room for alternative views to emerge. To use unadjusted gestures and responses when a researcher engages in conversations with organisational members is a craftsmanship that the researcher and organisational member co-construct together as they communicate (Cunliffe, 2002a). Unadjusted gestures and responses emerge out of the conversation when both parties are sensitive to each other and the surrounding milieu and are reflexively open to explore and generate desirable local realities that the organisational member believes are meaningful.

1) Bring attention to something that has struck people or moved them
2) Move about in the meshwork and construct new connections
3) Move from the abstract to the concrete
4) Work with existing metaphors
5) Work on bringing a desirable future closer to the present
6) Persist to stay in the meaning vacuum

Bring Attention to Something That Has Struck People or Moved Them

When a researcher and an organisational member want to introduce unadjusted responses in a research conversation, a relevant place to start is to bring attention to something that has struck or moved the organisational member and try to arrest or pause these moments (Shotter, 2010; Cunliffe, 2002a, 2002b). Often, when people are struck by something, they have caught themselves in a situation that means something to them but which they do not know how to handle.

Before the conversation, the organisational member has likely discussed the challenge with others from within the same local 'somewhere' whose action guiding anticipations and assumptions are similar. Their language, intonations, and observations are therefore also similar and, as a result, they often re-construct the organisational dilemma as they communicate. The researcher brings with him or her a non-organisational anchoring from a different local 'somewhere' that identifies different action guiding assumptions and anticipations that enable both researcher and organisational member to engage in conversations where other aspects and perspectives of the dilemma can be explored.

In the following excerpt, Christian, the CEO of a medium-sized Danish consultancy firm, discusses one of his co-directors who is finding it difficult to relinquish the daily management of a department he directed for a short period of time. Christian explains how important it is that the co-director return to his old job and focus on the overall strategy of the company, one pivotal reason being that the co-director has become increasingly demotivated in his job; the employees from the department that he temporarily managed are also displeased with his leadership.

In the excerpt following, Christian and I initially generate adjusted responses to co-construct an understanding of why it is better for the co-manager to return to his prior job, and a sense emerges that Christian is struck by this incident for other reasons as well. In an attempt to bring that sense into the conversation, an unadjusted response is presented at the end of the excerpt.

Christian (C): 'I'm struggling a bit with my co-director; I can't seem to get him to – oh.'
Mette (M): 'Get him to let go?'
C: 'Yes, to let go and also to reinforce his part of the organisation.'
M: 'Does he feel the same?'
C: 'Well, we're getting there. It's a process for him, I'm working on it. My CFO and I are both pushing him gently. The challenge is that I want him to be removed from the daily

management, but it's difficult because he has to want it, too. If I just remove him, I won't have him working for me anymore, and I really don't want to lose him at the top-management level, especially strategically.'

M: 'Based on what you're telling me, it doesn't sound like he finds [that option of leaving daily management] very appealing. At least, not right now.'

C: 'No, he doesn't, but the fact of the matter is that he was hired to do strategy work. When he initially had to take over [the daily management], he really didn't want to.'

M: 'Does he mention that he misses the other aspect, focusing on strategy?'

C: 'No, but I really need him there. He's really strong strategically; he's a strong implementer.'

M: 'And a good discussant for you; I seem to recall you've said previously?'

C: 'Yes, yes.'

M: 'Who do you discuss things with when he's not there?'

C: 'Go fish.'

M: 'Go fish?' (Laughter)

C: 'I don't have anyone else. That's another reason why it's important to me, why I need him. A CFO can help you along the way, but it will always be based on a financial perspective.'

(Research conversation 3, Christian)

The unadjusted response Christian and I co-constructed, 'Who do you have sparring discussions with when he's not available?' allowed us to explore the dilemma in a different way and understand why Christian was so moved by the situation; he no longer has someone within his local inter-act that he can discuss strategic challenges with, which frustrates him. As we explored this different facet of the dilemma, we both complexified our thinking. We came to realise that the desirable future here and now was not only one where the co-manager and the employees were more motivated, but also one where Christian and his co-manager were capable of engaging in strategic dialogues with each other.

As Christian and I explored the dilemma, we also came to realise through co-constructing unadjusted responses that Christian could deal with the dilemma in other ways, as it no longer only involved the co-manager and the employees' motivation, but Christian's ability to engage in discussions about the company's strategy together with the co-manager. By reviewing the dilemma, it also became possible to better relate to it and engage in other conversations about it where other understandings and actions can emerge.

Move About in the Meshwork and Construct New Connections

As presented in the previous chapter, an organisational meshwork consists of multiple local inter-acts where different and even contradictory actions and understanding coexist. Organisational problems and dilemmas are often co-constructed across these local inter-acts. People within one local 'somewhere' are struck by how people within another local 'somewhere' understand or act in a given situation and find it challenging to engage in joint meaning construction with each other. Consequently, people often turn to others within their local inter-act to construct meaning and, as their generalised action guiding assumptions and anticipations are co-constructed by themselves, it is relatively easy to construct meaning and agree on how to move forward.

What people often 'forget' in the process of co-constructing local meaning is that the way they move within their local 'somewhere' must mesh together with how people in other local 'somewheres' decide to move forward. They forget that the way they gesture, respond, and act can become easily entangled in the problems they so eagerly want to solve (Cunliffe, 2002a; Shotter, 2010). In the following excerpt, I converse with Laura, head of the Department of Regional Development in one of the Danish Regions. She explains some of the internal challenges her department is facing because of a restructuring process.

Laura explains how difficult it has been for her and the other departments to cooperate with a particular department, primarily because Alex, the manager of that department, does not want to cooperate in any way. Each time the department managers meet and discuss how to coordinate between them, Alex does not participate. Without Alex's presence, it becomes extremely difficult for the other department managers to evaluate the flow of the assignments, and they constantly attempt to take Alex's preferences and disinterest in cooperating into consideration. As Laura and I converse about the situation, the possibility to be radically present emerges, and we begin to notice that the way we gesture and respond in adjusted ways around the problem begins to re-construct it. Laura and I then generate an unadjusted response that enables us to explore what we could co-construct if we began to gesture and respond differently:

Laura (L): 'As I am telling you all this, I can hear how much it concerns me. It really concerns me as well as my colleagues.'

Mette (M): 'How can you turn it around in a way that allows you to comply with the new centre structure and not only with him, so you make room for yourselves?'

L: 'Yes, it cannot continue like this. It really taxes all of us, and I'm sure it also taxes Alex. Maybe that's what we should do.'

M: 'Use the re-structuring to make it more obvious what you need from Alex's department if cooperation is going to succeed.'

L: 'I think that is really great input. Yesterday we talked a lot about all of the things we don't believe can happen. Maybe it's better we start talking about and defining what we need and figuring out how to do it.'

(Research conversation 2, Laura)

As Laura and I paid attention to our language and the meaning we co-constructed, we realised that we ourselves play a part in the becoming of the meshed problem that Laura wants to solve (Cunliffe, 2002a). As the unadjusted response, 'How can you turn it around?' emerges, Laura and I invited each other to reorient and relate to ourselves differently (McNamee, 2000). As we explored our gestures and responses, we noticed new connections and other ways to act and construct meaning. What this excerpt illustrates is that if a researcher and an organisational member change their way of communicating and acting, they can embrace multiple ways to construct meaning and act. Only if researchers and organisational members are sensitive to each other and the alternative aspects and perspectives that emerge as they communicate here and now can they speak and act them into being.

The small changes in gesturing and responding emerge from the curiosity from two people (Laura and I) who live in different local 'somewheres.' As the previous excerpt shows, being curious, present, and sensitive to the conversation enabled Laura and me to jointly gesture and respond in new ways that neither could have accomplished alone (Shotter, 2010).

The generated change may appear minor, but small changes can be significant here and now in the local inter-act, where Laura lives every day. The challenges in coordinating with Alex's department presently tax Laura's and the other department managers' energy in their everyday practice. As mentioned earlier, the past and the future are re-constructed or de-constructed in the present as people converse, act, and generate relational meaning. This means that the small changes in how Laura and I gestured and responded created new possibilities to relate and reorient ourselves differently regarding the dilemma with Alex (Cunliffe, 2002a; Shotter, 2008).

By gesturing and responding differently, Laura and I help each other to stop treating the dilemma as an issue of everything Laura and the other managers could not do in order to be considerate of Alex's demands. By moving around in the meshwork, new understandings began to emerge, and it became possible to co-construct what Laura and the other managers could do by engaging in different ways of communication and action.

Move from the Abstract to the Concrete

A researcher may occasionally have a conversation with an organisational member that moves the member to discuss an abstract idea. The conversation does not deal concretely with the realm of what people can do here and now; on the contrary, the conversation stays at a normative level, which as such is not an issue. However, as mentioned previously, life is experienced in unique here-and-now encounters within a local 'somewhere' of the meshwork and not on an abstract level. I therefore suggest using unadjusted responses to move from the abstract level to a focus on how people act and speak within the concrete conversation in which they are participating. The way the researcher and organisational member communicate and act enable some practices and understanding to emerge. They should explore if the way they take part in constructing the meshwork leads them in the ways they find advantageous at the given moment (Cunliffe & Shotter, 2006).

The following excerpt is from another conversation with Laura. During the conversation, she describes the effort she made in allowing the employees in her department to have partner discussions since it contributes to their well-being; they solve their tasks more efficiently and constructively when they engage in conversations about their job with a colleague. In the process of her everyday practice, Laura forgets, however, that she also needs someone with whom she can discuss things. We therefore explore on an abstract level the benefits of having a coach with whom to converse. To shift closer to the concrete and local inter-act where Laura lives her life and explore how life could be different if she had a coach. Laura and I use unadjusted responses.

Laura (L): 'So I've thought about it several times, and I think I ought to have a coach, someone who could give me some supervision and be a communicator about work. I could do it, undoubtedly. I just don't do anything about it. I know I ought to, and I hear others around talk about seeing a coach regularly.'

Mette (M): 'What do you think holds you back?'

L: 'I don't know. It's just me stopping myself. Maybe I think that time is better spent on something else, but I should do it. I'm sure it's the right thing to do, not only for me; the whole organisation would benefit from it if I did it.'

M: 'What would the organisation look like in a year if you started talking with a coach?'

L: 'It wouldn't look worse, that's for sure. We can only gain from it, and it's just me who isn't doing anything about it.'

M: 'Do you think your leadership and your everyday practice would be different if you began to include others in your thought processes?' (Laura clears her throat) 'You make yourself available to so many people. What if someone was available for you?'

L: 'Personally, I would gain from it tremendously, that's for sure. In relation to how I solve my tasks, too. It has always been my saying, and not only in relation to leadership: it's always beneficial to discuss a matter with someone else before acting on it.'

M: 'What would it take for you to say, "This is it. It's time for me to call a coach"?'

L: 'I actually think I'm almost there. It's completely ridiculous. I just have to pull myself together, that's it.'

(Research conversation 3, Laura)

Unadjusted responses such as 'What do you think holds you back?' 'What would the organisation look like in a year if you began talking with a coach?' and 'What would make you say, "This is it. It's time for me to call a coach"?' do two things: they first make the idea more concrete by coupling it to concrete activities in the local inter-act where Laura lives and explores how other people within the local inter-act would respond to this change in practice. They also enable Laura and me to engage in imaginary talk and put into words how we here and now believe the organisation would look if Laura had been visiting with a coach for some time. In this process, we incrementally begin to explore how the desirable future would look if Laura called a coach. We do not engage in this exploration due to the solution that Laura should call a coach. We engage in this talk to move from generalisations to concrete stories and possible activities. Furthermore, we begin to talk in practice instead of talk about practice (Cunliffe, 2002a; Shotter 2010). This shift embraces the generativity and ontology of language and confirms that there will always be alternative ways Laura can live if she and I are attentive to what emerges as we communicate. Talk has a moving effect (Shotter, 2010), but not an effect either researcher or organisational member can or should try to control. The shift emerges when a researcher and organisational member are sensitive to the differences expressed and pursue them.

As Laura and I conversed, we moved closer together like wayfarers without a predefined goal. Whether Laura decides to call a coach afterwards or not is not the purpose here and now. The current purpose is to use unadjusted responses to explore the multiple ways Laura can move forward and co-construct how each is desirable and within reach on a more concrete level; what that leads to belongs to another here and now.

Work with Existing Metaphors

As previously mentioned in the chapter, a researcher can, when he or she and the organisational member are radically present in a conversation, use different metaphors to question what is taken for granted and imagine new desirable futures (Cunliffe, 2002b). People use metaphors as a natural part of communicating to help them create juxtaposing images of what is and what is not allowing them to instantaneously reduce complexity (Cunliffe, 2002b). Metaphors are within a relational constructionism perspective understood ontologically, meaning they are not used to discuss reality. Realities and metaphors are constructed as people discuss and generate certain understandings and initiate given actions (Cunliffe, 2002b).

As metaphors are talked into being and in the local 'somewhere' people live, they rapidly generate certain ways of gesturing and responding that enable people within a local 'somewhere' to construct certain taken-for-granted assumptions metaphorically (Cunliffe, 2002b). The metaphors, therefore, occasionally limit people's ability to construct meaning in other ways; they invite given juxtapositions that people within a local 'somewhere' come to assume and do

Exploring Unadjusted Gestures 55

not question. If by using unadjusted responses a researcher invites an organisational member to exchange known metaphors and an unadjusted response is being pursued, the researcher and organisational member can create space for creative discussion; they open up the possibility of juxtaposing different elements and therefore enable different understandings to emerge.

In the following excerpt, Christian and I discuss how he, as part of an ongoing strategy process, is very preoccupied with solving the organisational core of the consultancy firm. Christian is convinced that if he recognises the core he will detect how the company, via the core, can increase its financial growth and market share. As Christian and I consider the core, we realise that 'core' is a metaphor that demands a very concrete and specific content, which is difficult for us to articulate. Christian and I, therefore, use an unadjusted response as a way of introducing a different metaphor to explore other possible ways to move forward:

Christian (C): 'What I have as my big challenge is how I can increase our growth. What is our core? I'm very preoccupied with finding our core. This is where I believe our biggest growth potential is. It revolves a lot around understanding the people we're cooperating with, what their undetermined needs are, what they want to try out. We need to understand their needs, what makes them happy, what conditions they operate under, and when they are successful in order to try and think like they do. This is where we have to stand out. It's that process, all of those stakeholders who have a saying. We have to have a profound understanding of their everyday experiences and their success criteria.'

Mette (M): 'How can you co-create with them? That's where it starts to get interesting.'

C: 'Yes, and the whole process that leads up to it. That's what I'm working on figuring out; getting to the core of it. Then it will be easier to begin adding things from there.'

M: 'You have to have a playground for ideas. How much do you experiment?'

C: 'We're experimenting now. We are trying to create playgrounds, but we don't have a master plan for playgrounds.'

M: 'But a part of it is also to try out different things. Think about where it takes you and what works.'

C: 'At the risk of being accused of being an optimist, I think a lot of what we're doing actually works.'

(Research conversation 4, Christian)

During the conversation, Christian and I used an unadjusted response and introduced the terms 'playground' and 'experiments', which are less concrete and allowed us to communicate in other ways that juxtaposed different ideas. As we made this change in metaphors, the linkage to the company's everyday practice suddenly emerged; it became possible to see how their existing everyday experiments and co-constructing co-operations with their customers were a way to incrementally move forward and generate knowledge on how to increase their financial growth and market share. The metaphors 'playground' and 'experiments' were not introduced because they were the correct metaphors to replace the term 'core'; they were introduced and further explored because Christian and I at this point could make them meaningful. The way we introduced them provided us with more tangible ways to advance.

Work on Bringing a Desirable Future Closer to the Present

As presented earlier in the chapter, people live in one unique here-and-now encounter at a time. Certain memories of the past and future are either reconstructed or altered depending on how people jointly construct meaning and initiate actions. The future a person may move towards can be one they find undesirable and want to avoid; based on existing action guiding assumptions, anticipations, and what is taken for granted, he or she can often become caught in local meaning structures. What is assumed makes it difficult for people within the same local 'somewhere' to be reflexive and co-construct other understandings.

In the second inspiration point, Laura and I initially gestured and responded in ways that played an active part in the becoming of the meshed problem we wanted to solve (Cunliffe, 2002a). As we began to use the unfamiliarity between each other's assumptions as a resource to articulate the unadjusted responses, we began co-constructing different ways to move forward. In the conversation here, I move these ideas forward and focus on how, by using unadjusted responses, it becomes possible to not only invite people into seeing a larger picture but also into seeing the part they are playing in the reality they are critiquing (Cunliffe, 2002a). This also makes it possible to discuss what they believe to be a desirable future as well as how they in the here and now can redirect their expectations regarding other people's responses (Shotter, 2010).

In the following excerpt, I converse with Paul as he explains how difficult it has been to engage in strategic dialogues with the region's General Health Board. As mentioned at the beginning of the chapter, regional General Health Board members have withdrawn a strategic decision regarding the regional hospital and Paul has had other negative experiences with them. In this excerpt, Paul describes how the regional General Health Board members have withdrawn an earlier agreed restructuring of the local hospital and the consequences this had on their cooperation.

Paul (P):   'In September, the General Health Board approved a new management structure. I was then asked to meet with the Regional Council and was told that I cannot implement the new management structure. It's really frustrating. I get a bit irrational because they present me with arguments like, 'Why don't you just make a clinic?' I mean, we've been through all of this for a long time and there are good arguments supporting the structure we agreed on. I simply don't understand it. I feel I've had some constructive dialogues with a lot of the people at the top, so I really don't know how we ended up here. That is also why my big challenge has been how I can engage in constructive strategic dialogues with the top management about this hospital.'

'But they broke a psychological contract. We have to rely on each other and know where each other stand. I'm an optimist. I've taken part in constructive strategic dialogues. If not, I wouldn't have been able to sit in my chair these last ten years. It presupposes that you share detailed knowledge about how you run a hospital and that you're able to generate common ideas about how to succeed. It's all process. I'm having a dialogue meeting with the small Governing Board this month.'

Mette: 'How are you going to act during this meeting?'
P: 'In my darkest hours, I wish the meeting wasn't taking place at all because I have these images of the last meeting [where the restructuring was withdrawn]. And it wasn't good at all.'
M: 'So, you have some work ahead of you to build some positive images. What would have to happen during that meeting to make you leave it with a feeling that a step in the right direction has been taken?'
P: 'We would have to communicate in a civil way. That's what it's all about. It's like being on one of those critical political debate programs where the host just ignores what you are saying and jumps to the next question before you manage to answer the previous one. Then you stand there thinking, "When is this going to stop, so I can leave and get back to my work?"'
M: 'And that's not the purpose of these meetings. What could have you have done right then and there to change the situation?'
P: 'I don't know.'
M: 'It is quite interesting because it could easily happen again next time if you don't change your course of action.'
P: 'Yes, and I don't . . . I don't quite have a plan for how to deal with it.'
M: 'If you want to move away from how things were last, you might have to let go of something you're familiar with and that you rely on to get closer to where you want to be.'
P: 'Yes. I'm with you part of the way.'
M: 'What makes you disagree?'
P: 'To get there, I'd have to work on myself. I'd have to stop being so stubborn. I have to work on that.'

(Research conversation 2, Paul)

Initially, Paul talked about how he anticipates the upcoming meeting with the regional General Health Board will be unproductive. Paul and I easily agreed, by using adjusted responses, that the regional General Health Board had made unreasonable decisions and could not be trusted. However, instead, we explored Paul's desire to engage in strategic dialogues with the regional General Health Board. We thus engaged in a reflexive conversation by exploring an unadjusted response: 'So you have to work on constructing some positive images?' This question was used to briefly pause the immediate reflex and instantaneous construction of meaning and instead begin to imagine reflexively what the future would look like if Paul and I, here and now, engaged in a strategic dialogue with the regional General Health Board. As we explored how to bring this potential future closer to present here and now, it became clear that there were no existing taken-for-granted assumptions or meaning structures that we could spontaneously rely on as we communicated. We entered unknown territory, sensitive to each other and the other possible meanings we might co-construct. In the process of anticipating a new future, Paul and I were also reflexive about how he contributes to co-constructing the organisational dilemma he wants to get out of: 'Well, I'd have to stop being so stubborn. I have to work on that.' The purpose of this reflexive exploration was not to attribute blame but to be reflexive about the dilemma and explore if the actions being carried out support generating a reality that is desirable at the given moment.

Persist in Staying in the Meaning Vacuum

In the previous chapter, it was stated that sometimes the simple task of counting to ten slowly and letting time work its wonders can help a researcher and an organisational member want to move into unknown territory. It can also be a help to be incrementally reflexive about how a researcher and an organisational member have multiple ways of constructing meaning and moving forward. In order to embrace the unknown, it is important that a researcher, as a resourceful conversation partner, sensitively respect and question what is being taken for granted. The purpose of this dualistic practice is for the researcher and organisational member to engage jointly in a social-poetic creative discussion about the here and now in meaningful new ways that allow new ways to move forward to emerge.

As previously mentioned, using unadjusted responses and exploring jointly what up until now has been taken for granted as reality within a local 'somewhere' can call for persistence. The researcher can introduce this type of persistence into the conversation. If both the researcher and organisational member want to continue exploring what is being questioned and presently stay in the meaning vacuum, they must support that persistence as well as endeavour to get a sense of how the world would look from there by co-constructing it.

Exploring Unadjusted Gestures 59

In the following excerpt, Christian and I jointly question what has been taken for granted until now within the local part of the meshwork where Christian lives. This conversation emerges from the conversation due to a sense that Christian cannot find a meaningful way to solve some challenges the organisation is experiencing with public housing by relying on what those within his local 'somewhere' already know, take for granted, and anticipate.

Christian (C): 'I want to move some fence posts here. We're working with the public housing sector where all the social problems are just piling up, and what can we do about them? Is it because no one has focused on public housing for a while? How can you deal with that problem? It's that kind of uncertainty, being faced with a challenge that I don't have an answer to.'

Mette (M): 'You have all the answers where you're positioned right now.'

C: 'How we can increase our growth? I don't have the answer to that.'

M: 'If you keep spending time and talking with the same people, you will continue to reach the same conclusions. You need to spend time and discuss this with other people.'

C: 'That's a very good description; I understand what you're saying. We do a lot of analysis and none of it, so far, has told me something I didn't know upfront. The analyses don't indicate new ways of moving forward. There's no solution that I didn't see coming. Even if we did make deeper [analytical] dives, maybe the solution isn't where we're looking right now.'

M: 'The questions you're raising are based on your perspective of reality. You've positioned yourself organisationally in a way where people give you the answers they know you want to hear. The closer the answers are to your perspective of reality, the safer they feel.'

C: 'Yes.'

M: 'And your board cannot challenge you.'

C: 'No, they cannot.'

M: 'If you want to move forward, you need to find someone who will challenge you from inside the organisation. Otherwise, it will be like the conversations you have with your coach where you explore a lot of wonderful ideas, but nothing ever happens.' (eight seconds pause)

C: 'Yes. Now we're getting somewhere. The challenge you're presenting is a new one. I haven't been challenged like this before.' (Laughter)

M: 'But you have to do this. Otherwise, you'll be stuck.' (ten seconds pause)
C: 'Where the hell am I going to find someone who dares to really shake things up who doesn't feel subject to my conventions?'

(Research conversation 5, Christian)

Notice how the conversation was characterised by longer pauses and a joint acknowledgement that if Christian stays within the same organisational patterns and only constructs meaning with people from his local 'somewhere,' it becomes challenging to engage in reflexive and social poetic conversations with people in other local 'somewheres.' These conversations are necessary if the consultancy firm wants to deal with the public housing problems they see. Acknowledgement emerged as Christian and I jointly explored unadjusted responses such as, 'If you want to move forward, you need to find someone who will challenge you from inside the organisation' and – momentarily – stayed in a meaning vacuum. Christian and I did not rely on what was assumed anywhere. We allowed each other to dwell in the unknown for a moment until something began to emerge and became more apparent than we then could express in words and images (Shotter, 2011).

It is important to emphasise that to be in a not-knowing position and question what is taken for granted is a bold move. To coordinate multiplicity and move forward from a point of uncertainty and embrace that meaning is never given. This space is porous and belongs to the present here-and-now encounter and is difficult for many to acknowledge, though it is possible. Being a resourceful conversation partner with a non-organisational anchoring that introduces both adjusted and unadjusted responses can be a great support. A researcher and an organisational member can – like Christian and I in the excerpt – engage in conversations where they proactively embrace each other's different local inter-act and can engage in reflexive, socially poetic, imaginary, and creative discussion about a possible future. This future can be based on how the researcher and organisational member each and jointly pay attention to different meanings, take other things for granted, embody unlike action-guiding anticipations and assumptions, and live in disparate local 'somewheres.'

Concluding Words about Using Unadjusted Gestures and Responses When a Researcher Wants to Engage in Research Conversations with Organisational Members

In this chapter, I have presented what can be termed 'unadjusted responses.' I have also presented glimpses into how to engage in conversations with organisational members and explore jointly unadjusted gestures and responses. It can be argued that to become a resourceful conversation partner, a researcher and an organisational member must use both adjusted and unadjusted responses. The conversations that engage the practices presented here are in many ways similar to the everyday conversations people normally engage in. The difference in research conversations is that researchers work actively with complexifying thinking, being radically present to one another, and using their differences to open up social poetic conversations.

To use unadjusted responses in conversations is to take part in reflexive, radical, and social-poetic dialogues where the researcher and organisational member jointly generate new understandings and practices and value the differences between them. They persist to move as not-knowers as they jointly construct local knowledge and meaning here and now that they cannot construct alone. In many ways it is similar to balancing on the head of a pin; there is no manual or method to follow. Both manual and method emerge simultaneously as both researcher and organisational member remain sensitive to each other and the organisational dilemmas and solutions they are exploring.

To accept that the researcher's and organisational member's local knowledge are necessary but insufficient can be challenging. By reflex, people spontaneously and instantaneously construct local solutions that they come to take for granted and anticipate will solve a problem. That is why unadjusted responses cannot characterise a whole conversation; resourceful conversation partners need adjusted responses as well.

To constantly pause and question what people think they know is not an easy task. Not only must people acknowledge their own co-constructive part in finding a solution to their problem, they must also acknowledge and embrace that what they thought was the answer was only one of many possible and meaningful answers. What might be the most challenging aspect of this is that this acknowledgement does not only characterise research conversations; it involves every conversation people engage in. To acknowledge and embrace this is to change one's mindset regarding how people live.

To engage in these conversations requires a researcher to 'relinquish the control we often feel we need to have over our research and be responsive to our co-collaborators' (Ripamonti et al., 2016: 5). It becomes a delusion that the researcher can control the conversation and ensure that the organisational member presents the right answer to his or her questions (Cunliffe, 2002a; Shotter, 2010). Because of a researcher's theoretical anchoring and years of experience, he or she also lives in a local 'somewhere.' What is taken for granted and understood as real there is as local to the researcher as it is anywhere. It, therefore, must also be questioned and altered in the unique here-and-now conversation. What counts as reliable, relevant, and essential is 'to be found within the intertwined nexus where all those involved in a situated difficulty interact with each other' (Shotter, 2010: 281). A researcher does not discover anything during these research conversations; the researcher and organisational member jointly construct new local understandings and actions that they believe are meaningful ways to move forward. In that process, you rework what you as the researcher previously thought you knew.

This also raises the question: can these conversations be considered research? If you ask me, I believe they can. Gesturing in adjusted and unadjusted ways during research conversations are practices in a research process that is meshed, local, here and now, conflux, and co-constructed. Research and the construction of knowledge are contextual, local, relational, and dependent on who generates it. A researcher must be present in unique here-and-now encounters; what is written afterwards in reports, journals, chapters, and conference papers is a differently co-constructed knowledge that locally, relationally, and contextually has to be meaningful then and there, which will be explained in Chapter 8.

References

Cunliffe, A. L. (2002a) Reflexive Dialogical Practice in Management Learning. *Management Learning*, 33 (1), 35–61.

Cunliffe, A. L. (2002b) Social Poetics as Management Inquiry—a Dialogical Approach. *Journal of Management Inquiry*, 11 (2), 128–146.

and Managing. In: Rafaeli, A. & Pratt, M. G. (eds.) *Artifacts and Organizations*. London, Lawrence Erlbaum Associates Publishers, pp. 119–137.

Gergen, K. J. (2009) *Relational Being: Beyond the Individual and Community*. Oxford, Oxford University Press.

Gergen, K. J. (2010) Co-Constitution, Causality and Confluence Organizing in a World Without Entities. Draft for: Hernes, T. & Maitlis, S. (eds.) *Process, Sensemaking, and Organizing*. Oxford, Oxford University Press.

Gergen, K. & Thatchenkery, T. (2004) Organization Science as Social Construction Postmodern Potentials. *The Journal of Applied Behavioral Science*, 40 (2), 228–249.

McNamee, S. (2000) The Social Poetics of Relationally Engaged Research. In: Deissler, K. & McNamee, S. (eds.) *Phil und Sophie auf der Couch: Die Sozialepoesietherapeutischergesprache* [Philosophy in therapy: The social poetics of therapeutic conversations]. Heidelberg, Germany, Carl-Auer_SystemeVerlag, pp. 146–156.

McNamee, S. (2012) From Social Construction to Relational Construction: Practices from the Edge. *Psychological Studies*, 57 (2), 150–156.

McNamee, S. (2015a) *Listen to me!* Keynote presentation at the 3rd International Conference on Dialogical Practices—Humanizing Human Practices. 23rd–25th September 2015, Kristiansand, Norway.

McNamee, S. (2015b) Radical Presence: Alternatives to the Therapeutic State. *The European Journal of Psychotherapy and Counselling*, 17 (4), 373–383.

McNamee, S. (2016) The Ethics of Relational Process: John Shotter's Radical Presence. In: Corcoran, T. & Cromby, J. (eds.) *Joint Action: Essays in Honour of John Shotter*. Oxon, Routledge, pp. 89–101.

McNamee, S. & Hosking, D. M. (2012) *Research and Social Change—a Relational Constructionist Approach*. New York, Routledge.

Mead, G. H. (1934) *The Philosophy of the Present*. London, The Open Court Company Publishers.

Mead, G. H. (1974) *Mind, Self and Society from the Standpoint of a Social Behaviorist*. Chicago, Chicago University Press.

Ripamonti, S., Galuppo, L. Gorli, M., Scaratti, G. & Cunliffe, A. L. (2016) Pushing Action Research Toward Reflexive Practice. *Journal of Management Inquiry*, 25 (1), 55–68.

Shotter, J. (1996) 'Now I Can Go On': Wittgenstein and Our Embodied Embeddedness in the 'Hurly-Burly' of Life. *Human Studies*, 19 (4), 385–407.

Shotter, J. (2008) Dialogism and Polyphony in Organizing Theorizing in Organization Studies: Action Guiding Anticipations and Continuous Creation of Novelty. *Organization Studies*, 29 (4), 501–524.

Shotter, J. (2010) Situated Dialogic Action Research Disclosing 'Beginnings' for Innovative Change in Organizations. *Organizational Research Methods*, 13 (2), 268–285.

Shotter, J. (2011) Knowledge in Transition: The Role of Prospective, Descriptive Concepts in a Practice-Situated, Hermeneutical-Phronetic Social Science. *Management Learning*, 43 (3), 245–260.

Shotter, J. & Billig, M. (1998) A Bakhtinian Psychology: From Out of the Heads of Individuals and into the Dialogues Between Them. In: Bell, M. & Gardner, M. E. (eds.) *Bakhtin and the Human Sciences: No Last Words*. London, Sage, pp. 13–29.

4 Engaging in Relational Action Learning Processes
A Way to Make Sense of Everyday Relational Management Practices

Mette Vinther Larsen and Jørgen Gulddahl Rasmussen

Introduction

In Chapter 4, there is a shift from one-on-one conversations as have been presented in the two previous chapters to conversations, or group inquiries, between several leaders and two researchers. The focus of this chapter is to present a way, jointly with researchers and a group of leaders from non-competing organisations, to make sense of how everyday management practices are understood and dealt with over a period of time. The purpose is to present an inquiry that enables researchers to co-construct knowledge together with a group of leaders from different companies regarding how they make sense of and deal with unexpected emerging opportunities and couple such processes with their mundane daily practices of management.

This type of inquiry has been used in several research projects. In those projects, it was observed that the leaders who participated did so very actively. One reason for this may be that the conversations between these leaders and between the researchers and leaders make it possible for them to explore quotidian challenges and seek for new answers. For researchers, this manner of inquiry makes it possible to engage in conversation on what resources leaders draw upon to solve everyday challenges and how they jointly address these problems and the possibilities related to them.

This chapter begins by presenting some of the preconditions of these conversations before more direct exploration into how this type of inquiry can be applied in six steps. How the authors developed the inquiry and the process will also be discussed. There are several ways to begin, and every other inquiry will differ methodologically from the inquiry we have initiated.

Over the last several thousand years, since Sun Tzu in 500 B.C. and Socrates in 400 B.C., management has been studied, and it is expected to be studied for many years to come (Sharfritz et al., 2005). Some might perhaps say that 'enough is enough,' but there continue to be important areas to study which centre on collaborative knowledge-generating processes among researchers and practitioners alike (Ripamonti et al., 2016).

From a relational constructionism perspective, managing is presently synonymous with accepting and embracing that the future is unknown and that many challenges and possibilities will unexpectedly and continuously emerge. The everyday practices of an organisation are shaped by and depend on how members of that organisation jointly make sense of them. What goes on among an organisation's competitors, customers, suppliers, legislators, and even its employees may be easy at times to understand and predict, but other times practices and processes can hit leaders unexpectedly and with great impact as if they were a bolt of lightning.

Organising and managing within an organisation are concurrently filled with routine operations: How does the organisation function? How are services and products developed, produced, and delivered? There are many micro-activities that require employees in different departments to generate correct ways of handling operational tasks, to resolve and refine the way customers are treated, how suppliers are corrected, and how other leaders engage in solving tasks that cross internal boarders within the organisation. The handling of such tasks is analysed by Mintzberg (1973), who begins by introducing the concept of 'emergent opportunities', where the focus is on what comes unexpectedly to an organisation as well as its leaders and employees (Mintzberg & Waters 1985).

The word 'inquiry' is used to characterise a method of conversation. Inquiry sums up a number of activities in the form of conversations with the intention of constructing different interpretations between a group of leaders and researchers on how to understand organisational challenges. To support these conversations, studying documents, web pages, and other written material is important; it is the conversations, however, that are key in constructing knowledge concerning the field of management practices.

To concentrate on how emergent opportunities are understood and integrated into the shaping of an organisation, it is important to underline the significant way in which these opportunities are interpreted and managed as its leaders communicate. The way leaders jointly construct meaning about the opportunity and move forward is in line with relational constructionism and may greatly impact the well-being and competitiveness of a firm. The processes of 'discovering' emergent opportunities, how they form in the communication within the firm and among its leaders, how they meet and are integrated into daily activities, and how they become part of the overall strategy of the firm are the main research questions addressed in the inquiry presented and discussed in this chapter.

Among the ideas presented elsewhere in this book are multiple ways processes and actions can be understood and dealt with that depend on how people communicate and construct meaning together. Being able to support multiple meanings enables leaders to become more reflexively aware of the various ways that co-constructing meanings and actions supports different possibilities for the organisation.

The inquiry presented in this chapter works actively to include various voices by bringing leaders from different local 'somewheres' or 'local worlds' together to jointly share their different interpretations of emergent opportunities and local understandings in order to meet and make room for new understandings to be co-constructed as the leaders communicate. It is an important part of the inquiry to listen to several voices and how people's experiences constructed such voices.

To work with this particular kind of inquiry is to accept that everything is in a constant flux. There is no way a researcher can know beforehand what will be interesting to explore; one does not need to know what to explore to facilitate reflexive and relational action learning conversations. What seemed true before may not seem true afterwards. Whatever position the observer has accepted is important in defining his or her truth. This is natural for both the participating leaders and the researchers.

The Foundation of an Inquiry

The ontology behind an inquiry into these phenomena is based on relational leading, communication, and language (Larsen & Rasmussen, 2015). The main elements in an inquiry are related to the epistemological basis of knowledge in that sense. This is not only an inquiry to help understand emergence and coincidence but also to ascertain how coincidences are constructed, experienced, and used in organisations. In this way, an inquiry focuses on the relationship between leaders and organisations, employees and other leaders, along with an ongoing polyphony.

In this inquiry, two different types of researchers have collaborated: the company leaders who have vast resources on specific management practices, and the researchers who possess a responsibility to support the construction of knowledge during the conversations with those leaders. In this way, the inquiry can be built on co-research between both leaders and researchers.

One practice with which a researcher can introduce the foundation of an inquiry is to ground one's work in a 'becoming and dwelling perspective' on life instead of a 'being and building perspective' (Chia & Holt, 2006; Heidegger, 1951; James, 1909; Tsoukas & Chia, 2002). This is a view that is referred to in other chapters; it interprets the world as constantly changing, not as something planned but always occurring (Chia, 2013).

There is great interest in interpreting those aspects of management and leading that seem to constantly change what is taken for granted in an organisation, or 'a local world,' instead of interpreting change as something done structurally by leaders as rational planning individuals. To understand management, leading, and daily life within an organisation, the inquiry presented focuses on what is taken for granted, which centres particularly on the emerging and unexpected experiences and changes within the organisation.

Observing an organisation through a becoming perspective tends to focus on the small changes leaders and employees not only experience but also actively take part in together. In this context, becoming denotes an ongoing construction process that constantly changes the organisation and the world around it by changing how everyday activities are accomplished. This can be microscopic in work routines and daily collaboration, but occasionally, great revolutionary changes can impact the entire organisation. In the becoming perspective, an organisation never ceases to change.

The most important inspiration this inquiry draws upon is relational leading, or relational being, with its influence on activities that occur, ideas that emerge, and communication constructed between researchers and participants (Gergen, 2001; 2009; Gergen & Gergen, 2004; Hosking et al., 1995; Larsen & Rasmussen, 2015). Those who participate in these inquiries become 'constructed' as persons, leaders, and employees through relational communication. This denotes that conversations that occur in the present, the future, and the past are interpreted from the perspective of this moment. In this manner, the inquiry has something in common with what is referred to as a 'localist view,' but is here further developed in a constructionist direction (Alvesson, 2003).

This understanding of life within organisations and between organisational members is supplemented with a methodological inspiration that comes from researchers who study leadership from a relational perspective (Cunliffe, 2001; Cunliffe & Eriksen, 2011; Hosking, 2010; Uhl-Bien, 2006). Two books that are useful are McNamee & Hosking's (2012) on methodological aspects and Larsen & Rasmussen's (2015) on theoretical background.

This way of inquiring requires constructing knowledge by studying communication between leaders as well as leaders and their employees, how this communication forms ideas and interprets emerging experience, the management of these ideas, and their integration into the ongoing becoming and formation of the organisation. From this perspective, the entire organisation, or, as Karl Weick states, the entire organising, consists of the myriads of relations that are in action at the actual moment (1979).

To view organising as relational forms, the next dimension in an inquiry is to see organising as a 'meshwork' (Czarniawska 2013; Ingold 2008; 2011; Larsen 2013). Organising can be interpreted or illustrated as a large number of lines running in different directions, side by side, intersecting each other and moving in constant processes. This is one way to interpret the everyday activities of any organisation. The meshwork perspective emphasizes that it is impossible to follow and understand every line and the immediate effect of them crossing each other; there is simply not enough time or resources to study them all. It is inspiration drawn from conversations with leaders and their employees that directs what lines to illuminate in the specific research project.

This inspiration also underscores that an employee or a leader only function within and observe some lines, but not all; this makes an inquiry focus on the different local views that are emerging for different local groups within the meshwork. To participate and become a part of this meshwork is a researcher's responsibility in order to contribute to the conversations that take place in the interaction between leaders and researchers. To do this, not only adjusted responses are important (see Chapter 2); unadjusted responses also need to shape the conversational process (see Chapter 3). The intention behind this is to develop knowledge into the interaction between leaders and researchers on how practical managerial activities can be interpreted differently and brought to life through conversations based on adjusted and unadjusted responses.

Practical Inspiration

To be practical means to bridge the field of study, e.g. management and leading, and the inquiry as easily as possible. There are different guidelines on how to act as researchers, how to interpret and encourage the steps taken by participating leaders, how to interpret oneself as a researcher, and how to collaborate with leaders and researchers. To study management from such a perspective is, as shown previously, based on the interpretation of a large amount of data. Data on how management is conducted according to the inquiry are, in principle, useful, but to find and interpret all data is impossible. Such data might report on financial turn-over, product sales, production processes, marketing activities, personnel, strategies, daily decisions and activities, and conversations in 'every corner' of the firm. Everything a researcher gains access to should be assessed for its potential as data for the specific inquiry.

In order to develop what direction to follow in data construction, as well as how to interpret how such data is constructed and integrated into daily management within a firm, it is important to recognise a researcher comes from 'the outside.' To come from the outside with a non-organisational anchoring may indicate, even when we have important qualifications on the theories and models of leading and organising, that a researcher has insufficient knowledge to make useful interpretations. One might even take the position that using theories and models from a textbook world could direct inquiry in useless ways. To study managerial practice is not about studying theories on leading, but is an attempt to interpret the practice.

These are processes where researchers, as carefully and respectfully as possible, engage in conversation with leaders to participate in a process that not only constructs new knowledge on management for research purposes but also constructs new practical knowledge for the leaders and their organisations. It is through such conversations regarding possible futures for participating leaders and their organisations that the knowledge on what management can become is constructed.

For this reason, the inquiry presented in this chapter involves not only researchers but the practising leaders as well. A leader may, from a relational perspective, be interpreted as a kind of co-author, as may the researcher (Alvesson & Sköldberg, 2009; Shotter & Cunliffe, 2003). Using this method, both researcher and leader can collaborate and inquire into how managerial practices are defined based on how they each, in various ways, make sense of an incident.

The purpose is for the researcher to make room for 'generative moments' with the leader to jointly share and question how they each understand and act based on what is assumed within their local 'somewhere' or local world (Ripamonti et al., 2016; Shotter, 2010). This practice can support moving knowing and practicing closer to one another by making room for collaborative and reflexive dialogues between leaders and researchers; generative moments can help interpret mundane activities that take priority and understand how shaping the organisation is managed on a daily basis.

To understand the significance of everyday, practical opportunities, the inquiry takes inspiration from a practice-oriented way of learning called 'action learning' (Pedler, Burgoyne & Brook, 2006; Pedler, 2016). It is a practical method developed to improve leaders' skills by inviting them to work in small groups and systematically analyse and discuss each other's challenges that stem from their daily managerial work (Revans, 1983).

According to its founder, action learning is not a technique but an idea and a philosophy (Revans, 1981; Pedler, 2016; xxi). From this perspective, action learning is the inquiry used by researchers as a broad frame for conducting conversations that construct new knowledge on the practices of management. This way of working has inspired researchers to invite leaders from different companies to jointly analyse the challenges they experience in managing and study these challenges within a relational framework (Larsen & Rasmussen, 2013).

From the beginning, the action learning way of studying management was founded on a realist ontology and has even been discussed in connection to critical realism (Burgoyne, 2009). As mentioned previously, however, this is not the direction of the inquiry presented in this chapter; the collaboration between leaders and researchers is instead understood as a process of co-constructing new and, in the moment, unique knowledge on management. This co-construction is achieved through a reflexive process based on conversations that interact closely with the practical, hands-on processes that involve leaders every day.

The combination of education and action are very important in leading. The way researchers work with action learning is inspired by reworking original thoughts that adhere to relational constructionism. This requires underlining the ontological position of language as researchers attempt to make room for reflexive dialogues among leaders (Ripamonti et al., 2016).

The inquiry presented in this chapter uses the idea of gathering a number of leaders to present and discuss what they interpret as practical challenges in their different firms at the time of the meeting. The inquiry presented is not founded in any kind of realism, but such meetings between leaders and researcher consist of interpretations that enable them to co-construct knowledge of what they reflect upon and observe (Larsen & Rasmussen, 2014).

In that process, we as researchers organise the framework and co-generate the opportunities and challenges that are explored; they play an integral part in co-constructing meaning and possible ways of moving forward. By bringing leaders from different local 'somewheres' or local worlds together, facilitators act as 'a catalyst in helping practitioners question their (and their own) taken-for-granted assumptions and actions as a means for generating new and alternative interpretations and responses to common problems' (Ripamonti et al., 2016). This process calls for researchers to make an active attempt to jointly engage in dialogues and question our ways of making sense. It is also important that we engage in new ways of linking theory and practice and make room for polyphony as we engage in the reflexive action learning dialogues and subsequently publish the results (Cunliffe, 2002; Ripamonti et al., 2016).

Using Inquiry in Conversation

This section approaches how to use inquiry, including general guidelines concerning with whom to use inquiry, the number of participants to include, and what one should know before beginning one. Also presented in this section is an example of inquiry process including the six steps leading from the beginning of the inquiry to the end. In the practical world of management, there are neither beginnings nor endings; rather, there are only continuous actions. Each inquiry develops its own ways of handling constant change.

What is key to engage in such inquiry conversations are researchers who are willing to listen, participate in conversations with leaders, and implement practical activities coupled with the research. A small number of leaders, approximately four to five from different firms, are needed. The firms involved should not be in direct competition with each other or be closely related to each other through contracts or other professional commitments. The chosen leaders must not be nervous or hesitant to present and discuss important practical challenges with a small audience of leaders and researchers. These leaders must also be willing to have their presentations of managerial challenges published anonymously in journals and articles for a larger public.

In order to embark on action learning processes using this inquiry, researchers must possess a basic knowledge of firms, management, and social science methodologies and an extensive willingness to listen and participate open-mindedly in conversations on constructing knowledge on management. The practical work then required is depicted on the following pages.

If researchers are willing to conduct this type of research inquiry, there are several ways to contact and engage leaders in a research project. The following points present one way that you as a reader can allow yourself to be inspired when you develop your own relational and reflexive action learning group process. Remember that the inquiry is generated relationally; the single parts of it are presented in the following steps:

1) Make preliminary contact with an industry association
2) Invite the participating firms
3) Meet with the leaders from the participating firms for the first time to construct the first case story
4) Hold the first relational and reflexive action learning meeting/seminar
5) Co-construct data for the next relational and reflexive action learning meeting/seminar
6) Conclude the relational action learning process

Preliminary Contact with an Industry Association

We have chosen one way to start the research process that has proven to be successful on several occasions, particularly in the interaction between what is taken for granted and what emerges. The first decision concerns which industry is interesting to study. By choosing a specific industry, participating leaders are saved the effort of explaining the specific, practical information about their own industry to each other.

After choosing an industry, it is important to locate the regional or national managing director of the trade association it belongs to. A managing director not only possesses considerable knowledge of the companies within the industry and its leaders; he or she is often interested in participating in other close-up studies of how the industry is working aside from the general and more statistically oriented studies the association itself often produces.

Invite the Participating Firms

The first official step in collaboration between the researcher and the director of an industry is in the introduction letter that outlines the research project to the members of the association. Before the following letter was written, a meeting took place between the director of the industry association and the researchers in order to define the details of the investigation, such as their interest in diversity in management and exploratory solutions. The director of the association arranged the initial contact between multiple interested firms by phone.

Once this had been arranged, the researchers waited for a response from the firms; five firms quickly responded. The researchers then proceeded to arrange meetings with the four of the five firms that were very interested.

Aalborg University
Date: February 20, 2014

Strategic Management in Fashion Companies
There is no doubt that the interplay among market development, management, and design are relevant and key subjects in your company. As researchers in firm development and strategic management, such interplay is of the utmost interest to us. It is the internationalisation in selling cloth designed by small Danish fashion companies that has particularly caught our interest, and we see a need to expand upon existing knowledge.

We, through our research, want to enlarge existing knowledge within this area by approximating ourselves to concrete daily managerial decisions, activities, routines, and interactions between management, design, and marketing. We especially want to do this in collaboration with a small group of small firms that in the future wish to be characterised as focused on developing their share of the international market. In addition to this, the management must have an interest in knowing more about how to become successful and why.

We are two researchers from the Department of Business and Management at Aalborg University – Professor Jørgen Gulddahl Rasmussen and Associate Professor Mette Vinther Larsen – who, for the last several years, have done research on strategic management in close collaboration with the management in the wind and fashion industry. Our latest research (2012–2014) involved five small firms that supplied software and hardware to the renewable energy sector.

Previous to that (2008–2012), we managed a project that included four firms within the Danish Association of Fashion and Textiles. We have included a statement from one of the participants, CEO [xxx], from that project.

The collaboration with [firm xxx] and the other participating firms resulted in the publication of the book Strategisk ledelse som meningsskabende processer, by Mette Vinther Larsen & Jørgen Gulddahl Rasmussen (2013), published by the Jurist and Økonomforbundets Forlag.

We would like to invite you to collaborate with us over the next few years. On a regular basis, three or four times per year, we would visit your firm to follow its development. In between those visits, we would hold seminars with the leaders of the participating firms where we would address general questions concerning markets, management, and design.

When we take a point of departure in this project and the above-mentioned assessments, we can ensure that the management in each firm will develop strategic ideas for interactions between market and design, address and discuss questions on organisational and managerial challenges, and provide feedback regarding the firm's routines.

This project would be funded partly by donations and partly by Aalborg University. The Danish Fashion & Textile Association will be an active participant in creating contacts as well as hosting seminars and other activities. In return, the participating firms must provide space for our quarterly visits as well as make leaders, designers, and marketing specialists available for brief conversations. In addition to this, one or more leaders must meet for the quarterly seminars, which are arranged for all the participating and noncompeting firms for two to three hours.

More information about the projects is available by emailing Mette: mvl@business.aau.dk or Jørgen: jgr@business.aau.dk or by contacting CEO [xxxx] by phone.

Enclosed: Letter from CEO [yyy]
(signed) Mette Vinther Larsen & Jørgen Gulddahl Rasmussen

Figure 4.1 The Introduction Letter

Meet with the Leaders from the Participating Firms for the First Time to Construct the First Case Story

To begin the actual inquiry, there are two possible ways to invite the participating leaders to take part of the inquiry where polyphony is more interesting than predefined answers, heterogeneity is more interesting than homogeneity, and several right solutions are more interesting than one right solution.

One way to introduce this concept is to gather the leaders from all the firms for a first seminar to outline the assessment of the situation at the individual firms and present the entire layout of the research project. A seminar is approximately a half- to full-day meeting where leader and researchers can participate in the conversations on equal terms. Another way the researcher can begin is to visit each individual firm to present the inquiry in detail to its respective CEO, whom he or she would involve, and together construct the first assessment of the present situation at the firm. Both starting points are possibilities.

It is important that the researchers participate in the conversations throughout the entire project. We do not use the word 'interview' because the inquiry is not based on interviews, but on conversations. We and the leaders are, as mentioned previously, two equal participants in the conversations. The researchers contribute by making the practical framework and being inquisitive, while the leaders reflect on the current circumstances of the firm. What we and the leaders must agree upon is a mutual inquiry into ongoing day-to-day management. What happens afterwards is steered by the process constructed by the two partners.

It is important that, from the beginning, the researcher presents and gradually helps the leader to practice this mutual inquiry in a field of practical management. Every participant including leaders and researchers plays an active role in this research process based on their curiosity. It is also important to underscore that every conversation must resemble daily practice as closely as possible, not only through the examples used but also through the language used. It is a researcher's obligation to learn the words and language used by the leaders involved. It is not an obligation for the leaders to learn any of the formal language of management theory.

To work with relational conversations means accepting that these conversations are constructed between invested participants who wish to benefit from them. These participants also maintain constant interest in discovering and influencing where the conversation is headed. Intentions are necessary to participate in the conversation, and the conversation impacts those intentions. A conversation is a line in a meshwork that can advance in many different directions. The aim of the inquiry is to construct jointly how day-to-day management is interpreted, and it is important to be open to many possibilities.

This does not mean that both the researchers and the leaders cannot raise questions or comment using adjusted and unadjusted responses, but the conversation must concern the actual story about the current managerial situation told by the leader. Leaders help develop the line in the meshwork by explaining the circumstances based on their experiences. Researchers follow the story and share their own experiences when it relates to the story. Together, both participants reflect on the story during the conversation.

The following extract was taken from a conversation between the authors and two CEOs at one of the firms. The two leaders had tried unsuccessfully to hire an agent for the Italian market and rather humorously attempted to evaluate the relationship between academics and practising leaders. The conversation is a follow-up on a conversation from a previous meeting.

Researcher 1: 'What about Italy – What came from that?' (Executive 1 and Executive 2 both start laughing)
Executive 1: 'My friend Luigi [the unsuccessful Italian agent].'
Executive 2: 'He disappeared completely. It was strange; the man had contacted us himself. He had driven up here [from Italy] and held a meeting with the company in Kolding that he worked for. He is clever. He has a university degree.'
Researcher 1: 'But we have already told you that [a university degree] does not vouch for anything.'
Executive 1: 'No, those university people.'
(Recorded at a company visit August 27, 2015)

The excerpt from the conversation indicates that the inquiry targets rather small day-to-day activities to build mutual interest in why such mundane activities may be important to understanding the inner workings of management. The dialogue can also be used to highlight that humour and informality within conversations are important.

To follow such mundane day-to-day lines in the meshwork requires flexibility. In this way, the inquiry can be guided by what in social science is often called 'flexible method', which means that the story is followed by commentary and questions with the intention to view the story in a reflective perspective. This does not require preparing questions before entering the conversation. The inquiry does not allow a researcher to demand that his or her questions be answered. Instead, the inquiry must build upon a keen interest in participating in the ongoing process here and now and constructing knowledge regarding the concrete processes of management. Both researchers and leaders must develop a mutual interest in understanding the processes of management.

The following example is a conversation between the authors and two top executives from another firm regarding the challenges that emerged from a situation concerning international currencies when doing business. The US dollar had increased its value more than European currencies, but their suppliers in China required payment in US dollars. Furthermore, their customers paid for the finished products in the devaluated European currencies. This brief extract demonstrates that conversations are continuously adapting. Even the two executives who decided together how the firm should tackle this rather difficult challenge use the conversation to reflect upon what to do.

Executive y1: 'We should have raised our prices.'
Executive y2: 'No, I don't think so. There could have been severe consequences.'
Researcher 2: 'Do all of your competitors have the same problem?'
Executive y1: 'Some, of course, had currency transactions that were more favourable than ours. And because of that, they could choose to take market shares by keeping the prices low and then wait to raise their prices. But that [raising prices] would be silly, in my opinion. You'd have to raise your prices just when everybody else has stabilised theirs.'
Executive y2: 'Yes, it wasn't the right time.'
Executive y1: 'But I know that is what [a specific competitor] has done. They have made efficient currency transactions and not raised their prices. So, they are peeing in their trousers right now.'
Researcher 2: 'One might say that an efficient currency transaction is when it is possible to reach the next decrease in that currency.'
Executive y1: 'Yes.'
Executive y2: 'But has [the specific competitor] not increased their prices?'
Executive y1: 'That was what they said.'
(Recorded at a company visit August 20, 2015 [p. 18])

This extract is an example of how management can 'learn' in practice by reflecting on how to proceed as well as evaluate, from an everyday process, an important emergent process challenge about changing currencies.

To develop a collaborative conversation with the intention of constructing new knowledge is the overall purpose of visits to each individual firm. The first visit contains a conversation between the researcher and the leader, normally with the CEO as the primary participant, and often a tour around the firm. Visits also include conversations with other leaders and employees selected by the CEO with the intention of deepening the researcher's knowledge on how management is conducted within the firm.

Such conversations in all participating firms are inputs for the upcoming seminar. To construct useful material that can serve as input for the seminar in an efficient manner, the inquiry must be built from the recordings of the conversations in the individual firms to construct a case. The recording of one conversation might easily result in a transcript of more than twenty printed pages, and each visit produces approximately two or three conversations. Multiply these proceedings by the number of firms involved, and it becomes too much for a CEO to read before a seminar. Thus, the authors developed a case consisting of three to five pages summarising the visit with each firm.

A case must be constructed and written by the researcher using transcripts from the conversations held with the respective firms. A draft for a case is then mailed to the CEO for corrections, supplements, and approval. When it is approved, it is mailed together with the other cases to all participants of the research project, including the managing director of the trade industry association. The document must be received two to three days prior to the following seminar in order to give all participants time to read the cases before the seminar begins.

The First Relational and Reflexive Action Learning Seminar

The main purpose of the relational and reflexive learning of the seminar does not end in one definite result; it instead attempts to explore many perspectives taken from the practical experiences of skilled leaders. In this way, such a seminar contains a number of different but equal questions, ideas, suggestions, and practical solutions. A seminar can be compared to a meshwork where a number of different and changing perspectives are shared and discussed among the participants.

The following extract is a copy of the introduction of the case description from one of the firms in the authors' inquiry. It focuses on how to create a brand that is in line with a firm's intentions. This particular theme was the CEO's main priority to be resolved in the initial visit to the firm a few weeks before. The extract shows the writing style the authors used to construct an input out of the recorded conversations.

Case Company Z, December 2014

This case is based on a conversation between [CEO in Company Z], Jørgen, and Mette, December 17, 2014

> **How does one support brand development so that it moves away from selling products to selling the lifestyle and the adventures the brand originally included?**
>
> The company owns something quite extraordinary. Its style represents something in the selection of colours, the designs it has, and the quality of its goods. The company operates within a niche where there are only a few competitors. Up until now, we have not been able to unfold this in an efficient way; too much of communicating in the company has revolved around taking care of salespeople, agents, shop assistants, PR agents, etc. They haven't been able to sufficiently understand and communicate the lifestyle and the philosophy behind the brand.

At the same time, the employees of the company have been much too busy finding, training, and keeping agents motivated.

First paragraphs of a five-page case on Company Z, used as input for the seminar January 8, 2015.

The action learning seminar included four company inputs like the one depicted previously. The seminar took place in a meeting room belonging to the industry trade association. It is common to use space at the trade association unless one of the firms requests that the participants visit its location so that the other CEOs might experience some material details of the firm. The seminar is divided into sections of time so that each firm is designated a section. In the letter shown in Figure 4.1, the duration of a seminar was planned to last two to three hours. In the inquiry, this was extended to six to seven hours per the participating CEOs' request. Thus, at the seminar, each case section lasted approximately one and a half hours.

The cases are descriptions of what the individual firms experience as important and challenging. It builds on conversations that are one to three weeks old and are a part of the input for the seminar. As a supplement to each case, the CEO makes a short introduction that may focus on another important subject that has emerged between the conversations in the firm and seminar. The inquiry allows this because constructing practical knowledge on management must build on the special interests at the present moment and what is important to the individual firm.

It is also important for the other CEOs to discuss perspectives they find most relevant to every single case. They are encouraged to raise questions, present what they see as practical solutions, and reflect on the challenges in a case or in the oral presentation of the individual challenge. It is the authors' experience that this leads to the most fruitful and open conversations on management. This also means that the inquiry does not encourage participants to say, 'But at the last seminar you said . . .' If old experiences are reintroduced into the conversation, it must come from a CEO, not from the researchers. The reason for this is that the inquiry was developed to focus on the here-and-now situation.

The conversation on the challenges of each firm can, from a relational perspective, be seen as an exchange of messages and adjusted and unadjusted responses where the leaders and researchers put forward gestures and responses. It is important to encourage the leaders to be proactive in the conversation in order to keep them within the challenges they experience. It is a polyphonic process that occurs in the moment when it concerns future desires or the present interpretation of earlier experiences. It is up to the leaders to define how they want to move understandings generated further and initiate actions in their respective organisations.

From the beginning, it is important to encourage every participant to enter into discussion, which is not difficult; the leaders want to use their experiences to help resolve their own case as well as the cases presented by the other leaders. The researcher's responsibility is to help build space for the conversation to use some of the many possibilities, which lie in different interpretations, intentions, and ideas. It is not a process with any intention to create consensus.

Another of the researcher's obligations is to make sure to keep the time schedule, participate when it seems useful, and take care of the recording equipment. Keeping to the time schedule can be the most difficult task; if it becomes too difficult, it should be addressed by all participants. One solution might be to extend the seminars from three hours to five or six hours; seven hours should be the absolute maximum time for the seminar.

The recording is transformed into a transcription of maximum ten pages, which is mailed to all participants as a means to recollect the seminar. This might lead to comments via email to the researchers from one of the leaders; the sender is either answered directly, or the subject is brought up in a general form to all participants, dependent on the subject raised. It is important to follow up quickly on such communication as this keeps the research project running in between seminars and firm visits. The inquiry functions through many forms of communications; the more intense the communication, the more efficient the knowledge construction.

One of the important advantages of the seminars and the communication processes that follow them is the many different questions, comments, and ideas that are developed during and after the seminar. It is given by a polyphony of voices, often unharmoniously, because the inquiry intends to construct different interpretations. It is the different interpretations being built during the conversation that make it possible for all participants, both leaders and researchers, to construct broader and more facetted pictures of what management is. To play with more than one idea of an everyday management process is the advantage and not the disadvantage of this method.

Co-construct Data for the Next Relational and Reflexive Action Learning Seminar

There are several alternatives concerning follow-up visits to the individual firm that should each be considered. One criterion for what to choose is how the different alternatives in the actual situation support the polyphonic process of constructing a wide array of different perspectives, interpretations, and meanings.

One way is to continue visiting with one or several of the leaders and employees. Another is to have one researcher visit a firm for a day or two. The purpose of a longer visit is to get a different impression of daily life in the organisation. Such a visit must be presented from the start to employees in the firm by the participating leader; thus, employees will not think their performance is being measured or they should spend all their time talking to the researcher. It should be clear to everyone that the project is on leadership and that notes should be taken. Recordings or videos should not be made of these visits.

The material from a longer visit is only used by the researchers; due to his or her tight schedule, the participating leader receives a draft of the case to be used at the next seminar. It is also important that the questions during the visits are not seen as directed toward measuring anyone's efficiency or personal life within the firm; themes and conversations are strictly directed toward understanding the everyday managerial processes. Any critique or severe disagreement must be dealt with by the researcher with the utmost delicacy.

A third way to 'visit' firms is to email questions or tasks to the participating leaders. One example to cause the leaders to reflect between visits and seminar was written the following way:

> [Before the next seminar], we want you to think of two managerial episodes that are significant to you. They need to revolve around a situation where you, your employees, or your colleagues found it difficult to reach an agreement or solve a situation. These episodes are still present in your memory. Maybe they have not been solved, or you are not pleased with the outcome. There are two columns on the paper [we have emailed to you]; in the first column, describe this challenge so that everyone can understand it. The second column is a bit more difficult: it has to be used to reflect upon what this says about yourself, your management, and thoughts about your firm.
> (Message mailed to the CEOs in October 2015)

The idea behind this way of constructing knowledge is to involve the participants more actively in the research process in order to inspire them to handle this task, reflect, and interpret what they see as important emerging phenomena. This step constructs challenges for the next seminar 'directly' from the here-and-now field of management practices.

A fourth way to make conversations on the actual managerial challenges is to encourage the participating leaders to use their mobile devices to take photos that symbolise such challenges. It might be a picture of exchange rates to symbolise the challenge of changing exchange rates and increasing costs when paying Chinese suppliers in US dollars. It could also be a photo of an empty wall, symbolising a lack of ideas on what to do in 2017. A third example could be a number of empty office chairs symbolising a lack of qualified employees for certain important functions in the firm.

These different ways of conversation seem most suited when the research project is well underway. It demands trust between the participants and it demands that experiences are made based on conversations. It is also important to note that leaders, particularly of small firms, are more eager and accustomed to speaking than using more 'unusual' forms of communication; to meet in person with the researchers and other leaders leads more directly to conversation. Conversely, to use a variety of forms of conversation lays the ground for sharing different perspectives and views.

Conclude the Relational Action Learning Process

Having up to eight seminars and approximately the same number of firm visits during the entire period of the inquiry makes it possible to follow a large number of coincidences and emerging phenomena and observe how they are constructed and interpreted. Some of them result in important new creations in the form of new products, entrance into new markets, new personnel, and new types of organising processes. Others have a much shorter lifespan and seem forgotten from one seminar to the next. Using this method, the last category is as important as the first; each is seen as lines in the meshwork that constantly form and reform the firm.

Experience teaches that there must be a certain number of meetings to develop trust, a common agreement in order to work together as co-researchers, and sharing mutual impressions of each other's firm. There must be opportunities for the individual leaders to work together on projects not directly belonging to the research project, such as improving websites, confronting banks, or influencing how national industry fairs are managed.

Using a flexible method makes it possible to both prolong an inquiry and, to some extent, shorten it. Even though the period can be flexible, it is of utmost importance for the researchers to construct data in the here and now during the entire inquiry process. A researcher must accept that there is no defined finishing line for challenges; a challenge and how it changes is understood in perspective for the period of time it is studied.

The duration of an inquiry is defined from its inception between leaders and researchers. In our last three projects, we decided that the duration should last approximately two years. In some cases, it is possible to shorten an inquiry's period of time. When the inquiry is nearly complete, the researcher should end the process with a special learning seminar. This seminar is unique because it functions as a challenge for both the participating CEOs and the researchers, who choose what they view as important findings from the project's two-year duration and present them not as results or answers, but as questions and challenges. The last seminar is divided into a number of 'exercises' that encourage the CEOs as well as the researchers to interpret what they learn from it.

The final seminar should highlight the concept of leadership as a process of continuous action and learning for leaders as well as researchers, and highlight that no answers are permanent, merely steps towards new questions. Leaders should recognise that each emerging phenomenon is new and constructs challenges that have not been interpreted before; their ability to reflect upon them polyphonically is important. For researchers, it is important to recognise that what they interpret from their research are more than answers, but questions that will hopefully offer input into the ongoing process of understanding management for both practitioners and scholars.

Output from the Reflexive Action Learning Process and Its Relational Direction

As the inquiry builds on flexibility, there is no reason why the interpretations of managerial activities derived from the conversation should not be brought into conversations with the leaders immediately after the inquiry has been launched. Practice analyses already begin in the form of conversations at the initial firm visits and during the seminars. Often, one or more of the leaders will try out ideas that have been addressed as themes at seminars as part of their daily activities. For over a century, seminar conversations have been seen as informal and embedded learning processes that can be analysed by pragmatic researchers (Dewey, 1907; James, 1909); there are similarities between how they are analysed 'at home' and the ideas of situated learning (Lave & Wenger, 1991, Wenger, 1998).

Another question remains to be answered regarding how such conversations can be transformed into papers, dissertations, journal articles, and textbook knowledge. The research activities are case studies not only because the input for each seminar is referred to as a case. Each process, from the construction of a coincidence to the inception of a new product or communication process, can be interpreted as a case. In addition to this, the conversation often draws on more than one of these coincidences; it binds actions and understandings together in a polyphony and in this way constructs a larger meshwork of leading. These conversations, and how researchers convey them in writing, are constructions made by a group of experienced professionals, e.g., leaders and researchers who can detect more than one truth, who will attempt to apply what they have learned to perform better as leaders, and who are accustomed to developing practical knowledge together with others.

Researchers and leaders must also acknowledge how language changes the world, a perspective that dates back to Wittgenstein (1953). It is similar to leaders' practical use of language in their efforts to market and persuade their employees to change routines and ways of working. The definition of language can be coupled with what side of the ravine the 'linguistic turn' is seen (Alvesson & Kärreman, 2000). The inquiry presented in this chapter has actively worked with many different voices by bringing leaders together from different 'local worlds' to jointly share their different interpretations of opportunities through using different local understandings to generate new understandings as they communicate. These understandings may make a significant difference in the well-being and success of a firm.

Acknowledging this also means acknowledging how knowledge is constructed between people (Larsen & Rasmussen, 2015). This way of shifting priority from the individual to people acting together influences strongly the results and negates most of the modern Western world's understanding of 'the individual.' This changes the understanding not only of leadership but also research; it underscores the difficulties of concluding anything that has generic value outside the processes in its specific relations.

What becomes of using the inquiry? The inquiry establishes room for conversations that enable practitioners to better manage challenges that emerge in their daily responsibilities. The following excerpt is what they expressed during a seminar in January 2015.

Executive z: 'Grains of gold appear in such a meeting.'

Executive y2: 'It is really cool. I think it was the same the last time [we met].'

Executive w: 'You're going over some matters in your mind; matters you don't have or don't take the time [to explore] in your everyday life.'

Executive y2: 'We are handling many of the same problems and dilemmas, and then we hear that there are other ways to solve them.'

Executive x1: 'Instead of the usual talk at the office with your [business] partner.'

Researcher 1: 'You know how the scenario will go, and then you act according to what you anticipate the reaction will be. In here, you have less possibility of anticipating what will come.'

Executive y2: 'These types of problems often come up when you are busy or under pressure. Then it's, "How do we solve it?" You aren't open-minded enough to reflect, at least not like today, where we've taken a day away from the normal schedule.'

(Recorded January 8, 2015, in the closing moments of a seminar)

Through such conversations, leaders learn to construct cases and ideas on how to handle practice. The conversations and reflections in each case are practice for management. Each participant relationally constructs new polyphonic ideas in the moment on how to become reflexive in the world of practical management.

The difficult part of the process is to transform the interpretations constructed in the actual moment to letters and words. It is not only a 'lack of words' but language with its predefined meanings that creates an obstacle for communicating with others with different views of the world.

As the inquiry is founded on a relational perspective, it is clear that the results coming from this type of inquiry are input into an ongoing conversation between leaders and researchers. The results can, therefore, be evaluated from a perspective of usefulness in the processes to understand managerial activities. The results give input into new interpretations on what is taken for granted and construct an interest and engagement that produces energy for further work within the area.

References

Alvesson, M. (2003) Beyond Neopositivists, Romantics, and Localist: A Reflexive Approach to Interviews in Organizational Research. *The Academy of Management Review*, 28 (1), 13–33.

Alvesson, M. & Kärreman, D. (2000) Taking the Linguistic Turn in Organizational Research. Challenges, Responses, Consequences. *The Journal of Applied Behavioral Science*, 36, 136–158.

Alvesson, M. & Sköldberg, K. (2009) *Reflexive Methodology. New Vistas for Qualitative Research*, 2nd edition. London, SAGE Publications Ltd.

Burgoyne, J. (2009) Issues in Action Learning: A Critical Realist Interpretation. *Action Learning: Research and Practice*, 6 (2), 146–161.

Chia, R. (2013) In Praise of Strategic Indirection: An Essay on the Efficacy of Oblique Ways of Responding, *M@n@gement*, 16 (5), 667–679.

Chia, R. & Holt, R. (2006) Strategy as Practical Coping: A Heideggerian

Cunliffe, A. L. (2001) Leaders as Practical Authors: Reconstructing Our Understanding of Management Practice. *Journal of Management Studies*, 38 (3), 351–371.

Cunliffe, A. L. (2002) Reflexive Dialogical Practice in Management Learning. *Management Learning*, 33 (1), 35–61.

Cunliffe, A. L. & Eriksen, M. (2011) Relational Leadership. *Human Relations*, 64 (11), 1425–1449.

Czarniawska, B. (2013) *On meshwork and Other Complications Portraying Contemporary Organizing*. Göteborg: University of Gothenburg, GRI-rapport 2013:3.

Dewey, J. (1907) *The School and Society*. Chicago, IL, University of Chicago Press.

Gergen, K. J. (2001) *Social Construction in Context*. London, Sage.

Gergen, K. J. (2009) *Relational Being. Beyond Self and Community*. New York, Oxford University Press.

Gergen, K. J. & Gergen, M. (2004) *Social Construction—Entering the Dialogue*. Chagrin Falls, OH, TAOS Institute Publication.

Heidegger, M. (1951) *Wohnen, Bauen, Denken*. Included in: Vorträge und Aufsätze, Teil III.

Hosking, D. M. (2010) Moving Relationality: Meditations on a Relational Approach to Management. In: Bryman, A. et al. (eds.) *SAGE Handbook of Leadership*. Thousand Oaks, CA, Sage.

Hosking, D. M., Gergen, J. K. & Dachler, H. P. (1995) *Management and Organization: Relational Alternative to Individualism*. Aldershot, Avebury.

Ingold, T. (2008) *Lines. A Brief Story*, Oxon, Routledge.

Ingold, T. (2011) *Being Alive. Essays on Movement, Knowledge and Descriptions*. Oxon, Routledge.

James, W. (1909/1987) *Writings 1902–1910*. New York, The Library of America.

Larsen, M. V. (2013) *Strategizing Through Organizing*. Taos, World Books.

Larsen, M. V. & Rasmussen, J. G. (2013) *Strategisk ledelse som meningsskabende processer*. Gylling: Jurist- og Økonomforbundets Forlag.

Larsen, M. V. & Rasmussen, J. G. (2014) Strategisk ledelse som udnyttelse af tilfældet. *Nordiske Organisasjonsstudier*, 16 (3), 26–55.

Larsen, M. V. & Rasmussen, J. G. (eds.) (2015) *Relational Perspectives on Leading*. Basingstoke, Palgrave Macmillan.
Lave, J. & Wenger, E. (1991) *Situated Learning: Legitimate Peripheral Participation*, Cambridge, Cambridge University Press.
McNamee, S. & Hosking, D. M. (2012) *Research and Social Change. A Relational Constructionist Approach*. New York, NY, Routledge.
Mintzberg, H. (1973) *The Nature of Managerial Work*. Englewood Cliffs, NJ, Prentice Hall.
Mintzberg, H. & Waters, J. A. (1985) On Strategies, Deliberate and Emergent. *Strategic Management Journal*, 6, 257–72.
Pedler, M. (2016) *Action Learning in Practice*, 4th edition. Farnham, Grower.
Pedler, M., Burgoyne, J. & Brook, C. (2006) What Has Action Learning Learned to Become? *Action Learning: Research and Practice*, 2 (1), 49–68.
Revans, R. W. (1981) The Nature of Action Learning. *OMEGA*, 9 (1), 9–24.
Revans, R. W. (1983) Action Learning. Its Terms and Character. *Management Decision*, 21 (1), 39–50.
Ripamonti, S., Galuppo, L., Gorli, M., Scaratti, G. & Cunliffe, A. L. (2016) Pushing Action Research Toward Reflexive Practice. *Journal of Management Inquiry*, 25 (1), 55–68.
Sharfritz, J. M., Ott, J. S. & Jang, Y. S. (2005) *Classics in Organization Theory*, 6th edition. Belmont, CA, Thomson Wadeworth.
Shotter, J. (2010) Situated Dialogic Action Research Disclosing 'Beginnings' for Innovative Change in Organizations. *Organizational Research Methods*, 13 (2), 268–285.
Shotter, J. & Cunliffe, A. L. (2003) Leaders as Practical Authors: Everyday Conversation for Action. In: Holman, D. & Thorpe, R. (eds.) *Management & Language*. London, Sage.
Tsoukas, H. & Chia, R. (2002) On Organizational Becoming: Rethinking Organizational Change. *Organization Science*, 13 (5), 567–582.
Uhl-Bien, M. (2006) Relational Leadership Theory: Exploring the Social Processes of Leadership and Organizing. *The Leadership Quarterly*, 17 (6), 654–676.
Weick, K. (1979) *The Social Psychology of Organizing*, 2nd edition. New York, McGraw-Hill, Inc.
Wenger, E. (1998) *Communities of Practice. Learning, Meaning and Identity*. Cambridge, Cambridge University Press.
Wittgenstein, L. (1953) *Philosophical investigations. Philosophische Untersuchungen*. Oxford, Macmillan.

5 Polyphonic Inquiry for Team Development, Learning, and Knowledge Production

Lone Hersted and Charlotte Øland Madsen

Introduction

In the previous chapter, a dialogically based inquiry was presented that enables researchers to co-construct knowledge together with groups of managers from different organisations. In this chapter, we describe how we, as researchers, interacted with practitioners working together at an NGO as we co-constructed a polyphonic inquiry for team development, learning, and knowledge production, inspired by action research and the use of a reflecting team, originally deriving from systemic family therapy (Andersen, 1990). We were interested not only in co-creating knowledge with and in the team, but also in co-creating learning and knowledge production at an organisational level. In line with the other authors of this book, we build on social constructionist meta-theoretical ideas and write about our experience from a constructionist approach to research and social change. Our practice was developed and refined while working together with a team of advisers from an NGO for organic farming and organic food production located in Denmark. In line with the values of the organisation, a basic principle of this practice was to think and work in terms of sustainability, environmental care, and social responsibility.

We undertake research as a form of social action, as described by McNamee (2010), McNamee and Hosking (2013), and Gergen (2015). In this research paradigm, the researcher's role can be seen as that of a 'disturber', 'facilitator', and 'co-creator'. In this chapter, we describe and reflect upon how this practice took shape, share some examples from it, and explain the methodology and theory behind our practice. To a great extent, we draw inspiration from the Bakhtinian school as well as the transformative methods from the tradition of systemic family therapy (initially inspired by Gregory Bateson) developed by the Milan Group and further developed by Tomm and Andersen. We have transformed some of their ideas and working methods (Cecchin, 1987; Tomm, 1987, 1988) from a therapeutic context to an organisational context, with a focus on multiple perspectives, relationships, and dialogic processes. Concerning our action-research-inspired inquiry, we draw mainly on Gergen (2015), McNamee and Hosking (2013),

Gergen, (2009) and Reason and Bradbury (2008). Our thoughts concerning process and wayfaring are mainly inspired by Shotter (1993, 2010) and Ingold (2008, 2009).

Researching from a Future-Forming Perspective

The project was initiated at the request of the NGO. One of the authors of this chapter (LH) was approached by the project manager of the NGO and asked if she could assist the advisors in developing their practices and help them to become a knowledge-sharing team. The researcher agreed to help further this process, building on her experience of facilitating dialogically based reflexive processes and knowledge production in teams. The project became an opportunity to work further on the development of collaborative inquiry methods. They agreed that the other author of this chapter (CM) would join the process, primarily as an observing researcher who would observe and assist in documenting the process and the method applied. It was decided to work with the team of advisors and their project manager through six half-day sessions over a period of six months. The six half-day sessions were followed by individual interviews and a seminar with the team of advisors.

From our research perspective, this project was an opportunity for us to practice participatory research for social change from a 'future-forming perspective' (Gergen, 2015: 288), considering research as creative construction from a collaborative, dialogue-based approach. In line with Gergen, the authors believe that research and knowledge production can be developed together with practitioners in order to create social change, for instance through participatory research and action research. As Gergen argues:

> We live in a world in which religious and political conflict threaten the globe, governments are dysfunctional, communities are eroding, longstanding cultural traditions are evaporating, and we struggle with our relationships to our habitat – both natural and technological. It is time for the social sciences to channel their substantial resources of intelligence and ingenuity into creating more flourishing forms of living together.
>
> (Gergen, 2015: 307)

Gergen advocates new forms of research based on co-construction and knowledge sharing, where the production of knowledge becomes a resource for the people involved but also for others, both practitioners and scholars, around the world. He calls for 'research in which knowledge is acquired through the complex and creative process of constructing a successful practice. [. . .] When such knowledge is shared, it becomes a resource for others' (Gergen, 2014: 11).

Inspired by Gergen, Shotter, McNamee, Hosking, and other social constructionist scholars, the authors decided to experiment with and refine a dialogically based practice in an attempt to enhance reflexivity and development in the NGO. While working from a social constructionist understanding of action research, we invited the participants to co-construct knowledge together with us in a dialogical setting. Our aim was to develop a framework for collaborative reflexivity and knowledge construction while considering learning as a 'joint action' (a term borrowed from Shotter, 1993, 2010), where everybody in the process contributes to the reflexive process and builds upon each other's thoughts and ideas. From this perspective, learning can be seen as a process where participants play an active role in collaborative knowledge building. As McNamee points out:

> Once knowledge is viewed as a collaborative construction, it is seen as a relational achievement, not a private, cognitive process. To the constructionist, abstract information cannot be transmitted or internalized. Rather, what we take to be information (for example, knowledge and meaning construction) is relationally accomplished as people coordinate actions to produce meaning that is deeply connected to their histories. Therefore, knowledge is not merely accumulated in the mind of an individual; it is generated in the constant embodiment of people relating with each other.
> (McNamee, 2015: 339)

In this chapter, we explain how we interacted with practitioners during the task of developing and refining this inquiry. In a social constructionist paradigm, research is a relational and co-constructive process, and researchers are often seen as change agents. In this project, we wanted to soften the traditional role division between researcher and change agent. In line with McNamee and Hosking, we consider research to be an engaged unfolding in ongoing emergent relational processes shaped by minimal structures (2013: 59). In the project, we were interested in exploring the process of co-inquiry and wanted intervention and research to take place at the same time. The idea was to co-create a collaborative space for reflection and knowledge building through dialogue, where each voice in the process was valued and recognised. Furthermore, while recognising that we, as participants in any kind of research project, always take part in fluctuating or ongoing processes, we consider our research to be a situated and co-constructed process. This means that if the process had taken place in another context with another group of participants, it would have developed in a different way. In the last section of this chapter, we discuss the ontological and epistemological assumptions guiding the inquiry, and we elaborate on the very important ongoing ethical reflections we had as we developed and applied the inquiry in practice. First, however, we will present the relational inquiry as it developed during the process with the participants.

Problem Field

The advisors in the NGO were all involved in projects aimed at enhancing collaboration between organic farmers and their stakeholders in and outside their local communities. The funding for these new projects came from a private Danish foundation, Willum Fonden, which contributes financial support to initiatives working towards a better environment, in particular in the area of organic farming. Due to the complexity of this new type of project, the advisors were supposed to switch from the traditional role of advisor to the role of process facilitator. This meant that their traditional focus on giving expert advice to individual organic farmers had to be broadened, and a series of new and diverse perspectives had to be taken into account. The new role as process facilitator demanded new ways of thinking, relating, communicating, and leading, and posed a new challenge to the advisors. In particular, working on complex projects involving many different stakeholders with differing opinions, ideas, needs, and interests led to challenges, tensions, and conflicts. At the NGO's request, we agreed to help create a collaborative learning environment within the organisation that could support the participants in their reflexivity in order to develop and improve their decision-making processes for their projects in organic farming. Furthermore, we were asked to help the advisors move from an individual-based working culture to a more team-oriented culture, where knowledge sharing and relational reflection would become part of their daily practice. A stronger team culture was considered necessary to refine the project work and prevent the advisors from 'burning out'. A further aim was for the participants to develop skills in process facilitation, questioning, and reflexivity. In short, we were invited to initiate a movement among the participants from having the answers as advisors to asking questions as facilitators. This meant that they had to re-define their own professional identity construction. Initially, we reflected on this challenge as researchers, which led us to the following four overall research questions for the inquiry:

1) How can we share and create knowledge together from a relational and dialogue-based approach with the inclusion of multiple voices?
2) How can we widen the range of perspectives, inspire the participants to become more curious, and help them amplify their use of questioning, sharing knowledge and ideas, offering mutual feedback, and working from a more dialogically based orientation, instead of working as isolated individuals?
3) Would it be possible to move from an individual orientation to a more relational orientation and create a working culture in the team where collaborative reflexivity is treasured, practised, and considered important for the project work?
4) How can we, through a polyphonic inquiry, inspire the participants to experiment with new attitudes, new orientations, and new ways of relating to their surroundings?

When developing these four overall research questions, based on an initial conversation with the lead project manager, we found that they were mainly formulated from an academic researcher's point of view. In order to ensure that the participants could identify themselves with the project, we invited the participants to formulate their challenges and research questions in their own words. Rather than taking an *outside-in* perspective, we wanted to work from an *inside-out* perspective. Therefore, at the beginning of each session, the participants were asked to formulate their own here-and-now research questions. These were all oriented towards 'knowing how' rather than 'knowing what' (see Gergen, 2015). Here are some illustrative examples:

- How can I, as an advisor to the NGO, facilitate and support the process of generational handover from a farmer nearing retirement to the new generation of organic farmers?
- How can we engage stakeholders in contributing to organic agriculture on a Danish island that has already developed projects within the framework of sustainable energy forms?
- How can I, as project manager, facilitate a process whereby organic farmers collaborate and coordinate with conventional farmers when they share large swaths of land that is are influenced by many different political interests?
- How can we, as an NGO, support the formation of a whole new social farming community in the border region where organic farming initiatives can contribute to social welfare, such as the inclusion of disabled people?
- How can we rethink the concept of organic farming to encompass and actively involve many different stakeholders in a specific community and in our society in general?

We found it important to reflect upon this process of initially constructing an *outside-in* perspective (together with the team manager) and then integrating a series of *inside-out* perspectives from the team members themselves. It had to become a shared process of co-construction via ongoing dialogue. Therefore, at the beginning of each session, we had a dialogue with the entire team about the contract for the process. Luckily, there were no contradictions between the initial request from the project manager, our own research questions, and the research questions from the team members; in fact, these questions and expectations seemed to supplement each other and made sense to all participants.

Setup and Structure

In order to frame the process, we created a small community of learning together with the team (Lave and Wenger, 1991; Wenger, 1998). The team members met with each other and their project leader once every month for a whole day. We were invited to facilitate the morning sessions (three hours each) at six meetings for a period of six months. Our research draws mainly on participation and field notes from these six-morning sessions. In addition, six weeks after the end of this process, individual semi-structured qualitative interviews were carried out with each participant. These interviews had a formative, evaluative purpose. Furthermore, the whole process was evaluated at a follow-up seminar with the entire team of advisors and their project manager, facilitated by one of the authors (CM). During the entire process, field notes were taken and individual interviews were audio recorded and transcribed in full. Instead of 'collecting' data, we prefer the term 'generating data', in accordance with the principal ideas of action research from a constructionist perspective, because we see data generation as a co-constructive process where research and intervention are closely interwoven and take place at the same time (see McNamee & Hosking, 2013).

The Inquiry

This section describes our participatory inquiry in more detail and presents an example from our practice. The group, consisting of six agricultural advisors and their project manager, mainly works on issues concerning the transition from conventional farming to organic farming. However, new and more complex tasks required new approaches to project management, involving many different and new types of stakeholders.

Instead of positioning ourselves as 'experts' and the advisors as 'objects to be studied or informants', we attempted to position ourselves in a 'not-knowing position' (Anderson, 1990) as process facilitators, and the advisors from the NGO were positioned as experts on their own practice, namely organic farming. Rather than being 'observers' of 'objects' or 'interviewers' of 'informants', we, as researchers, became co-creators of new ideas and knowledge production with the participants. We noticed that the advisors were used to being very isolated from each other and that they often encountered orientational difficulties in their 'wayfaring' (Ingold 2008, 2009). Obviously, they needed someone to share with. Some of them even expressed that they sometimes found themselves in a paralysed state and, in order to avoid conflicts, postponed important actions and decisions, which resulted in even more conflicts and problems. Their challenges seemed so complex that any attempt to practice linear project management would immediately fail. No cookbook could provide the participants with useful answers. More circular ways of thinking, relating, and communicating seemed to be necessary in order to succeed with these complex projects in organic farming. In order to help the advisors develop and refine their project work, we assisted them in creating a framework for collaborative reflexivity, knowledge sharing, and mutual feedback on challenges and possibilities related to their projects. In line with Shotter, it seemed to be a question of gaining a practical sense of 'how to go on' in many different situations and deciding on a line of 'action within it' (Shotter, 2009: 2). As researchers, we assumed the roles of 'disturbers', 'facilitators', and 'co-creators' in order to help the participants reflect collaboratively on their challenges so that they could find orientation and take action based on a more reflexive approach.

In other words, we were asked to help the participants in their 'wayfaring' in the foggy landscape of their new assignments. With inspiration from systemic and social constructionist practices, we applied the use of a reflecting team with elements of roleplaying concerning team members' past, present, and future experiences and actions. In this way, a relational training ground was co-created in order to enhance and refine reflexive processes within the team concerning future actions and the ability to move within the process, taking into consideration the notions of unpredictability, uncertainty, and changeability that characterise complex change processes with many stakeholders in ever-shifting conditions.

Ethical Guidelines

As mentioned in the introduction, our practice draws on principles from supervisory inquiries developed and described within the systemic and social constructionist tradition. In order to challenge the assumptions that are taken for granted and co-construct new insights among the participants and ourselves, we took our point of departure from three working principles described by Gianfranco Cecchin from the Milan Group. These three overall principles are closely connected and described by Cecchin as 1) curiosity, 2) irreverence, and 3) neutrality. In addition to these three principles, we added a fourth principle, namely the principle of polyphony (polyvocality) inspired by Bakhtin. These principles can be described as follows (for further explanation, see Cecchin, Lane & Wendel, 1992, 1994; Bakhtin, 1981, 1984):

1) By the term 'curiosity', Cecchin (1987) refers to the importance of always being curious and asking circular questions while formulating questions from many different perspectives, instead of making conclusions about the 'truth' on the basis of vague assumptions. Exhibiting curiosity is a matter of considering as many perspectives, possibilities, and ideas as possible.
2) The principle of 'irreverence' in a Cecchin et. al. (1992) understanding is about being irreverent towards the taken-for-granted assumptions of the participants (including the interviewer, the person in focus, and, in this case, the members of the reflecting team).
3) The idea of 'neutrality' (Cecchin, 1987) means not taking sides or allying oneself as a facilitator with any particular person or perspective, but rather remaining curious in order to understand many different perspectives and the logic behind them.

4) The idea of polyphony (polyvocality), inspired by Bakhtin (1984), is, in our practical use of the term, a reminder to recognise and take into consideration multiple voices and perspectives and to acknowledge diversity and multiplicity. For instance, while entering into dialogue with the reflecting team, we try to integrate the diverse voices of the many different stakeholders who are involved in a situation. In line with McNamee and Hosking (2013: xiv), promoting polyphony is a matter of ensuring a space for dissensus, complexity, and multiplicity.

Our concern with ethics in this kind of collaborative knowledge production will be explained in more detail in the two last sections, entitled 1) 'Withness' Thinking in Research' and 2) 'Ethical Reflections'.

Unfolding the Inquiry

As mentioned previously, the advisors were used to working on an individual basis without sharing knowledge or creating ideas together as a team. Due to the increasing level of complexity and challenges of their new projects, there was an evident need for the creation of a practice and a space for collaborative learning and reflection in the group (Wenger, 1998). Therefore, we were interested in finding out how we could work from a relational approach to reflexivity and knowledge building. Our wish was to create and develop a setup and a structure for dialogue within the team that could invite and enable reflexivity and knowledge building among the participants, a kind of reflexivity and knowledge building that could become enhanced and refined by the inclusion of many different perspectives, inspired by the Bakhtinian notion of 'polyphony' (1984). Based on these considerations,

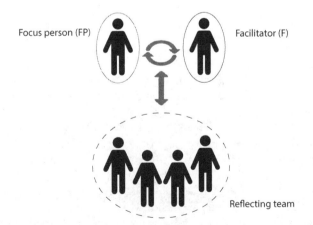

Figure 5.1 The Spatial Setup of the Dialogue Process

we decided to adopt a reflecting team method, inspired by, among others, Andersen (1991). We adapted this method to the needs of the team. The spatial setup for the process is visualised in Figure 5.1 and will be explained, with examples, later in the section.

In Figure 5.2, we show the different phases of each half-day session with the participants in a learning circle. In each session, one advisor assumed the role of focus person (FP) and presented his or her project and his/her own research question. The focus person changed from session to session, so that everybody achieved insight into each project and the challenges related to that project. At the beginning of each session, we took time to follow up on the previous session before switching to a new focus person with a new theme. In this way, new reflexivity and learning were enhanced. All six advisors and their project manager played an active part in the sessions, which was important for enhancing their identity as a team with knowledge sharing and co-construction of knowledge as part of its daily culture. Following is a more detailed description of each phase. However, we remind the reader that this description is not a recipe but a set of guidelines.

In the following sections, we will describe the different phases in more detail and provide some case-specific examples.

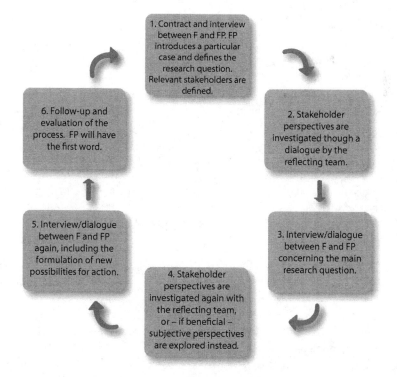

Figure 5.2 A Typical Dialogic Session

Phase 1: Contract and Interview/Dialogue with the Focus Person

In the first phase of each session, one of the participants (the focus person) was invited to explain his or her current project to us and the reflecting team. One of the researchers (LH) served as a facilitator in this process by asking questions mainly inspired by Cecchin (1987) and Tomm (1987, 1988). This initial process of the inquiry was designed not only to provide the facilitator and the other participants with the necessary basic knowledge of the project, but also to explore the story of the focus person, as told by him- or herself, 'from within' the complexity of an ongoing situation (Shotter, 2009: 8). The initial interview often became centred on the here-and-now challenges of the project, and the focus person was asked to pinpoint what he or she particularly wanted to investigate with help from the facilitator and the reflecting team. During the initial conversation, this explicit theme was turned into a research question by the focus person him- or herself (as described previously). The focus person was asked to point to the most important stakeholders for the project and explain a little about these stakeholders and their backgrounds. Each member of the reflecting team was given the task of identifying with a specific stakeholder perspective and listening to the interview between the facilitator and focus person from that specific perspective. In this initial phase, the facilitator and the focus person had a dialogue based on a series of questions. Often the questions were formulated along these lines:

- What is the major vision of this project? Why is this project important?
- What do you consider to be the major challenges in your project – now and in the longer term?
- Who are the stakeholders of the project? And what are the relationships and connections between them?
- How do the stakeholders construct their realities at meetings? How do they position themselves and others?
- What does the world look like from their perspective? What aspect of the project would be particularly important for them? How could they eventually contribute to (or detract from) the process going forward?
- Are there any tensions or conflicting interests among the stakeholders?
- What should you be particularly aware of? Are there any pitfalls to take into consideration?

As illustrated previously, these types of questions focus not only on the many individual voices or stakeholder perspectives but also on the relationships and connections between them. Working from a constructionist approach, we shied away from a primarily individual focus to a more relational-responsive understanding of project work. Furthermore, we tried to help the advisors see themselves as forming part of the tensions and conflicts emerging in the projects and assist them in breaking out of undesirable communicative and relational patterns. In the following sections, we will illustrate our practice with an example of the relational-responsive processes and the dialogue that emerged during a session.

Case Example from Phase 1

In the first phase of the session, a new project was presented by one of the advisors, Benny (focus person). His project concerned the possible acquisition of 477 hectares of land by a consortium of both conventional and organic farmers. The land was owned by the Danish state, and the consortium was led to believe that this piece of land would be put on the market for sale. Both conventional and organic farmers were leasing this land from the state and had their cattle grazing in this area. Some of them held a meeting and decided to invite all the lessees of the land to join them in this consortium, with the purpose of making a shared bid on the land. In phase 1, Benny reported that the land had been sold from one ministry to another without an official round of bidding. The farmers were frustrated with this new development because they were relying on the land to fulfil official environmental regulations for farming concerning the treatment of manure. They were now at an impasse and decided to keep the consortium running and to put in a shared bid on the lease of the land, thus continuing the current practice of grazing their cattle on the land. A further recent complication of the situation was that the use of the farmland for grazing might not be possible in the future if the Ministry of the Environment were to decide to flood the area and return it to its original state.

Examples of questions asked by the facilitator in phase 1 and the subsequent dialogue:

Facilitator (F): 'What is the main task of the NGO in this project?'

Benny (B): 'To help the farmers continue their practice of grazing their cattle on the land. But there are several different possibilities. Maybe the lease period can be extended because one farmer has a contract that is one year longer than that of the other farmers, and we may, as a part of the legal process, be able to keep up the practices of all farmers' cattle grazing on the land for another year. However, I'm not sure this is the best direction for the consortium right now. Another possibility is that the government may decide to cut off the layer of turf and return the area to its original state as a bog so it can become a tourist attraction. There are many different interests at stake, and the farmers need us to help them with their project.'

F: 'What kind of help would you appreciate from the team today?'

B: 'I would appreciate shared reflection on the potential conflicts, which can be described as a "Pandora's box", both between the conventional and organic farmers in the consortium and between the consortium and the external stakeholders. I need the help of my team to formulate an action plan here and now.'

The dialogue between Benny and the facilitator continued in this way for a couple of minutes. When asked by the facilitator, Benny explained that he would like to hear the different voices of the reflecting team address the following research questions:

- What should my [Benny's] role be as a project manager in this complex landscape, from the perspective of the NGO for organic farming and organic food production? What should/could be offered in terms of assistance and resources from the NGO?
- What are the potential consequences of changing from buying to leasing the land?
- Whom could we consider contacting for legal advice? Is it possible to extend the lease agreements for another year because of a binding legal agreement with one of the farmers? And would such an idea be in the interests of the consortium consisting of both organic and conventional farmers?
- How can I [Benny] and the reflecting team sketch a provisional action plan for this project?

After formulating these research questions, the dialogue continued. Benny pointed out five important stakeholder perspectives:

- The organic farmers
- The conventional farmers
- The forest ranger (representing the state owners)
- The mayor (representing the local municipality)
- The Ministry of the Environment.

In this phase, Benny's reflection process on his project took centre stage. He had the time and space to tell the story, and he invited his colleagues on the reflecting team to reflect upon the case from different angles. By telling his story to others, Benny was able to construct pivotal questions concerning possibilities for future actions on the project and to identify key stakeholders with whom he had to interact and negotiate. This led to a future-forming perspective in the storytelling process, aided by questions from the facilitator.

In the following section, we move to phase 2, where the team members were invited to join the reflection process.

Phase 2: Dialogue in the Reflecting Team from Different Stakeholder Perspectives

In the second phase of the session, the reflecting team members were asked to reflect on the story and talk from specific stakeholder perspectives, as defined previously. Without previous planning, the team members identified so strongly with their stakeholder perspectives that the dialogue turned into a little roleplaying scenario. This roleplaying was not planned by the facilitator but emerged during the process when the participants became inspired by each other. As can be seen in the following excerpt, one of the advisors, Sylvester, played the role of a conventional farmer and had to convey perspectives on the case accordingly, which for him was a very unusual stakeholder position. By working with multiple voices of stakeholders in this way, new perspectives and horizons were explored. Simultaneously, each participant reflected upon his or her own practice and the practice of his/her colleagues.

In the following excerpt, we will take a closer look at some of the utterances that members of the reflecting team made while identifying with the different stakeholder perspectives.

Case Example from Phase 2

In the following example, we show how the advisors on the reflecting team changed their subject positions and engaged in a sort of roleplaying scenario. The utterances are from the participants, who were taking different stakeholder perspectives (roles). The different voices illustrate the polyphony:

Organic farmer (OF):	'We want action now because of the threat of coming bidders for the lease of the land.'
Conventional farmer (CF):	'The mayor must be interested in supporting the conventional farmers' interests in this case.'
Mayor (M):	'Is it possible to divide the consortium up between conventional farmers and organic farmers?'
OF:	'We need to apply pressure now to get the land; then we can argue about the distribution of it.'
Forest ranger (FR):	'We need a politically acceptable solution – one that is easy to administrate. A clear plan: that is what is important to us.'
CF:	'As conventional farmers, we are out of the picture, as it was agreed that the land should be organic farmland.'
M:	'We would like to talk to the farmers. If they could buy the land, it would be fine with us.'
OF:	'We have no shared interests in this with the conventional farmers.'
FR:	'It's not for sale. It could possibly be rented, but this will only be possible for the organic farmers. The conventional farmers must be phased out.'

M: 'We think this is a fantastic possibility!'
FR: 'How can you exploit the area? It's not okay to break the rules!'
CF: 'We don't want to graze cattle on the land; we want to spread manure from our pigs. From our perspective, we don't think it's fair that we were not allowed to place a bid on the land.'
FR: 'It's not possible for you to buy the land!'
CF: 'We are considering leaving the consortium and suing the state for breach of contract. Some of us have 1,000 pigs and we are dependent on being able to spread the manure.'
M: 'You haven't played a proper part in the political game!'
CF: 'The municipality has not been paying attention to this [problem].'
FR: 'You [conventional farmer] haven't been proactive enough.'
M: 'We haven't had access to the state of affairs. But is it at all legal for organic farm animals to graze in areas fertilised with manure from conventionally bred animals?'

And so on.

As seen in the example previously, in this phase different voices were invited into the dialogue process and they illustrated the polyphony of the case. The complexity of Benny's initial case story was intensified with the exploration of the different stakeholder perspectives. The roleplaying enabled the reflecting team members to abandon their own taken-for-granted perspectives and explore other views. In phase 3, Benny is invited into a new reflection process concerning his case.

Phase 3: New Interview/Dialogue between the Facilitator and Focus Person

In the third phase, a new dialogue between the facilitator and the focus person (Benny) took place, with the purpose of exploring the challenges from *within* the project. In all the projects we worked with in this NGO, there were many relational tensions and conflicts at stake. In this third phase of the session, the focus person was asked to walk around the 'relational landscape' together with the facilitator. The aim was to explore different stakeholder positions and thereby challenge foregone conclusions and taken-for-granted assumptions about the perceived relational tensions and conflicts in the case. The following questions seemed to be very helpful in this phase:

- When you listened to all these voices on the reflecting team, what struck you?
- What do you think is at stake for the involved partners? How do the different stakeholders view the situation, in your opinion?
- What foregone conclusions or taken-for-granted assumptions are implicit or explicit among the involved partners and may be held by you, as well?

- What arguments, logic, feelings, and values are at stake?
- What significance does the particular use of language have in the process? Do you remember how people talked together at your last meeting with the stakeholders?
- Do you see any patterns in these ways of relating to each other?
- What could you and the stakeholders do to break out of these patterns?
- What could you do to strengthen the relationships among the participants?
- How could you involve and engage the stakeholders even more in the project? How can you contribute to their commitment to the process?
- What kinds of resources, knowledge, or expertise do you need right now in order to proceed? Would it be helpful to involve any experts, e.g., for legal, financial, or specific technical matters?
- Who else do you need to be in dialogue with, e.g., significant politicians or specific organisations?
- Are there any possibly important players that you haven't thought of yet?
- What can be learned from this episode/conflict, and what kind of awareness does it point to now and in the future?

Case Example from Phase 3

This example shows how the new interview/dialogue between the facilitator and focus person opened up further reflection on his project. The dialogue between the stakeholder positions in the roleplaying session prompted new reflections. After a longer session with the reflecting team, the facilitator asked the focus person, 'What kinds of reflections do these perspectives among the reflecting team open up?'

Benny (B):   'I predict a mess on the board of directors of the consortium. We need to sort out all this confusion. The next step I'm going to take is to talk with a woman who is a professional advisor from the National Centre for Agricultural Counselling and try to find out what we can achieve in new negotiations.'

Facilitator (F):   'The farmers on the board seem to have a relationship of mutual dependency, which seems to function. Could you eventually build on this? It seems like all of you need to coordinate and collaborate. What do you think about this way of seeing it?'

B: 'We need to create a common plan/strategy, without any deals under the table. For instance, we could make a five-year plan together.'

F: 'How could you tell a story that represents all the stakeholders in the group? By, for instance, using a language of multiple voices? How, in your practice, can you work with the inclusion of many different voices?'

B: 'While working for the NGO, of course, our main focus is on organic farming, but we have agreed to include all the farmers in the association. The main vision for the association is that the land should be cultivated from an orientation of organic farming.'
F: 'But it seems like all the stakeholders are dependent on each other.'
B: 'Yes, but we cannot just fold our arms and wait.'
F: 'So what do you think about the future of the project?'
B: 'I need to recap and elaborate new proposals for the upcoming meeting. The situation has changed, and I wonder whether the original project formulation still works or if it will need adjusting.'

In phase 3, the conversation between the focus person and the facilitator was orientated towards the future. Aided by his own storytelling and the roleplaying session, Benny was able to navigate the landscape of his case in a different way, grasping future possibilities for action. The conversation led Benny to new reflections on how to proceed as project manager.

In phase 4, the colleagues on the reflecting team were invited to provide their reflections on how Benny could eventually proceed with the project.

Phase 4: Dialogue in the Reflecting Team from Different Stakeholder Perspectives

In this phase the colleagues on the reflecting team were asked to reflect upon the originally formulated research questions and the subsequent conversation between the focus person and the facilitator. This time it was decided to abandon the specific stakeholder perspectives in order to open up further reflection. The reflecting team members were asked to take their own subject positions as professionals and to offer their own perspectives on the challenges described by the focus person. This meant that phase 4 involved the team members' own experiences and knowledge concerning the topics brought up in the session. Furthermore, they offered information about relevant persons in their professional network who could possibly provide Benny with some legal, agronomic, and financial expertise in relation to the project.

Case Example from Phase 4

An excerpt from the dialogue within the reflecting team is presented as follows. As mentioned previously, the reflecting team members were asked to contribute their own thoughts and ideas as colleagues of Benny.

Steven (S): 'It sounds like you need to contact H. H.' [a counsellor from the state]
Chris (C): 'I agree. She [the counsellor from the state] acts as a representative for both organic and conventional

Polyphonic Inquiry 101

	farmers and has the authority to make the politicians listen to her.'
S:	'You need to explore the potential conflict between the conventional and the organic farmers in the consortium. Will they be able to collaborate?'
Benny (B):	'Wouldn't it better to let the professional counsellor give her point of view on this, through her professional insight?'
Helen (H) (project manager of the entire team):	'I think it would be good to develop a shared strategy for the consortium, one that can integrate diverse interests.'
S:	'We also need to consider our own interests in this matter. Should we work to cultivate the interests of both organic and conventional farmers, or should we be part of a plan to outmanoeuvre the conventional farmers?'
B:	'It is the consortium's vision for the land to be organic farmland, and that's why we have been asked to take part in the process.'

In phase 4, the dialogue between Benny and the other team members developed into a process of knowledge sharing, but they also explored different possibilities for action. Together, they started co-constructing new pathways. In the process, Benny, as a relative newcomer to the organisation, was invited into the network of contacts of the other team members.

In phase 5, a final dialogue with Benny was initiated by the facilitator and supported by comments from the reflecting team, with the purpose of developing possibilities for future actions concerning the project.

Phase 5: Final Interview/Dialogue between the Facilitator and Focus Person

In this phase of the session, we used questions that could contribute to expanding the perspectives even further. Typical questions were:

- How could this project develop from a broader perspective? What are the potentials? Could others learn and gain inspiration from it? Whom might you involve? What kind of story would you like to tell about the project next January? What kinds of stories could ideally be told by the stakeholders and other players involved in the project?
- How can you and the partners who are involved formulate a vision in which all the significant stakeholders can identify themselves?
- What kinds of alternative ideas and approaches that we haven't thought of yet could involve the surrounding community, local institutions, or organisations in a positive way?

Excerpt from phase 5:

Facilitator (F):	'How can you follow up on this?'
Benny (B):	'This palaver in the boardroom should become visible.'
F:	'What do you think about the idea of inviting a colleague to the next meeting?'
B:	'Yes, that would probably be beneficial.'
Steven:	'Yes, because Benny would not probably be able to see or grasp it all.'
F:	'I just try to imagine the scenario . . . Could you possibly take a time-out during the meeting and share with each other?'
B:	'Sure.'
Helen:	'Your approach is important. Who could assist you? Maybe Sylvester would be the best option in this case.'

Thus, in phase 5, a set of reflections on future actions was co-created. The idea of involving a colleague, Sylvester, was one option among others. Together, the group coordinated a vision for the future of the project.

Phase 6: Group Follow-up and Evaluation

In phase 6, the whole team was invited to weigh in on how they experienced being part of the process.

Case Example from Phase 6

In this final stage of the session, the entire team was invited to follow up on the session and evaluate the outcome from a here-and-now perspective. One by one, all participants expressed their thoughts on the session and what they had learned from it.

Facilitator:	'What did you think of this session?'
Sylvester:	'The most important thing has been that some of us in the final phase stepped out of our roles and became more "ourselves".'
Kathleen:	'The conversation led to some points that I hadn't thought of before. It is like talking and thinking at the same time. Many possible scenarios were explored.'
Helen (The project manager):	'That is also the way I see it. We investigated the problems in ways that surprised me.'
Sylvester:	'For instance, when you want to try to understand how a conventional farmer thinks, then you have to identify with his perspective.'
Facilitator:	'What does it mean to you that you can use the resources and experiences of others on the team?'
Benny:	'There is really a lot to work with! Everybody came up with some important perspectives from their roles.'

The team members reflected upon how they had experienced identifying with different stakeholder perspectives and then shifting back to become more 'themselves' again during the session. The attempt to identify oneself with the role of a conventional farmer had obviously made an impact on Sylvester. For Kathleen, the process had led to new insights that she had not considered before. Similarly to Kathleen, Helen found that it had contributed to seeing the case in new and surprising ways. Likewise, Benny found that the dialogue had brought about new perspectives in relation to his case.

Brief Analysis of the Session

As can be seen in the excerpts from the dialogue from different stakeholder perspectives, Benny's description of the project as a 'Pandora's box' is convincing because the more knowledge we achieved concerning the project, the more complicated it became. Every time we tried to see the project from a different stakeholder's perspective, it became more complex. There were tension and potential conflicts within the consortium between organic farmers and conventional farmers. The change from land purchase to lease agreement had thrown the entire process into a whole new frame of reference. The many voices represented by the reflecting team developed into a sort of roleplaying scenario. Benny concluded that the next board meeting for the consortium would be pivotal to the process, and that he needed to be well prepared for potential conflicts.

Furthermore, as requested by the facilitator, we discussed the idea of including another team member, Sylvester, as a companion. The idea was that he could be present at the coming meeting with the stakeholders so that Benny could have someone to share and reflect with before, during, and after the meeting. As can be seen from the examples, the methodological setup gave the participants a chance not only to explore their cases from their own perspective, but also, because of the division into stakeholder perspectives, to see the case from multiple perspectives. They were invited to walk around in the foggy landscape of the case with their colleagues, exploring the polyphony of stakeholder interests. An additional benefit of this inquiry was that the whole team of advisors became engaged in Benny's project and began exploring it from *within* the case by taking different stakeholder perspectives. By engaging in the process and contributing to it with their knowledge, experience, and imagination, new knowledge and new possibilities for action were co-created. By taking part in Benny's story and sharing the experiences and viewpoints, the session became a relational learning experience for each person in the room.

Follow-up Conversation

A week after our session, Benny and Sylvester took part in a board meeting with the stakeholders of the project. In the following session with the team members, a month later, we had a follow-up conversation with the purpose of intensifying the learning from the process and trying to understand what had happened afterwards.

In this follow-up conversation, Benny and Sylvester expressed their satisfaction with the events that had unfolded during the board meeting. The potential conflicts had not dominated the meeting, and both organic and conventional farmers were engaged in the continuation of the idea of the consortium placing a shared bid on the rental of the land. Benny reported that he had spent considerable time after our previous session preparing for the meeting and that it had been of great help to him to have Sylvester present at the meeting. There was only one short altercation between an organic farmer and the chairman of the consortium, a conventional farmer. The organic farmer asked the chairman about a newspaper article in the local press in which the chairman had expressed his concern that the land would be rented entirely by organic farmers. The chairman defused the situation by saying that the journalist had exaggerated his comment. The dispute was then put to rest. Benny now saw the importance of inviting professionals with expertise in legal and economic issues to examine the project and advise the consortium on how to proceed.

When asked by the facilitator, 'To what extent did the supervision contribute to the way in which you conducted the meeting?' Sylvester answered: 'It can't be directly transferred, but it's also important to think things through before such a meeting; it might have been the preparation, the thinking it through that made the meeting a success.' Benny added: 'Thinking it through matters. At the board meeting we started out with a roundtable presentation of all the viewpoints in the consortium. Sylvester and I had agreed not to bring up the possible themes of conflict, and I must confess that I spent a lot of time worrying about these conflicts and, in the end, none of them came up.'

After this briefing by Benny and Sylvester, the facilitator invited all the team members to a shared reflection on the learning process for this specific case:

Benny (B):	'It's nice to have two colleagues participating in the project, because it gives you an opportunity to learn in a different way.'
Steven (S):	'Yes, these two won't learn anything without talking together. We're all like that. You need an observer from the outside and you need some feedback.'
B:	'Yes, and it was nice to take a "time out" with Sylvester during the meeting to discuss how things were going.'
Helen (H) (the team leader):	'We could adopt this for the other projects. Please let me know in the future if any of you need assistance with difficult meetings.'

Facilitator (F):	'You are all used to working alone as experts. On a team, it's important to prioritise time to share and enable learning processes.'
Kathleen (K):	'It's important to have someone who can see what's going on during the meeting, because you can't look them all in the eye.'
H:	'All our projects are vulnerable.'
S:	'It's important to have another professional opinion. You don't learn anything from running these projects on your own.'
K:	'It's important to ask questions to get to know what's going on. You need to forget about your professional expert positioning and engage in dialogue instead.'
B:	'And it's important for keeping motivation up during the project. To keep it moving!'
S:	'It motivates the people with whom we work to be able to change things. The thing that annoys me is that we don't always have the energy to play with them in the super league. We have a role to play as an organisation primarily by communicating the goals and dreams of all these visionary people taking part in our projects.'

Brief Analysis of the Follow-up Conversation

While focusing on the method of the inquiry combined with the reflections from within the process, the authors found it interesting that both Benny and Sylvester expressed their relief that the board meeting did not end in open conflict between the conventional and organic farmers. They attribute this, in part, to the amount of preparation they did before the meeting, inspired by the dialogues and roleplay with the reflecting team in the previous session.

The concern expressed by Benny that the meeting might eventually turn into a 'Pandora's box' of conflicts motivated Benny and Sylvester to prepare for the meeting and coordinate how to ensure that all the board members would be invited into dialogue and feel that their voices were heard in the meeting – and in the decision-making process. They also chose to begin the meeting with the presentation of a visionary plan for the whole project and to tell the board members that they were all important stakeholders in this vision. Looking beyond the initial relief and the success of the meeting, interestingly, Benny and Sylvester chose to focus on constructing a relational and dialogic invitation when starting the meeting. Additionally, they found it important to be careful in constructing their own subject positions because, from a stakeholder perspective, they could be seen as biased in favour of the organic farmer stakeholders. Both Benny and Sylvester believed it had been important that they attended the meeting together. In their evaluation of the project, they both emphasised the value of having been able to break with the regular pattern of working alone and recognised the necessity of learning from each other and providing mutual support.

We believe that this move from working alone, on an individual basis, to entering into closer relationships with colleagues helped the participants in their learning and working processes. Having someone to reflect with before, during, and after a meeting seemed to be an approach that worked well for them. This practice of relational interaction could easily be implemented for other projects if needed. Kathleen's comment that, in these cases, 'It's important to ask questions, to get to know what's going on. You need to forget about your professional expert positioning and engage in dialogue instead', is also interesting. This utterance indicated that she had reflected upon her own role in her professional tasks, and perhaps recognised that she herself needed to change her subject position in order to make progress. These and other comments showed how the participants, when sharing their cases through dialogue, were able to learn from each other. It also showed that such a session is relevant not only for the person in focus, but also for the other participants, who are actively involved through their participation on the reflecting team.

Six Months Later

Six months later, one of the authors of this chapter (CM) conducted individual semi-structured qualitative interviews with each team member in order to obtain insight into the learning outcomes of the participants. The following analysis focuses on how Benny now retrospectively constructs his work with the consortium of both conventional and organic farmers.

Benny: 'The interesting thing will be if the consortium is able to stay together on this project and if it will be able to contribute to a vision of farming that is useful for the community, not just enabling the continuation of grazing for their cattle. For me, it has been a crazy thing to start up. I am not an agronomist myself; I am originally an organic farmer and a schoolteacher. I think they had to see if I was able to do the job, but I now feel that I have gained their respect and that they trust me.'

Reflecting on the skills of the farmers on the project, Benny now sees his own role as a process facilitator and coordinator helping the farmers to reach a higher level of reflection, as well as teaching them to incorporate business skills into communication and processes.

However, Benny said in the interview that he finds his own role in changing the perspectives of the local councils, municipalities, and ministries the most interesting part of the project. As he puts it:

Benny: 'The most exciting thing is trying to make them think out of their frameworks and boxes. The local city councils have drawn up huge plans, and they just do not know how to execute them. I really hadn't realised this before now, but in the larger context of all these projects, we [the counsellors] contribute to the wriggling and changing of some of these conventional frameworks and assumptions.'

Reflecting on the participatory inquiry and the collaborative learning practice, Benny says that he has found this work very inspiring. In general, he thinks that he and his colleagues need to be able to understand the stakeholders of the projects and find out how to communicate with them. He said, 'You need to have a lot of empathy and be able to read their minds and the situation. Then you need to form a picture, and they might have diverging opinions and interests, but you have to be able to navigate through this while maintaining a helicopter view of the overall direction you want this to go.'

Benny described how he has enjoyed having a partnership with one of the other advisors, Sylvester, on his project. This partnership contributed to the project advancing in the desired direction and allowed them to discuss situations as they emerged during the process. He pointed out that this partnership kept the process energised. He explained that working together makes them less vulnerable as advisors, for instance, if one of them has time constraints or when unforeseen things occur. Benny added that the dynamics of the group of advisors have greatly contributed to his learning curve, and that the conversations in the group have helped advance his project and have given him new tools and perspectives on how they could work on such a project. As he said: 'Working together on the team means that we are equipped to do this. The supervisory model works.'

Benny expressed in the interview that the multi-voiced dialogic process carried out in the supervisory session, the current dialogues with Sylvester and other colleagues, and the interactions he has had with the stakeholders of the project have together contributed to a successful outcome.

In the following section, further methodological reflections that we as researchers have made during the process are presented.

Reflections on the Inquiry

This section turns our attention to our initial research questions and reflects upon the processes of the inquiry from a general viewpoint.

- How can we share and create knowledge together from a relational- and dialogue-based approach, with the inclusion of multiple voices?

As described at the beginning of this chapter, each session was co-constructed with the participants, and sometimes the reflections among the multiple voices on the reflecting team developed into a sort of roleplaying. We find it interesting to see how roleplaying can contribute to inspiring the multi-voiced dialogues undertaken by the participants.

By immersing ourselves with the participants in the relational flow of meaning creation, the processes unfolded as we were all walking around in 'somewhat foggy surroundings' (term used by Shotter, 2009: 3). The process encouraged the group members to find their own way in this bewildering landscape of new circumstances in which they found themselves. The process outlined many different possible pathways, and as co-constructors of the inquiry, we emphasised the need for further dialogic explorations in the group, not just finding 'the appropriate path to follow', but continuing to explore the emerging possible ways to see (or construct) the 'landscape' and act on a reflexive basis.

Retrospectively, the process of project management in the NGO was and still is an ongoing process with many new bends and turns along the path. Some processes were deeply influenced by unexpected developments in the surrounding context, like suddenly encountering a deep gorge along the path. Every time something changed, the participants involved had to deliberate about new ways to cross this gorge. As researchers and co-creators of the dialogue processes described previously, we noticed that the participants not only explored the landscape of their individual projects, but also explored and built on ideas from their colleagues. Through the dialogue sessions, the resources of the different group members were shared and further developed, and a network of 'knowing subjects' emerged in the process. It was a matter of enabling each team member to share and build knowledge in a 'joint action' (Shotter, 1993, 2010). It was not only a question of achieving new insight into each individual project, but also of co-constructing meaning with the overall objective of developing new and sustainable pathways for organic farming and new perspectives for the NGO.

- How can we broaden the range of perspectives, inspire the participants to become more curious, and help them amplify their use of questioning, sharing knowledge and ideas, offering mutual feedback, and working from a more dialogically based orientation instead of working as isolated individuals?

Reflecting on the practice of involving a multi-voiced reflecting team, we see the inquiry as an invitation to take part in dialogic exploration of how different stakeholders of a project might have different worldviews and ideas that could enrich and develop the projects or, in the worst case, obstruct the projects. It was interesting to see how the participants, by identifying with stakeholder perspectives different from their own ways of thinking, were forced to reflect on their own foregone subject positions and taken-for-granted assumptions. This opened up new ways of reflecting and questioning one's own role as project manager. Furthermore, the participants became aware of reflecting on 'myself-in-relation-to-others', which can be defined as reflexivity of the second order (Cunliffe, 2002a). This level of reflexivity led to new ways of interacting with the others on the projects, new ways of relating, listening, and inviting to dialogue (as opposed to a monologue-based approach). Seen from a learning perspective, the project supported and strengthened the participants as reflexive practitioners and dialogue partners. We experienced this learning process during frequent time-outs, where the group entered into critical and creative reflections concerning their projects and the relationships involved. As Schön (1987) might have put it, they began practising *reflection-on-action* in order to enhance their *reflection-in-action* in future actions.

- Would it be possible to move from an individual orientation to a more relational orientation and create a working culture within the team where collaborative reflexivity is treasured, practised, and considered as qualifying the project work?

Initially, the idea of advancing towards a more relational orientation within the team seemed like a waste of time to one of the participants. Being part of a time-pressured organisation, where each member had multiple tasks, it was difficult, in the beginning, for one of the team members to see how these sessions could contribute to solving current problems in their projects. However, as the process developed, in the final evaluative interview each of them expressed that they had come to depend on the group for competent feedback on their projects. The initial scepticism experienced by one of the participants can be seen as a part of a learning process, where we challenged the taken-for-granted ways and classical expectations of 'problem solving'. By encouraging relational teamwork, and in particular by imagining future scenarios, we saw how the reflexive processes 'before the fact' (Shotter, 2016) became highly important. These kinds of reflections allowed the members of the group to explore their difficulties and projects together, and to explore the shared knowledge of the whole team rather than relying on the permission and single judgement from the official project manager to continue with the projects on their own.

- How can we, through polyphonic inquiry, inspire the participants to experiment with new attitudes, new orientations, and new ways of relating to their surroundings?

When working with dialogue as a method for 'relational responsiveness' (Shotter, 1993, 2010) for new and complex working fields and new ways of seeing situations, new possibilities for acting emerged. It became clear that the task of facilitating these kinds of processes is mainly about paying attention to relational processes and (as McNamee and Hosking emphasise) making space for dissensus, complexity, and multiplicity (McNamee & Hosking, 2013: xiv).

Our approach to research and organisational learning as described here draws on principles of both externalising and internalising the voices of others, which enable the participants to identify with others and, in this way, come to an understanding of the different logics and values at stake in a complex process involving many different stakeholders. Due to the divergent and convergent phases of the process, complexity was unfolded and reduced with the assistance of the facilitator and the reflecting team. The amplifying and reducing of complexity took place in different divergent and convergent stages of the process.

Bakhtin (1981) presents both centrifugal and centripetal phases in this kind of dialogic process, and we were aware of these processes throughout the project. The success of the approach depends to a certain extent on 'responsive facilitation', but also on the willingness to share and construct experience and knowledge within the team. In this way, co-constructing and sharing responsibility for the process enables it to proceed in a generative and creative way. Another very important factor is the matter of time resources available for each project. It was our impression that all the members of the team were deficient in time resources, as if the time had been underestimated from the early project planning process onwards. This seemed to be an overarching challenge for all of the NGO's projects related to organic farming. All the counsellors and the leading project manager seemed to have very stressful working conditions, which, of course, can negatively affect opportunities for reflexivity and learning.

In conclusion, there are many possibilities and perspectives for continuing this kind of organisational learning and research practice, working from a polyphonic principle towards collaborative reflexivity and meaning-making in order to enhance and refine future actions, practices, and ideas.

'Withness' Thinking in Research

This section presents our reflections on the positioning of the researcher as inspired by social constructionist ideas on ontology and epistemology. How can researchers as 'disturbers', 'facilitators', and 'co-constructors' immerse ourselves in the flow of the dynamic world we are studying, and how can we reflect upon the processes of the inquiry from our position as co-constructors? Earlier in this book, the methodological themes based on relational constructionist meta-theoretical premises have been touched upon (see Chapter 1).

How does one work as a researcher from *within* the inquiry processes? How can a researcher come to embody an ongoing subject position both during and after the inquiry? How can a researcher become a co-constructor of the inquiry by acknowledging that he or she takes part and constructs meaning influencing other people's lives? How can a researcher develop 'relationally responsive' practices while working 'with' people instead of 'about' people (Shotter, 2005a: 17)?

In our approach to research, we apply the idea of 'withness' thinking (Shotter, 2005b) and explore how the practitioners can unfold their own ideas and co-construct knowledge in new and innovative ways by adopting an approach that encourages dialogue, collaborative reflexivity, and a particular way of listening to the others and the 'othernesses' around us (Shotter, 2009). This inquiry has been inspired by action research seen from a social constructionist orientation, and the practice was carried out and shaped in a dialogic process with a group of advisors with various backgrounds within the field of organic farming. The idea was to work with the advisors from a participatory inquiry perspective, while considering that the traditional object-subject division between researcher and research participant would be counterproductive. Instead, the authors based the research project on the idea that all participants could be creators of knowledge and should be invited into these processes. This inquiry aimed to invite all participants into a shared learning process that offered the opportunity for sharing, reflecting, and constructing knowledge together through dialogue.

It was challenging to develop and refine an inquiry that allowed the advisors from the NGO to develop their reflexivity and gain a practical sense of 'how to proceed' by working pragmatically with the 'here-and-now best way to go' (Chia & Holt, 2009). Furthermore, we aimed to inspire them to reflect on future strategies on a long-term basis, through the idea of creating sustainable relationships with their working partners and other stakeholders. While acknowledging that the 'here-and-now best way to go' always emerges in the moment, and can be challenged by the unpredictability of the situation, this kind of inquiry process can be seen as an attempt to explore the 'landscape of possibilities' (Shotter, 2009: 3). Based on emergence and flux as fundamental conditions, our approach was very explorative, requiring a responsive and curious attitude from everyone that allowed us to constantly adjust our course and move *with* our surroundings while discovering new pathways. As Shotter describes it:

> For, coming to act in a way that seems to be *for the best* in a particular situation is not something we can decide upon simply within ourselves; we must turn towards the now new situation to which we have chosen to relate ourselves, and open ourselves to being spontaneously responsive to it – if we can do that, we will find that various crucial happenings will occur quite spontaneously in the complex processes at work in the 'popping up' of alternatives.
>
> (Shotter, 2009: 4)

The aim of the developed practice was to enhance the reflexivity among the participants concerning their own role as project managers and to enable the group to become a learning team. By developing and facilitating processes that encouraged the practitioners to actively dwell in different situations and explore complex circumstances from *within* prior to acting, this became a future-forming approach, which differs significantly from the simpler process of 'problem solving'. Based on these ideas, we designed a framework for the reflexivity processes to unfold in order to let the complexity of the ongoing situations reveal themselves from *within* (Shotter, 2009). Through collaboration, new pathways for future actions were imagined and discussed.

Reflections on Research Ethics

As a researcher and facilitator, one may occasionally find oneself in an ethical dilemma, asking oneself how to proceed. In this final section the ethical reflections we had while developing and refining our practice are explored. Ethical issues are important to address before, during, and after research is conducted. As described earlier, one of the researchers (LH) had the role as facilitator and the other (CM) had the role of process observer and interviewer in the final evaluation and during the final seminar. This relationship and division of roles made it possible to engage in joint reflection upon the processes after each session and during the preparation for the new session. In the following paragraphs, we will present the overall ethical assumptions from which we have worked within the project and reflect upon the research process. Furthermore, we will elaborate on some of the difficulties that may arise when employing an inquiry or practice as described in this chapter.

The inquiry presented in this chapter rests upon the idea that we all engage in social communities where shared experiences and judgments are socially constructed. However, these experiences and judgments can never be seen as 'certain' or 'correct'. This is one of the cornerstones of social constructionist research, and for us, it meant that we engaged with the NGO from a 'not knowing' position (Anderson, 1990). We were careful not to construct ourselves or to be constructed as occupying an expert role. First of all, we insisted on being curious about the polyphony of voices expressed during the dialogue sessions with the NGO. In our practice, this meant asking open-ended and very often circular questions (Tomm, 1987, 1988) and allowing all voices to be heard.

While carrying out this practice with the NGO, the authors were constantly aware of and reflected upon our own role as co-constructors. We reflected on and discussed how we interacted and co-constructed identities with the team members of the NGO. Together with the participants, we were engaged in the processes and bore equal responsibility for how they developed. Through dialogue and concurrent evaluations with the participants we found the best way to proceed from *within*.

This engagement in the process means that research ethics must be a very important and integrated part of practice. In what follows, the ethical reflection process the authors undertook when applying and refining the inquiry in practice is described. Hosking and Pluut (2010: 63–64) point out that reflexivity on our own role as researchers in qualitative research can be identified in three discourses: the first discourse is focused on 'minimising bias', the second on 'making bias visible', and the third, which is aligned with social and relational constructionism, concerns the importance of ensuring 'on-going dialoguing'. When opting to apply 'on-going dialoguing' during the research process, ethics are closely related to the situation and to practice. Rather than an objective yes-or-no answer to ethical questions, reflecting on ethics becomes a way of practising and being in relation with others. In our practice, the authors found it important to be aware of the following:

1) How can we best work with the concerns formulated by the NGO project managers themselves? By constructing our own roles as 'disturber', 'facilitator', and 'co-creator', it was crucial for us to maintain a curious and 'not knowing' positioning and not to fall into the expert role. We found it important to be curious not only concerning the process and the projects from the perspective of the NGO members, but also to be aware of our own constructions. After each session, we (the authors) discussed our own constructions and ways of understanding what was going on in the process. We were aware that the understanding we had of the sessions were seen from our own perspective. Furthermore, each session was evaluated immediately after the process through dialogue with the participants and after the six sessions had taken place (as described previously).

2) As a part of our ongoing dialoguing reflexivity, we aimed at being irreverent towards our own and others' taken-for-granted assumptions about events, relations, and circumstances in the process. Herein lies the foundation for development and learning (Gergen, 1994). This meant that we attempted not to accept and reproduce interlocked social constructions, but rather to keep looking for nuances and keep unfolding the complexity of the theme or the specific situation.

3) During the inquiry process, we attempted to be sensitive to and aware of conflicting wishes and power dynamics in the sessions. It was important to challenge degenerative ways of interacting by inviting the whole group into the session, not privileging some voices over others (Gergen, 1994; Hersted and Gergen, 2013). Our basic working principle for the sessions was to ensure room for multiple voices to be heard and ensure the practice process was respectful and in accordance with the wishes of the participants.

4) It was also important to avoid stereotypical identity constructions of others and of ourselves, including persons who were not physically present in the session (for instance the stakeholders). If such a thing occurred, we questioned the language game (Wittgenstein, 1953) and invited other language games or asked questions that opened up further facets of identities. Relatedly, we worked as much as possible from a second-order reflexivity level by encouraging the participants and

ourselves to reflect from a relational perspective, on *myself-in-relation-to-others* (Cunliffe, 2002). It was also important for us to apply circular questioning (Tomm, 1987, 1988), which directs attention towards relationships and invites new perspectives on a given topic, for instance by asking, 'How do you think person X experiences the situation?' Or, 'What do you think is important for person Y in order to engage in the project?' These kinds of questions are important when the focus person gets stuck and is only capable of seeing a situation from his or her own perspective.

5) Additionally, we continuously invited the participants to look at challenging situations from a meta-perspective in order to help them in creating (and co-constructing) a broader contextual understanding of their work, for instance by asking, 'What kinds of interests from the ministry influence this project and how?' Or, 'How do you think this project will influence the local population?' Or, 'How do you think these ideas correspond, or perhaps conflict, with the strategy of the municipality?'

6) If the participants were stuck in a situation related to their project, it was helpful to assist them in catching sight of new openings and possibilities and to reflect with them on possible new pathways and initiatives for future actions. Furthermore, recognising and encouraging even small initiatives in their project work leading in a generative direction was important.

These points of research ethics have functioned as reflective resources and concrete practices in our inquiry. Engaging with others in an inquiry like this is not a matter of following a recipe, nor is it a matter of having the right 'technique'. Rather, such an inquiry works by incorporating different approaches and ethical reflexivity as helpful *resources* before, during, and after the process (McNamee, 2009). Ongoing reflexivity is crucial for success in practising collaborative knowledge production as described in this chapter. We emphasise that it is always pivotal to continuously reflect on one's own ethical responsibility in the process, asking oneself questions like, 'What kinds of constructions am I co-creating with the participants in this moment?' 'Is this the best possible way for the whole group or community to move forward?' and 'Are there voices that have not been heard yet?'. We consider that these ethical considerations are vital in any kinds of action research and participatory research projects.

References

Andersen, T. (1990) *The Reflecting Team: Dialogues and Dialogues About the Dialogues*. New York City, W. W. Norton & Company.

Anderson, H. (1990) Then and Now: From Knowing to Not-Knowing. *Contemporary Family Therapy Journal*, 12 (3), 193–197.

Bakhtin, M. M. (1981) *The Dialogic Imagination. Four Essays by M.M. Bakhtin*, Holquist, M. (ed.). Austin, University of Texas Press.

Bakhtin, M. M. (1984) *Problems of Dostoevsky's poetics*, Emerson, C. (ed. & trans.). Minneapolis, University of Minnesota Press.

Cecchin, G. (1987) Hypothesizing, Circularity, and Neutrality Revisited: An Invitation to Curiosity. *Family Process*, 26 (4), 405–413.

Cecchin, G., Lane, G. & Wendel, A.R. (1992) *Irreverence: A Strategy for Therapists' Survival*. London, H. Karnac (Books) Ltd.

Cecchin, G., Lane, G. & Wendel, A. R. (1994) *Cybernetics of Prejudices in the Practice of Psychotherapy*. London, H. Karnac (Books) Ltd.

Chia, R. & Holt, R. (2009) *Strategy Without Design. The Silent Efficacy of Indirect Action*. Cambridge, Cambridge University Press.

Cunliffe, A. L. (2002) Reflexive Dialogical Practice in Management Learning. *Management Learning*, 33 (1), 35–61.

Gergen, K. J. (1994) *Realities and Relationships. Soundings in Social Construction*. Cambridge, MA, Cambridge University Press.

Gergen, K. J. (2009) *Relational Being. Beyond Self and Community*. Oxford, Oxford University Press.

Gergen, K. J. (2015) From Mirroring to World-Making: Research as Future Forming. Winner of the 2014 Essay Competition, Independent Social Research Foundation, London, UK. *Journal for the Theory of Social Behaviour*, 45 (3), 287–310.

Hersted, L. & Gergen, K. J. (2013) *Relational Leading: Practices for Dialogical Collaboration*. Chagrin Falls, OH, Taos Institute Publications.

Hosking, D. M. & Pluut, B. (2010) Reconstructing Reflexivity: A Relational Constructionist Approach. *The Qualitative Report*, 15 (1), 59–75.

Ingold, T. (2008) *Lines. A Brief Story*. London, Routledge.

Ingold, T. (2009) Stories Against Classification. Transport, Wayfaring and the Integration of knowledge. In: Baumford, S. & Leach, J. (eds.) *Kinship and Beyond: The Genealogical Model Reconsidered*. Oxford (UK), Berghahn Books.

Lave, J. & Wenger, E. (1991) *Situated Learning*. Cambridge, Cambridge University Press.

McNamee, S. (2009) Postmodern Psychotherapeutic Ethics: Relational Responsibility in Practice. *Human Systems: The Journal of Therapy, Consultation & Training*, 20 (1), pp. 57–71.

McNamee, S. (2010) Research as Social Construction: Transformative Inquiry. *Saude & Transformacao Social. Health & Social Change*. Florianopolis, 1 (1), 9–19.

McNamee, S. (2015). Radical Presence: Alternatives to the therapeutic state. *European Journal of Psychotherapy & Counselling*, 17 (4), 373–383.

McNamee, S. & Hosking, D. M. (2013) *Research and Social Change. A Relational Constructionist Approach*. New York, Routledge/Taylor & Francis.

Reason, P. & Bradbury, H. (eds.) (2008) *The SAGE Handbook of Action Research. Participative Inquiry and Practice*. London, SAGE Publications Ltd.

Schön, D. A. (1983) *The Reflective Practitioner: How Professionals Think in Action*. London, Temple Smith.

Shotter, J. (1993) *Conversational Realities: Constructing Life Through Language*, 1st edition. London, SAGE.

Shotter, J. (2005a) *The Short Book of 'Withness'-Thinking*. London, KCCF.

Shotter, J. (2005b) 'Inside the Moment of Managing': Wittgenstein and the Everyday Dynamics of Our Expressive-Responsive Activities. *Organization Studies*, 26 (1), 113–135.

Shotter, J. (2009) *Movements of Feeling and Moments of Judgement: Towards an Ontological Social Constructionism*. Paper presented at the Constructing Worlds conference, Taos Institute and MacMann Berg, 20th–23rd August, Denmark, [Online, July 17].Shotter, J. (2010) *Social Constructionism on the Edge*. Chagrin Falls, OH, The Taos Institute Publications.

Shotter, J. (2016) Undisciplining Social Science: Wittgenstein and the Art of Creating Situated Practices of Social Inquiry. *Journal for the Theory of Social Behaviour*, 46 (1), 60–83.

Tomm, K. (1987–88) Interventive Interviewing, Part I, II, and III: Part I in: *Family Process*, 26, 3–13. Part II in: *Family Process*, 26, 167–183. Part III in: *Family Process*, 27, 1–15.

Wenger, E. (1998) *Community of Practice: Learning, Meaning and Identity*. Cambridge, Cambridge University Press.

Wittgenstein, L. (1953) *Philosophical Investigations*. Oxford, Blackwell.

6 Doing Relational Research through Roleplaying

Lone Hersted

Introduction

The previous chapter described how researchers interacted with practitioners in the field of organic farming based on a multi-voiced inquiry for team development, learning, and knowledge production with inspiration from action research. The current chapter sheds light on the development of a participatory inquiry for learning and knowledge building based on *roleplaying*. This inquiry also used a reflecting team, as described in the previous chapter, but emphasis was now placed on roleplaying involving experimentation with language games and bodily interaction. The practice described in this chapter was aimed at developing competencies in dialogue, relational awareness, critical self-reflexivity, and collaboration among employees and leaders working in a public institution for neglected children and adolescents. It has been developed and described from within the movement, which is often referred to as the 'dialogical turn' (Flecha et al., 2003) or the 'relational turn' (Donati, 2011). The practice is rooted in a constructionist stance and is inspired by action research and arts-based research.

This chapter explores a specific project, which took place in a twenty-four-hour care centre for neglected adolescents between the ages of twelve and eighteen. The empirical research part of the project was carried out for a period of one and a half years. The adolescents lived at this institution because they had been removed from their parents due to social and psychological problems. During their childhood, they had often experienced serious breaches of trust in their relationships with other people, so we were interested in exploring and training *generative* ways of communicating and relating in the organization, in particular among the employees and the leading group.

This project's basic underlying assumption is that processes of dialogic coordination, which are at work in the continuous process of organising, are central to organisational collaboration and the development of fruitful relationships. As Austin (1962) pointed out, we do things with words, and through conversations we co-create our social realities. In our relationships we co-construct scenarios that can move in either a *degenerative* or a *generative* direction. This idea builds on Gergen's (2009) work and it will be unfolded later on in this chapter. In this inquiry, using language is considered an action, as a 'doing', and the important challenge is whether our ways of communicating can, for example, inspire and motivate people or increase tension, conflict, and alienation. Wittgenstein pointed out that we communicate through our participation in different language games (Wittgenstein, 1953). Unfortunately, sometimes we get caught in these language games and we become stuck in repetitive and predictable communicative patterns; thus, the question is this: how can we change the language game?

Informed by the dramatic arts, this chapter presents a transformative practice where alternative ways of communicating and relating as living, responsive, embodied beings are explored in a playful, collaborative-learning setting. As a researcher with a professional background in theatre, consultancy, and family therapy, I do not make a hard distinction between being a researcher, facilitator, and co-creator. I prefer the overall term 'reflexive inquirer'. This conception is in marked contrast to the notion of the researcher as an 'objective observer', which has traditionally been the research ideal in the positivist tradition, whereby the dichotomy between researcher and researched is clearly marked. However, the relational or social constructionist approach towards research questions the researcher's positioning as 'the expert'. In a constructionist understanding, there is no hard distinction between research and work for social change, and what is usually considered 'data' is seen as a co-construction and can assume many different forms (Gergen, 2015). As McNamee and Hosking (2013) write:

> All research intervenes in the lives of those who participate, as well as in the lives of the researchers themselves. This means that professionals who work in fields focused on social change, such as health and human services, organizational development, education, and community development, are researchers just as much as they are change agents. Similarly, researchers are change agents; they are not simply scientists making discoveries about the world; they change the world as they examine it.
>
> (p. xvi)

In a social/relational approach to research, the researcher is often seen as a change agent, a co-creator, and sometimes even as an artist. Gergen (2009) and other postmodern scholars acknowledge that all research is a constructed narrative. Gergen advocates for alternative approaches to research, for instance, by use of poetry, novel writing, music, theatre, dance, sculpting, etc. We see many creative attempts to include these elements in the arts-based research movement, for instance in the works by Eisner (1997), Barone and Eisner (2012), Butler-Kisber (2002), and Norris (2009), as well in the participatory research projects carried out by Michelle Fine during the last fifteen years.

Not only does the relational/social constructionist approach embrace hybrid forms of research, it also questions the division between the researcher and the researched as well as the separation between inquiry and intervention, process and outcome, data collection and data analysis. Rather than *collecting data*, constructionists talk about generating data. Some scholars (not only constructionists) even question the term 'data', pointing out that everything can be seen as data (Brinkmann, 2014). McNamee (2014) argues for research with a focus on relational processes since they construct our worlds:

> Traditional researchers are curious to discover how to understand the world 'as it really is' and how to discover 'new knowledge' about that world. Yet, if our view is a relational constructionist view, the 'thing' (or entity) we are examining is the interactive processes of people in relation with each other and their environments. We are curious about what sorts of worlds can be made possible through particular forms of interaction, particular ways of talking and acting. Thus, the focus on relational processes that construct our worlds is understood as something very different from the focus on discovering how the world is.
>
> (p. 75)

Thus, from a constructionist viewpoint, knowledge construction is mainly seen as a product of a relational process, building on specific language games and discourses. A social or relational constructionist approach to research opens new ways of conceptualising and engaging in research. As McNamee explains, 'Thus, for the constructionist, the "doing" of research can take many forms. Each is, as mentioned earlier, a different language game. And, different language games construct different understandings of the world' (McNamee, 2014: 82).

While working from a social constructionist paradigm, the idea of the project was to position the participants as co-creators of knowledge in roleplaying sessions informed by living dialogues with a reflecting, multi-voiced team. Inspired by Shotter, we saw this as an attempt to do 'research from within'. In line with Shotter, I am critical of separating living process into separated units and putting them into categories. Rather than examining objects and phenomena at a distance, I am interested in creating knowledge from within a practice together with the participants from a process-oriented view. Also inspired by Shotter (2005c), we could describe this practice as relational, responsive processes in resonance and involvement *with* participants as co-constructers of knowledge. Shotter (2005c) argues for a living involvement, a 'thinking-from-within' or 'withness' thinking, in contrast to what he defines as 'aboutness' thinking. Building on Bakhtin's writings, Shotter suggests that the researcher installs themselves 'within the moving' using engaging ways and advocates for an 'active, spontaneously responsive kind of understanding' (Shotter, 2005c: 589–90).

Understanding Dialogue as Coordinated Action

My initial contact with the institution where I ended up doing research was during a two-day workshop where I was asked to help a team solve some major internal conflicts. I noticed that there was a high level of tension, not only in the specific team but also within the entire institution. Distrust, tension, and conflict existed between the adolescents and the staff, between different staff members, between the staff and the leading team, and inside the leading team as well. Thus, I wondered whether it would be possible to enhance the dialogic and relational competencies among the people working at the institution. Would it be possible to do a larger research project working with the development of dialogical competences, for instance, through the use of roleplaying? I presented the idea to the leading team and the employees, and they all agreed that it would be an interesting experiment and supported the idea.

The basic objective was to explore and refine a collaborative learning and knowledge-building practice for the enhancement of relational and dialogical competences, which is inspired by Dewey's (1916) concept of learning-as-practice and communities of practice described by Lave and Wenger (1991) and Wenger (1998). The idea was to enable the participants not only to become reflective practitioners (Schön, 1983; 1987), but furthermore, to inspire the participants to transform the social worlds and relationships in which they took part. Building on the constructionist idea that our communication is constitutive for our social world, the practice should pay special attention to the use of language as well as the bodily dimensions of communication. The project was guided by the assumption that we can reflect and create knowledge together in dialogical relationships, and benefiting especially from the many different voices in a group. As mentioned in the introduction, an important inspiration for our practice has been Gergen's notion of generative and degenerative scenarios (2009), as described in the following:

> In a generative scenario, the participants build on each other's contributions. As one might say, the conversation 'goes somewhere.' There is learning, creativity, and often a sense of delight. [. . .] Most disruptive, however, are the degenerative scenarios. These are scenarios that move toward animosity, silence, or the breaking of a relationship altogether. They may begin subtly, but unless they are terminated at some point, relations will suffer significantly. So will the organization.
> (Hersted & Gergen, 2013: 26–27)

If people do not pay attention to these degenerative scenarios, they can easily and rapidly develop into undesired repetitive patterns (Pearce & Cronen, 1980: 225–240) or dangerous dances (Gergen, 2009: 111), where conflicts escalate and the participants become alienated towards each other.

Participants might even position themselves and the other in specific 'corners', leading the conflict to possibly explode. However, Gergen (2009) reminds us that these patterns or 'dances' are relationally constructed, and he emphasises our ability to be creative and change the scenarios. These scenarios are not fixed or given by nature. Gergen (2009) states, 'Together, we stand as creators of the future. The question is whether we can locate new and compelling steps, moves that will enable us to leave the dance floor before disaster strikes' (p. 111). People are constantly coordinating their actions and co-creating scenarios, and seen from a constructionist perspective, people are always making choices. As proposed elsewhere, the more familiar you are with the variations, the more options you have for moving in the conversation (Hersted & Gergen, 2013: 28).

From a relational approach, dialogue can be considered as a form of coordinated action. Metaphorically speaking, we invite our conversational partners into a 'dance', but we cannot control the outcome because we cannot predict how the other person will respond to our utterances. A constructionist-relational understanding of dialogue is in contrast to a representational-referential understanding, which is bound to the idea of transmitting messages from one individual to another. From a constructionist perspective, instead of transmitting messages from A to B and vice versa, we are co-constructing and coordinating a dialogue as we adapt our response to each other. Communication is shaped in the responsive interplay between the dialogue partners in a process of mutually moulding meaning and continuous coordination. As discussed elsewhere, Hersted and Gergen (2013: 9) argue, 'Our words are not containers of meaning sent from one mind to another; rather our words acquire meaning as they are taken up in ongoing interchange. Like a game of football, no single person is in control of the outcomes.' Meaning is co-constructed and coordinated in relationships. Or as Voloshinov (1929/1973: 103) from the Bakhtinian circle wrote, 'Meaning is realised only in the process of active responsive understanding. Meaning does not reside in the word or in the soul of the speaker or in the soul of the listener. Meaning is the effect of interaction between the speaker and listener.'

In this view, language is a way of *acting* in the world, not the *mirroring* of thought. Another important dimension of dialogue is *embodiment*. Building on earlier experience from the theatre world, I am particularly drawn to the bodily dimension of dialogue, and in this project, dialogue as an embodied social practice was practised. Drawing on inspiration from Shotter's (2014) concern about *embodied responsiveness*, we must be aware of the 'living bodily responses related to things that occur to us in our surroundings' (p. 16). Shotter (2014: 18) uses the term 'embodied ways of responding', concerning our spontaneous bodily reactions in relation to living beings, things, and occurrences. Shotter continues by arguing that people must try to be fully present and pay attention to what is happening in 'the living moment' (pp. 31–33). By listening to the response of our bodies and the interplay with our surroundings, we can learn about ourselves, others, and the surrounding world. The way in which we interact with other people and the way in which we express ourselves through our body become crucial for a relationship going forward. As Shotter points out:

> It clearly makes an enormous difference if we approach another person on meeting them with a clenched fist ready to strike or with an open hand ready to shake theirs. To do this, we must learn how to see what is around us 'in depth,' as offering us a 'space of possibilities' for our actions.
>
> (Shotter, 2005a: 42–43)

Therefore, as a reflexive inquirer in the project I attempted to be sensitive to multiple facets of communication, not only the spoken words, but also elements such as voice, tone, pitch, the rhythm of speech, body movements, gestures, and facial expressions. Embodied dimensions of dialogue are a significant part of this inquiry, a dimension that is often underestimated in communication studies in general.

In the following sections, the organisational context and the research inquiry will be explained in more depth and examples from the practice will be given in order to provide the reader with an overall idea of the project.

Organisational Context and Research Design

As mentioned earlier, the project took place over an eighteenth-month period at a twenty-four-hour care centre for adolescents (between twelve and eighteen years old). The institution was owned and operated by the local municipality. The project involved both the leaders and the employees of the centre (including pedagogues/social workers, schoolteachers, psychologists, secretaries, gardeners, and kitchen staff). Each group of employees participated in three days of training where they engaged in roleplaying with reflecting team, with the exception of one group that asked for one extra training day and the group of leaders, which received six days of training (three days in the initial phase and three days in the final phase of the project). In sum, the project is based on twenty-two training days with six different groups. With the exception of the leading group, which consisted of five leaders, there were between eight and ten participants in each group. The majority of the dialogue training sessions were recorded on video, except for cases where the participants did not wish to be recorded. Participants were assured of anonymity. Likewise, all participants were promised professional secrecy regarding the lives of the adolescents living at the institution.

After each training session, I reviewed the video recordings together with a student who had helped record the sessions. The aim was to learn from these recordings and qualify further research in the process. Special attention was paid to the communication as well as to the ways in which relationships were constructed among the participants (including ourselves as participants and reflexive inquirers). We listened carefully to the utterances of all the persons involved, observed the bodily expressions and reactions, and observed how participants (including ourselves) related to each other, interacted with each other, and co-constructed their identities and the identities of others during the process. Attention was also paid to the power dynamics among the participants and the level of engagement and enthusiasm displayed during the process. Some of these recordings were transcribed and analysed in depth. The entire research process was qualified by reviewing and reflecting on the video recordings.

However, due to the extent of the recordings (twenty-two working days from 9 a.m. to 3 p.m.) and due to the fact that the project concerned experimentation with, and development of, a participatory research practice for the enhancement of dialogic and relational competencies, we considered that a full transcription of all twenty-two working days would not be appropriate. Instead, emphasis was placed on the situated knowledge-producing processes we created together *with* the participants as co-researchers. Thus, the main work with the 'data' took place during the research process while we were working with roleplaying and a reflecting team. The participants themselves took an active part in analysing and discussing the presented scenarios and developing alternatives to these. In this way, the central part of the research was something we did together as a group. In accordance with constructionist ideas, intervention and knowledge building took place at the same time. Rather than 'collecting' data (as from more traditional research teaches), reflections and knowledge were co-created and generated collaboratively in an ongoing cyclical process (see Figure 6.2 presenting the phases in our practice). During the roleplaying sessions with reflecting team, multiple local realities were investigated and moulded in a collaborative process. As a recurrent principle, each scenario was approached from multiple stakeholder perspectives in a cyclical process where all participants took part.

In addition, to identify the potential effects of the inquiry, nine random representatives from different employee categories (e.g., administrators, team leaders, schoolteachers, pedagogues, kitchen employees, and secretaries) participated in focus groups at the end of the process to reflect upon their experiences. Three focus group interviews were held; they were audio recorded and transcribed in full. The utterances from these focus group interviews were divided into different categories according to their learning outcomes. In particular, emphasis was placed on outcomes such as acquiring bodily awareness, changing and expanding perspectives, developing critical self-reflection, and enhancing relational consciousness. These outcomes have been presented and discussed in my earlier work (Hersted, 2016; 2017).

Creating a Frame for Playing, Risk-Taking, and Reflexivity

When participants are not familiar with roleplaying, they may be anxious or afraid of showing their professional doubts and dilemmas in front of their colleagues or a researcher from the university. Some may even fear being judged as being unprofessional. Furthermore, for most people, it is quite challenging to reflect on, and question, one's own habits of communicating, and it is even harder to change these. This process requires that participants are willing to take risks and put their reputation at stake. Since these activities deal with transformative learning, it is crucial to co-create and establish a level of trust within the group, which is not always an easy task. In this context, a few clear guidelines can be helpful because they serve as a kind of emotional scaffolding, which enables the participants to take risks, experiment, and show their disorienting dilemmas. Here, risk-taking and playfulness are two sides of the same coin. In Vygotskian terms, the guidelines contribute to the creation of a frame, which allows participants to work from within and move beyond the zone of proximal development (ZPD) (Vygotsky, 1978; 2012). Therefore, as a process facilitator and reflexive inquirer, I emphasise the importance of creating a frame for playing, risk-taking, and reflexivity to occur. In order to create such a frame, a set of simple guidelines were defined, which helped the participants to both establish confidence and maintain focus on the task. This was very important, because the climate in the institution was often tense and the activity level was high, and therefore it was easy to become distracted by the surroundings characterized by a large number of disturbances. There was a need to create a psychological contract *with* the participants, an attempt to ensure that everybody in the process followed the agreed guidelines. For instance, if participants become distracted and lose their concentration, the working process is immediately affected, and the learning process becomes less intense. Or if participants become judgmental or start acting in a supercilious way towards one another, then the atmosphere becomes repressive and non-productive. Thus, the group agreed on a simple set of guidelines for being present, focused, confident, non-judgmental, and respectful towards each other and, as mentioned, all participants were ensured anonymity. These guidelines contributed to establishing a confidential zone, which allowed professional dilemmas to be explored and participants to be vulnerable. These guiding components gave space for new, playful experiments and creative ideas to emerge.

Challenging Habits and Institutionalised Ways of Communicating

Early in the project, I noticed that the organisational members often tried to solve the conflicts from an individualist approach by locating the 'problem' inside one or another person without recognising the relational aspects and their own part in it. The employees frequently classified the adolescents living at the institution using diagnostic terms or specific categories. For example, the girls who had problems with cutting themselves due to psychological and social challenges were categorised as 'cutters'. Others were categorised as 'Aspergers'. The employees tended to use what could be referred to as *institutionalised ways of communicating*, which were often impersonal and alienating. Instead of creating contact, confidence, and understanding, these ways of communicating seemed to create distance and polarisation. For instance, some of the employees used the terms 'inmate' and 'prisoner' to describe a young boy who had grown up in Denmark but had Middle Eastern heritage, and now lived at the institution. He had been involved in small acts of neighbourhood crime and was now seen as a person who 'had to learn how to behave in a right way'. However, when someone is positioned as an 'inmate' or a 'prisoner', the practice of punishment becomes legitimised. Nobody in the group questioned any of these terms before we initiated a dialogue about them while reflecting on a roleplaying session.

In order to maintain maximum participation in the roleplaying, the participants were asked to select challenging interpersonal episodes that they themselves had experienced at the organisation. These included challenges in relation to the adolescents living at the institution or to the parents of the adolescents, or in relation to colleagues, working partners, authorities, or external stakeholders. Thus, the roleplaying challenges that the participants presented were loaded with tension and reflected conflict and alienation within the organisation. These challenges can be seen in terms of what Mezirow (1994) calls 'disorienting dilemmas'. According to Mezirow (1991), a learning process should facilitate the appropriation of new perspectives. Through questioning and with the help of the reflecting team, the group explored the interpersonal episodes from new perspectives and tried out alternative scenarios by acknowledging the unique *otherness of the other* (Shotter, 2005a; 2005d). Often the roleplaying scenarios presented were divided into smaller sequences, whereby specific key utterances, intonation, movements, and gestures were questioned and acted out in alternative ways. The group could, for instance, repeat and highlight a short fragment, a gesture, or a sentence spoken in a particular way, or play the whole scenario again with new variations and a new outcome. In this way, the routine perspectives were de-constructed and alternative scenarios were developed.

Working Creatively with the Polyphonic Reflecting Team

At the beginning of each session, the group created a reflecting team in order to facilitate awareness of the communicative process in the roleplaying scenarios and the potentials for alternative actions available to the participants. The colleagues taking part in the reflecting team not only functioned as spectators but became active 'spect-actors', as described by the Brazilian theatre director Augusto Boal (1979; 1995), the pioneer behind forum theatre and forum play. Boal's idea of the 'spect-actor', inspired by German theatre director Bertolt Brecht, was supposed to activate the spectators and make them reflect on the scenarios. In Boal's approach to drama and theatre, the audience was invited to comment on the scenarios and to take an active role in order to change the presented scenario and, thus, be capable of changing their own social reality. Inspired by Boal, the members of the reflecting team were positioned as actively reflecting dialogue partners focusing on the role-playing scenarios enacted by their colleagues (see Fig. 6.1).

During the roleplaying, the team members observed, listened, and reflected from specific perspectives. This could be, for instance, the perspective of an adolescent, a mother, a father, a friend, a social worker, a pedagogue, a teacher, a leader, a union representative, or a politician. By observing the episodes from these different perspectives, the dialogues in the reflecting team become multi-voiced. Inspired by Bakhtin (1984), I have termed these 'polyphonic reflecting teams', whereby 'polyphonic' can be translated as 'multi-voiced'. During the process we moved from the past into the imagined future. The initial phase of a cycle typically focused on a past episode, a disorienting dilemma as experienced by one of the participants. However, in the construction of these past episodes and in our multi-voiced analytical attempts to understand them, we did not try to remain 'objective'. We were, of course, aware that the scenarios with the disorienting dilemmas were constructions based on the memory of the past.

In the next phase, the members of the reflecting team were invited to contribute with new ideas and alternatives to the presented scenarios, not from an abstract theoretical position, but from *within* the situation, as described by Shotter (2005b; 2005c; 2012), by exploring what we learned 'as we move around in relation to the others and othernesses we meet within the situations we inhabit' (Shotter, 2012: 135). This phase of the process was future oriented as we experimented with *possibilities not yet actualised* (Shotter, 2007). This can be termed a 'before-the-fact' inquiry (Shotter, 2007), because through imagining and experimenting with alternative

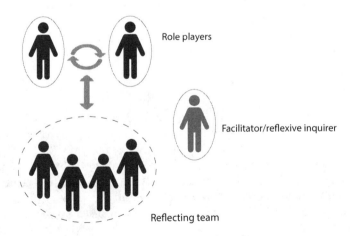

Figure 6.1 The Setup of the Roleplaying Session

scenarios, we co-created new understandings and action-guiding anticipations of a situated kind.

Our practice can be visualised as a learning cycle (see Figure 6.2) closely related to action research. At the same time, it is important to emphasise that this visualisation is a simplified model. In practice, these kinds of learning and knowledge building processes are characterised by non-linearity and a high level of complexity.

The reflecting team was encouraged to take a non-judgmental approach and show curiosity in a respectful manner. I reminded them to be careful in the ways they expressed themselves; for example, I asked them to use formulations such as: 'It strikes me that . . .', 'What makes an impression on me is that . . .', or 'I wonder why . . .' The role players were not obliged to follow the ideas of the reflecting team. The person who originally offered the episode (the disorienting dilemma) was free to choose what to do next. For instance, I may ask them, 'Now that you have been listening to the reflecting team for a while, is there anything that you have heard from them that makes sense to you or somehow inspires you?' or 'Is there anything from what you've heard that resonates with you or maybe even surprises you?'

The participants in the reflecting team were not only observing, listening, and dialoguing about the episodes, but were sometimes, as mentioned previously, moving (by invitation from the reflexive inquirer) into direct dialogue with the role players. Here, the method distinguishes itself from the systemic supervision method used and described by, for instance, Andersen (1991). In our practice, strict lines were not drawn between the reflecting team and the main persons in the process (in this case, the role players). On

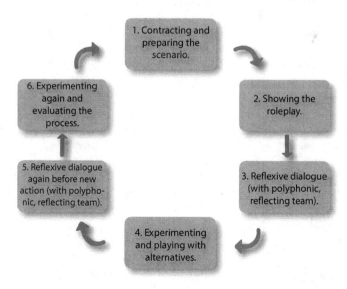

Figure 6.2 Phases in the Inquiry of Reflexive Roleplaying

the contrary, all of us were involved in the process and learning together through experimentation and play.

Sometimes a member of the reflecting team was invited to place themselves behind one of the role players and try to identify with this person. The reflexive inquirer asked, for instance, 'What do you think is important for X in this situation?' or 'How do you think X experiences the situation we just saw?' Thus, the participants were invited to imagine otherwise. The attempt was to enhance both *reflection-in-action* and *reflection-on-action* (Schön, 1983) as well as to train the ability to change perspective and identify oneself with the other.

From a social constructionist viewpoint, reflexivity can be seen as ongoing dialoguing in a relational process, critically and creatively questioning taken-for-granted assumptions and opening up to multiple local forms of life and to what might be possible (Gergen, 1994; Hosking, 2008). Rather than considering reflexivity as an entirely individual process, in our inquiry, reflexivity was conceptualised as a collaborative learning and knowledge building process by constantly asking questions and actively involving the reflecting team in the dialogues concerning past and future actions.

Cunliffe (2002) argues for incorporating reflexive dialogical practice in management learning as a way of developing 'more critical and responsive practitioners' (p. 39) and advocates for 'a critical self-reflexivity' or 'a second order reflexivity' (pp. 39–40). Second-order reflexivity differs from first-order reflexivity, which is more focused on being critical towards the generalised other (Cunliffe, 2002: p. 40). Cunliffe argues, 'Self-reflexivity [second-order reflexivity] is crucial because it is the basis for questioning the way we relate with others. By focusing on our own, often unacknowledged, representations of realities and working from within our experience, the impetus for change can be far more powerful than that mediated by externally imposed frames' (Cunliffe, 2002: 40). She also argues that learning is not necessarily emerging in structured and linear processes, but can be a messy process of making connections.

By actively involving the many different voices in the reflecting team, all participants were invited to reflect together and share responsibility for the learning and knowledge building process. Through the process, we tried to deconstruct and open up the disorienting dilemmas to multiple understandings. Contradictions, doubts, and new possibilities for action were discussed. By doing so, the reflexive dialogues were rendered more complex. In this way, the members of the reflecting team co-created learning and a *knowing-from-within* together with the role players through a dialogical process. Cunliffe and Shotter (2006: 235) refer to this kind of process as 'participatory ways of knowing,' based upon the verb 'knowing' rather than 'knowledge', whereby knowing can be characterised as 'unbounded, fluid, bodily sensed and often tacit, i.e., implicit in one's practices and expressions.'

The Researcher as Reflexive Inquirer

During this kind of process, the roles of the researcher are many, and the researcher is best seen as a reflexive inquirer. It is a matter of facilitating a nurturing frame for participation and helping participants to feel confident with the learning process (Hersted, 2017). Building confidence is crucial for participation, which means that a relationship built on mutual respect and recognition between all participants is central to learning. Furthermore, the reflexive inquirer must contribute with enthusiasm and engagement to the roleplaying practices. For many participants, working with roleplaying is an unusual approach to learning, and it is important that they believe in the possibility for positive outcomes. Most importantly, the reflexive inquirer must encourage the participants to develop new practices and a new consciousness. The reflexive inquirer must move *with* the participants and be careful not to impose their 'projects' or 'solutions' on them. The participants themselves must, as much as possible, discover their own ways of navigating while trying out new ways of communicating through the act of roleplaying. It may sound like a paradox, but on the one hand, the facilitator or reflexive inquirer must be humble and work from *within* the process, and on the other hand, he or she must be able to see the process from the outside, take initiative, formulate questions, introduce new language games and speech genres, and sometimes even act as a provocateur. It requires a sort of double perspective, which implies that the reflexive inquirer is able to observe the process from a second-order perspective and, at the same time, be a collaborative learner from *within*, who joins in the experimental learning journey.

In more concrete terms, the reflexive inquirer must inspire the participants to see the disorienting dilemmas from new and different perspectives and encourage them to imagine and to act out alternative scenarios where they experiment with different options for moving toward an active attentiveness to the process of relating. The reflexive inquirer cannot and must not manage the process, but can significantly contribute to it by drawing distinctions and highlighting specific aspects and details during the process. By asking questions, the reflexive inquirer can draw attention to specific aspects, invite participants to dwell on specific dialogic moves, and encourage reflection on alternatives. In this way, the reflexive inquirer has the task of ensuring that participants remain curious and reflexive as well as continuing to experiment during the process. Furthermore, it is important to ensure a playful learning environment.

As described elsewhere (Hersted, 2017), I drew on the systemic questioning inspired by Cecchin (1987), Tomm (1988), and Tomm et al., 2014) and, in particular, what is often defined as reflexive, circular questioning. This form of questioning has a relational orientation and invites participants to reflect on an episode from different perspectives and to imagine alternative scenarios. Thus, the reflexive inquirer may ask the role players directly: 'What would be important, do you think, for person X?' or 'How would Y respond to this if he or she heard your discussion?'

Questions that can be characterised as meta-questions can also be asked, such as: 'Do you notice some specific patterns in their communication?' 'What do you think characterises this language game?' 'What kind of relationship could you imagine instead?' 'How can we change the pattern?' The reflexive inquirer might also turn to genre questions, such as: 'If this were a movie, what kind of genre do you think is being played out here? For instance, a thriller, a melodrama, a comedy, a tragedy, or something else?' 'What other kinds of scenarios could they create together if X and Y started communicating in new ways?' or 'What kind of utterance could be the first helpful move towards an alternative way of communicating?' The reflexive inquirer is not an expert and does not have 'the right answers' or 'solutions', but through questioning and experimenting with alternative scenarios, the reflexive inquirer participates together with the participants in a creative learning process. Furthermore, it is important that the reflexive inquirer is sensitive and responsive to the needs of the participants and to the overall context, showing flexibility and readiness to adjust the practice during the process.

An Example from the Project

In the following excerpt, a concrete example will be presented in order to illustrate the practice. The example has also been presented as a part of my PhD thesis (Hersted, 2016).

Is not necessarily an easy task to break with old communicative patterns because it requires that we question our immediate reactions (based on reflex) in our relationships with others. When working with disorienting dilemmas, the reflexive inquirer gets insight into the 'backstage' (Goffman, 1959) of the organisation, and it happens now and then that the reflexive inquirer finds him or herself in a disorienting dilemma. One might ask oneself: 'Should I go further and insist here?' Or, 'should I let it go and change the subject?' 'What would the eventual ripple effects or consequences be if we moved closer to this conflict?' And, 'what could the consequences be if the group were to take another direction in the process?' One might feel tempted to bring one's own points of view into the dialogues, but the learning outcome will be better if the reflexive inquirer avoids giving direct advice, and instead uses questions that inspire the participants to reflect and come up with alternative ideas themselves.

During the entire process, the reflexive inquirer must be extremely patient and not put too much pressure on the participants, otherwise the learning can be blocked out. At the same time, the reflexive inquirer must question and challenge the taken-for-granted assumptions and communicative patterns

Relational Research through Roleplaying 131

that are present. It is a matter of finding a balance in being appreciative and challenging at the same time. Again, the reflexive inquirer must be sensitive to the zone of proximal development of the participant(s). Respect must be shown to all the participants in such a way that nobody feels that they lose face. The participants have to get along and be able to work together after leaving a session. They are bound together and depend on each other in the organisational community, and the reflexive inquirer has a responsibility to ensure that each session ends in a generative way. In this regard, it is also important to round off each session with an oral evaluation in the group. It is advisable to spend at least half an hour on this phase at the end of the day. The following gives a closer look at a specific case.

Case: William and Jennifer

A relatively new employee asked for help to create a better relationship with one of the girls living at the institution. Initially, he told us about an episode where the communication with the girl had gone very badly and had turned into a conflict. The situation took place during the daily room inspection. According to the employee, the girl's room was messy and she refused to cooperate in cleaning up her room. The employee found himself in a dilemma: How should he react in this situation? After he had told his story, I asked him to show it through roleplaying in as detailed a manner as possible. Together with a couple of colleagues from the team, he prepared the scenario (around fifteen to twenty minutes of preparation) and showed it to the rest of us. The reflecting team members were invited to listen to and observe the scenario from different perspectives: the perspective of the girl (Jennifer), the employee (William), a colleague, a manager, etc. The following presents a direct transcript from the beginning of the roleplaying scenario recorded on video. Some of the physical actions of the participants are described in parentheses, as these actions are considered just as important as the spoken words.

William (W):	(Knocks three times on the door to Jennifer's room)
Jennifer (J):	'Come in.'
W:	(Enters the room)
J:	(Continues sitting on her bed)
W:	(Approaches her, but almost starts vomiting while shaking Jennifer's hand, while saying) 'Hello, Jennifer.' (He remains standing and Jennifer remains seated on her bed. He avoids eye contact and looks at his watch, while saying) 'You have to get out of bed now. It's the middle of the day.'
J:	(Remains silent)
W:	(Visually inspects the room by turning his head). 'Just look at your room. Didn't you clean up yesterday?'

J: (Remains silent and looks down at the floor)
W: 'Listen, Jennifer. When people enter your room, it smells so much that you would almost think you've pooped in your bed. That is really bad. Are you hiding something here that is making it smell? Or is there a dead rat in here? It's absolutely terrible!'
J: 'Can't I just open the window and vent the room?'
W: 'Well, that would be a start. But we need to figure out where the smell is coming from. This smell isn't normal. What . . . could it be some of these clothes lying in here that need to be washed? When was the last time you washed your clothes?'
J: 'The day before yesterday.'
W: 'Well, then it's a shame that the clothes aren't placed in the closet instead of on the floor. So . . . at least you could start by doing that.' (He takes a look beneath her bed) 'What kind of bottles are those lying there?'
J: (Who looks terrified) 'What are you talking about?'
W: 'There are two bottles lying there. Will you please pick them up, because I'm an old man.'
J: (Picks up the two bottles and gives them to William) 'Well, it's just two bottles of soda.'
W: (Astonished, refuses to take the bottles) 'Soda? No, I sure don't want to touch them! Tell me, and now I'm asking you directly: do you pee in those bottles?'
J: 'No, it's just orange juice.'
W: (Even more astonished and apparently provoked, raises his voice) 'Orange juice? It looks rather thin to be orange juice!'
J: 'It's just orange juice!'
W: 'Well, I don't think you feel like drinking this, do you?'
J: 'No, it has been there for a long time, so I don't want to drink it.'
W: 'Well, I understand that, but I'm convinced that you've peed in these bottles, Jennifer. This is definitely not very tasteful . . . Why? There is a door right here . . . You can just walk out and pee. Or is it because you're afraid at night . . . or what's going on . . .?'
J: (looks down at the floor and remains silent)
W: (raising his voice) 'Well . . .?'

The employee stopped the scenario here and told us that this situation had turned into a conflict, but he did not wish to inform us about the details. As a facilitator of the process, I accepted this because I did not wish to put too much pressure on William. We agreed to focus on the scenario presented previously.

Reflections on the Case

In the episode transcribed previously, the room inspection ritual at the institution turned into a conflict. While talking about the presented scenario with the presenters and the reflecting team, I discovered that the employee, William, was a new employee and that he did not yet know the girl, Jennifer, very well. Before the group started examining the episode, he was not aware that Jennifer had a life story which, from her early childhood, had been characterised by violence from a brutal stepfather combined with an overwhelming fear of his behaviour.

After the first roleplaying session, during the conversation with the reflecting team, it was brought to light that for many years the girl had constantly escaped from her stepfather in the company of her mother. At the beginning of the session, William seemed to believe that the girl was simply bad mannered and needed clear instructions from adults. By asking the reflecting team members how the episode was experienced from Jennifer's perspective, the group gained more insight into her background and, little by little, began to understand the possible reasons why she might be afraid to go to the toilet during the night. The group also learned that in front of Jennifer's door the institution had installed a series of alarm bells that immediately sounded if she attempted to walk out the door.

Thus, by dialoguing with the reflecting team, tacit knowledge (Polanyi, 2009) about Jennifer and her circumstances was shared and new facets emerged. A team member informed the group that several times he had found the girl lying paralysed near the institution, for instance, in a ditch. 'It seemed like she was dead then,' he said, 'as if she has moved out of her own body'. Another team member told us that Jennifer, according to the report, had in her early childhood (since she was three years old) refused physical contact with others. At the same time, several team members explained that she used to run away from the institution and prostitute herself in the town.

The episode the group was exploring was that of a young girl with specific needs and relational challenges. It struck me that William had insisted on shaking hands with her (which was a ritualised convention at the institution), but at the same time, he had avoided any kind of eye contact with her. Apparently, Jennifer needed emotional support in order to feel safe. How then could the employee, in this case William, build up a trustful relationship with her? It was not only a matter of communicating in a more polite way, but also of taking the necessary time to meet the girl at 'eye level', being *with* her instead of yelling at her, and building up confidence little by little.

The group then tried to work with alternative possibilities to form an approach that was *being with* instead of *talking to* (Shotter, 2010). For instance, we experimented with an alternative scenario where William, instead of standing at the door, took a chair and sat down and talked with the girl in a soft and patient manner. We also discussed the importance of maintaining eye contact with the girl, which was rather difficult for William at the beginning. In short, it was not only a matter of finding the appropriate words (instead of blaming the girl), but also of working with the ability to relate in all aspects: wordings, intonation, eye contact, gestures, positioning, careful listening, etc. It was very much a question of paying attention to relational processes and being relationally responsive (and responsible) in a sensitive way.

Since William was a novice in a pedagogical working context, this learning session gave him a forum to try out different alternative scenarios and expand his repertoire of dialogic actions. The roleplaying setting offered him, with help and inspiration from his colleagues, a framework to try things out that he had neither imagined nor tried before, and it seemed to be an important learning process not only for him, but also for his colleagues. The participating colleagues seemed to recognise themselves in the episode and came up with useful and nuanced reflections while taking part in the reflecting team. Through experimentation and play with alternative communicative acts, everyone in the group learned and gained inspiration into the episode.

Overall Reflections Concerning the Inquiry

I found it important to explore the learning outcomes of our practice. Were there any signs that participants gained useful insight and competences from their engagement in the process? In order to learn about the learning outcome, three semi-structured focus group interviews were set up, each an hour in length with nine random representatives from the different employee categories. Some of the topics that emerged from these interviews were learning outcomes such as acquiring bodily awareness, expanding perspectives, and enhanced self-reflection and relational consciousness (see Hersted, 2016 and Hersted, 2017 for more details).

During the entire process, I was impressed by how convincingly and in detail the participants played their roles in the episodes. The participants themselves were also astonished to experience that they were able to do 'theatre' or 'roleplaying', and I observed that in the majority of the cases, they managed to play the roles quite well without overacting. In this kind of work, it is very important to avoid 'stereotyping' the other, but rather to be aware of nuances and multiple facets. The dedication and serious engagement among the participants was crucial to the process and helped us to progress and explore the dialogues with the reflecting team as well as experiment with alternative scenarios.

Over the course of the project, the participants opened up and revealed many episodes where tensions had escalated and turned into serious conflicts and, on some occasions, had ended with the use of force. As a reflexive inquirer, I was initiated into another social reality, similar to what Goffman (1959) would define as 'backstage', which differed significantly from what was presented on the official institutional website. The trust that we as a group constructed together was crucial for this to happen, and it would have been impossible to explore these delicate matters without it.

As a reflexive inquirer I was often embarrassed, and sometimes it was even difficult to bear the emerging insights. Working as a facilitator with roleplaying in a team of eight to ten participants who are not used to this kind of 'theatre work' is not always an easy task. It requires an augmented all-around relational awareness as well as a specific aesthetic sensitivity to the process. In this kind of work, the reflexive inquirer has to move on several tracks at the same time: being fully present in the process together *with* the participants and paying attention to details while, at the same time, keeping an awareness and overview of the process and paying attention to the organisational context. The reflexive inquirer must try to be sensitive to the responses and reactions of the participants and to the relationships developing in the process, find the right timing for each session, maintain dynamics, flow, and energy during the process, and encourage the participants to put themselves at risk.

This ability to open up was, for instance, crucial in the presented case, where William presented a disorienting dilemma. As a reflexive inquirer I noticed William's vulnerability and I asked myself how far we could go in this process and how William could maintain his dignity in his own eyes and in the eyes of his colleagues. How could I as a facilitator of the process relate to William in such a way that he would remain open to me and open to the risk-taking, playing, and learning process? Drawing on McNamee, the term 'radical presence' (McNamee, 2015) could be used as an ideal approach to be pursued. The idea of a radical presence builds on a relational understanding of our social worlds and pays an active attentiveness to processes of relating. McNamee states, 'Adopting a radical presence focuses our attention on the specificities of any given interaction while also allowing us to note patterns across interactions, across time, place, and culture' (McNamee, 2015: 377). Previously she explains that the idea of radical presence has to do with 'an exploration of broader relational and institutional contexts and the ways in which professionals and ordinary people alike can be responsive, present, and open to a multiplicity of life forms' (McNamee, 2015: 373). Drawing on McNamee's term, the entire group had to be radically present and take care of each other in the process of learning and knowledge building.

The training was envisioned to help the participants to develop their dialogical and reflexive competencies in order to create better relationships and prevent delicate situations from escalating into irreversible negative spirals. The attempt was to help them to reflect and be able to break with degenerative patterns, helping them become more resourceful conversational partners (Shotter & Cunliffe, 2003). Ultimately, I hoped to create organisational change. In many ways, our practice can be understood as an attempt to 'humanise' or 'sensitise' an organisation and encourage participants to find more lively and generative ways of relating to each other. The process implied questioning the taken-for-granted assumptions and routinized daily practices by discussing pedagogical and human values and amplifying perspectives and repertoires for action. To a certain extent, the goals were met in creating *transformative learning* (Mezirow, 2000) among the majority of the employees and leaders. Through roleplaying, the group was bodily, emotionally, and intellectually engaged, while discovering and learning 'in the making' that there are no universal formulas in this kind of work. The next paragraph explores some of the basic ethical considerations in our inquiry.

Relational Ethics in Participatory Research

A key concept in this study has been the relational ethics condensed in Shotter's term of 'withness' thinking (Shotter, 2008; 2010). This inquiry encourages us to understand processes from 'within' and to be 'with' the other person instead of positioning ourselves above (or beneath) the person. Instead of treating the other instrumentally (for instance by insisting mechanically on institutional rules) or as an object for fulfilling one's own goals, it is a matter of meeting the other with equity, thoughtfulness, and curiosity. In other words, it's a question of meeting and recognising the other as a unique person.

In our project, 'withness' thinking became extremely relevant, for instance, concerning how an employee approached a young resident, a parent, or a colleague, how a leader related to an employee and vice versa. Instead of labelling the other, it is important to seek acknowledgement and valorise the other's *unique otherness* (Shotter, 2005a). As described elsewhere, this requires an effort to be made in relating to the other person and talking *with* them, instead of talking *to* or *about* them. At the same time, it is a matter of developing a special awareness of thinking from *within* the unique situation and the context for the conversation, and from this position being able to sense and notice what is going on, what is on its way and what kind of new possibilities for action are emerging.

Closely related to 'withness' thinking is Bakhtin's idea of 'the unfinalised other' (Bakhtin, 1984: 63). According to Bakhtin, it would be unethical to *finalise* (or determinate) another person by defining who that person *is*, as if that person had a fixed identity. Drawing on Bakhtin's dialogism, one can say that dialogue avoids putting people into fixed identities, definitions, or categories and builds on the recognition of the other's unfinalisability. Bakhtin did not believe in an autonomous inner self, a core nucleus; on the contrary, he claimed that what one usually understands as a 'self' is polyphonic (multi-voiced) and that these multiple voices are born out of relationships (Bakhtin, 1981). Working with Bakhtin's dialogism, Frank (2005) elegantly states, 'no one person's voice is ever even his or her own; no one existence is ever clearly bounded. Instead, each voice is always permeated with the voices of others. Each voice resists and contests some voices, and it embraces others, but there is no one that could coincide with itself' (Frank, 2005: 968).

When finalising another person, alienation and distance are created and the possibilities of someone showing his or her polyphonic self are limited. From a Bakhtinian understanding, this is not a dialogic approach. When expressing ourselves, one expects others to respond or act actively, and others call us into response as well. In this way, our communication is never completed but always *becoming*. In this view of communication, it is important to be open and responsive in relation to the emerging and unpredictable conversation and also give others an opportunity to act responsively as well.

One may have anticipations concerning a relationship or a given situation but, as mentioned at the beginning of this chapter, one cannot predict the response of the other. However, one can develop one's relational competencies by using one's imagination. Through roleplaying one can be trained to identify with the other and imagine different sorts of responses from them before the response takes place. By doing this, one can become more resourceful in participating in living dialogues with others. Here, it must be underscored that it is not a matter of strategically planning conversations and meetings, but rather a question of talking with each other instead of talking to or about each other (Hersted, 2016; 2017).

Not only did the participants in the project play and experiment with different ways of communicating *with* each other, but I as facilitator and reflexive inquirer also had to work closely *with* them and meet each of them as a *unique other*. It is a challenge to show patience, recognition, and curiosity and to be fully present in the unique moments of creating together. This requires that the facilitator and the other participants pay constant attention to their relationships and the context, and that they demonstrate flexibility and an ability to improvise during the process.

This relational and contextual awareness can be summarised into the following basic ethical guidelines or recommendations:

- Always recognise the unique *otherness of the other* (term by Bakhtin and Shotter).
- Avoid the construction of closed identity conclusions (working from the Bakhtinian idea that one has *multiple* and *unfinalised* selves).
- Work *with* people and at the same time challenge and question the taken-for-granted assumptions and established truths (in the group and by oneself as a reflexive inquirer).
- Continue being curious, keep wondering and asking open questions.
- Always be creative and look for new openings in the dialogue.
- Avoid imposing initiatives on anybody but work *with* people in a *relationally responsive* way.
- Always respect a participant's wish not to participate in a roleplay. Be creative and offer other ways of participating, e.g., taking part in the reflecting team.
- Work with people from their zone of proximal development (Vygotsky).
- Ensure that all participants feel comfortable during and after the process.

In order to avoid typical pitfalls, and based on the practice, some general suggestions for readers who might consider using the inquiry of roleplaying with a reflecting team can be identified:

- It is crucial to create a non-judgmental atmosphere with mutual recognition.
- The reflexive inquirer and the participants must be very sensitive towards tension and conflict in the organisation and ensure relational responsibility and respect for everybody in the process.

- The reflexive inquirer must remain curious and be able to use different kinds of questioning types (coaching skills are a must-have for a good outcome) in order to open up new understandings. I have drawn great inspiration from the work of Tomm (Tomm, 1987, 1988; Tomm et al., 2014).
- Participants must help each other be fully present, even when only a few colleagues are present. It can sometimes be hard for participants to maintain focus during a longer session and therefore it is important to have a good sense of timing and to activate the reflecting team frequently in order to maintain the energy and motivation of all participants and to enable them to mutually inspire each other.
- The reflexive inquirer must bring energy into the process and possess a surplus of mental resources, particularly when the participants explore areas of conflict or subjects that make them vulnerable.

Conclusion

As this project suggests, dialogic roleplaying combined with a polyphonic reflecting team can serve as a significant tool in the development of dialogical and relational competencies for individuals and teams. The inquiry outlined here draws attention to the ways in which language is used in constituting reality, relationships, identities, and the creation of new opportunities in our social worlds. By adopting an explorative, experimental, and playful approach, this practice for learning and knowledge building was designed to increase discursive and relational awareness and to invite creativity in developing new and alternative possibilities for action. The project involved all the employees as well as the group of leaders in learning in order to create organisational change. The project has shown that this kind of practice is particularly successful when the participants themselves define the overall topics and guiding questions.

Furthermore, it is crucial for a positive learning outcome to create learning environments and knowledge building practices where the participants are recognised and appreciated as being individuals and professionals. These kinds of practices must be facilitated carefully and gently with sensitivity to the organisational context and the many different stakeholder perspectives. This project has demonstrated the potential in working with drama involving the whole body and all the senses. Not only did the participants develop competencies in dialogue, they also enhanced bodily awareness, self-reflexivity, relational consciousness, a change in perspective, and a stronger capability to identify with others.

This project used roleplaying both retrospectively in relation to past episodes and as an action-guiding inquiry. The results of the project are promising and can serve as inspiration within professional fields such as consultancy, the education of leaders and employees, and academic research. It is also important to note that the benefits of this inquiry go beyond organisational learning and can be expanded to the educational sphere, augmenting existing teaching and training practices. This study has aimed to experiment with an inquiry for simultaneously learning and researching, and there is no doubt that this approach, based on roleplaying, differs from many conventional research methods. However, from a constructionist approach, all research constructs the world on its own terms, and there is no research that is purified from human values, relationships, earlier experiences, etc. Seen from the perspective of action research (Reason & Bradbury, 2008), the inquiry presented here can be defined as a qualitative, explorative, and collaborative research inquiry.

In sum, roleplaying with a polyphonic reflecting team contained many different elements: play, imagination, identification, changing perspectives, multiplicity, meta-reflexivity, dialogue, embodiment, relational responsiveness, improvisation, experimentation, risk-taking, radical presence, collaboration, and co-creation. Engaging in this kind of practice involves all our bodily senses. Together, these multiple elements constitute a whole, integrated, and multi-layered approach which can be characterised as a synesthetic and collaborative form of learning and knowledge building.

References

Andersen, T. (1991) *The Reflecting Team: Dialogues and Dialogues About the Dialogues*. New York City, W. W. Norton & Company.
Austin, J. L. (1962) *How to Do Things with Words*. London, Oxford University Press.
Bakhtin, M. M. (1981) *The Dialogic Imagination. Four Essays by M.M. Bakhtin*, Holquist, M. (ed.). Austin, University of Texas Press.
Bakhtin, M. M. (1984) *Problems of Dostoevsky's Poetics*, Emerson, C. (trans. & ed.). Minneapolis, University of Michigan Press.
Barone, T. & Eisner, E. W. (2012) *Arts Based Research*. Los Angeles, Sage.
Boal, A. (1979) *Theatre of the Oppressed*. London, Pluto Press.
Boal, A. (1995) *The Rainbow of Desire: The Boal Method of Theatre and Therapy*. London, Routledge.
Brinkmann, S. (2014) Doing Without Data. *Qualitative Inquiry 2014*, 20 (6), 720–725.
Butler-Kisber, L. (2002) Artful Portrayals in Qualitative Research: The Road to Found Poetry and Beyond. *The Alberta Journal of Educational Research*, XLVIII (3), 229–239.
Cecchin, G. (1987) Hypothesizing, Circularity, and Neutrality Revisited: An Invitation to Curiosity. *Family Process*, 26 (4), 405–413.
Cunliffe, A. L. (2002) Reflexive Dialogical Practice in Management Learning. *Management Learning 2002*, 33, 35–61.
Cunliffe, A. L. & Shotter, J. (2006) Wittgenstein, Bakhtin, Management and the Dialogical. In: Hosking, D. M. & McNamee, S. (eds.) *The Social Construction of Organization*. Malmö, Sweden, Liber & Copenhagen Business School Press, pp. 226–241.
Dewey, J. (1916). Democracy and Education. In: Boydston, J. A. (ed.) *John Dewey: The Middle Works (1899–1924), Vol. 9*. Carbondale and Edwardsville, IL, Southern Illinois University Press.

Donati, P. (2011). *Relational Sociology. A New Paradigm for the Social Sciences*. London, Routledge, Taylor & Francis Group.
Eisner, E. (1997) The Promise and Perils of Alternative Forms of Representation. *Educational Researcher*, 26 (6), 4–10.
Flecha, R., Gomez, J. & Puigvet, L. (2003) *Contemporary Sociological Theory*. New York, Peter Lang.
Frank, A. W. (2005) What Is Dialogical Research, and Why Should We Do It? *Qualitative Health Research 2005*, 15 (7), 964–974.
Gergen, K. J. (1994) *Realities and Relationships. Soundings in Social Construction*. Cambridge, MA, Cambridge University Press.
Gergen, K. J. (2009) *Relational Being. Beyond Self and Community*. Oxford, Oxford University Press.
Gergen, K. J. (2015) From Mirroring to World-Making: Research as Future Forming. Winner of the 2014 Essay Competition at The Independent Social Research Foundation, London, UK. *Journal for the Theory of Social Behaviour*, 45, 287–310.
Gergen, K. J., Gergen, M. & Barrett, F. (2004) Dialogue: Life and Death of the Organization. In: Grant, D., Hardy, C. Oswick, C., Phillips, N. & Putnam, L. (eds.) *Handbook of Organizational Discourse*. 39–59, Thousand Oaks, CA, Sage.
Goffman, E. (1959) *The Presentation of Self in Everyday Life*. New York, Doubleday Anchor Books.
Hersted, L. (2016) *Relational Leading and Dialogic Process* (vol. 1). PhD thesis published at Aalborg University Press.
Hersted, L. (2017) Reflective Role-Playing in the Development of Dialogic Skill. *Journal of Transformative Education*, 15 (2), 1–19.
Hersted, L. & Gergen, K. J. (2013) *Relational Leading. Practices for Dialogically Based Collaboration*. Chagrin Falls, OH, Taos Institute Publications.
Hosking, D. M. (2008) *Can Constructionism Be Critical?* In: Holstein, J. & Gubrium, J. (eds.) *Handbook of Constructionist Research*. New York, Guilford, pp. 669–687.
Lave, J. & Wenger, E. (1991) *Situated Learning: Legitimate Peripheral Participation*. Cambridge, Cambridge University Press.
McNamee, S. (2014) Research as Relational Practice: Exploring Modes of Inquiry. In: Simon, G. & Chard, A. (eds.) *Systemic Inquiry: Innovations in Reflexive Practice Research*. London, Everything is Connected Press, pp. 74–94.
McNamee, S. (2015) Radical Presence: Alternatives to the Therapeutic State. *European Journal of Psychotherapy & Counselling*, 17 (4), 373–383.
McNamee, S. & Hosking, D. M. (2013) *Research and Social Change. A Relational Constructionist Approach*. New York, Taylor & Francis/Routledge.
Mezirow, J. (1991) *Transformative Dimensions of Adult Learning*. San Francisco, Jossey-Bass.
Mezirow, J. (1994) Understanding Transformation Theory. *Adult Education Quarterly*, 44 (4), 222–232.
Mezirow, J. (2000) *Learning as Transformation: Critical Perspectives on a Theory in Progress*. San Francisco, Jossey Bass.
Norris, J. (2009) *Playbuilding as Qualitative Research. A Participatory Arts-Based Approach*. Walnut Creek, CA, Left Coast Press.
Pearce, W. B. & Cronen, V. (1980) *Communication, Action, and Meaning: The Creation of Social Realities*. New York, Praeger.
Polanyi, M. (2009) *The Tacit Dimension*. Chicago, University of Chicago Press.

Reason, P. & Bradbury, H. (eds.) (2008) *The SAGE Handbook of Action Research: Participative Inquiry and Practice*. London, Sage.

Schön, D. A. (1983) *The Reflective Practitioner: How Professionals Think in Action*. London, Temple Smith.

Schön, D. A. (1987) *Educating the Reflective Practitioner: Towards a New Design for Teaching and Learning in the Professions*. San Francisco, CA, Jossey Bass.

Shotter, J. (2005a) *The Short Book of 'Withness'-Thinking*. London, KCCF.

Shotter, J. (2005b) 'Inside the Moment of Managing': Wittgenstein and the Everyday Dynamics of Our Expressive-Responsive Activities. *Organization Studies*, 26 (1), 113–135.

Shotter, J. (2005c) Understanding Process From Within: An Argument for 'Withness' Thinking. *Organization Studies*, 27 (4), 585–604.

Shotter, J. (2005d) Acknowledging Unique Others: Ethics, 'Expressive Realism,' and Social Constructionism. *Journal of Constructivist Psychology*, 18, 103–130.

Shotter, J. (2007) With What Kind of Science Should Action Research Be Contrasted? *International Journal of Action Research*, 3 (1+2), 65–92.

Shotter, J. (2008) *Conversational Realities Revisited: Life, Language, Body and World*. Chagrin Falls, OH, TAOS Institute Publications.

Shotter, J. (2010) *Social Constructionism on the Edge*. Chagrin Falls, OH, The Taos Institute Publications.

Shotter, J. (2012) Bodily Way-Finding Our Way into the Future. Finding the Guidance We Need for Our Next Step Within the Taking of Our Present Step. *Tidsskrift for Psykisk Helsearbeid*, 9 (2), 133–143.

Shotter, J. (2014) From 'after the fact' Objective Analyses to Immediate 'before the fact' Living Meanings. Draft for: *Culture & Psychology*, December 2014 (Available from ResearchGate).

Shotter, J. & Cunliffe, A. L. (2003) Managers as Practical Authors: Everyday Conversations for action. In: Holman, D. & Thorpe, R. (eds.) *Management and Language*. London, Sage.

Tomm, K. (1987–88) Interventive Interviewing, Part I, II, and III: Part I: *Family Process*, 26, 3–13. Part II: *Family Process*, 26, 167–183. Part III: *Family Process*, 27, 1–15.

Tomm, K., St. George, S., Wulff, D. & Strong, T. (eds.) (2014) *Patterns in Interpersonal Interactions: Inviting Relational Understandings for Therapeutic Change*. New York, Taylor & Francis Group/Routledge.

Voloshinov, V. N. (1929/1973) *Marxism and the Philosophy of Language*. New York, Seminar Press.

Vygotsky, L. (2012) *Thought and Language*. Cambridge, MA, MIT Press.

Vygotsky, L. S. (1978) *Mind in Society*. Cambridge, MA, Harvard University Press.

Wenger, E. (1998) *Communities of Practice. Learning, Meaning and Identity*. Cambridge, Cambridge University Press.

Wittgenstein, L. (1953) *Philosophical Investigations*. Oxford, Blackwell.

7 Analysing Organising as Dialogical Practices

Charlotte Øland Madsen

Introduction

The aim of this chapter is to describe and give examples of how to analyse research inquiries based on a social constructionist onto-epistemology with a focus on the ongoing social construction processes in organisations. Inspired by postmodern philosophies and social constructionism, the linguistic turn in the social sciences and organisational research has inspired new ways of analysing the interconnectedness of language and the ongoing construction of social reality (Alvesson & Kärreman, 2000a; Gergen, 1994). The idea that the ongoing construction of social realities and selves is embedded in dialogical practices has turned research attention to how these practices and processes can be studied (Cunliffe, 2002a; 2002b).

In this chapter research methods are described to suggest how in-situ dialogical practices can be analysed. Particular focus is placed upon how language is applied to construct versions of the social world we live in through social interaction and ongoing social meaning construction processes. The variety of ways in which these versions are constructed is hugely underestimated in conventional research (Alvesson & Kärreman, 2000b; Potter & Wetherell, 1987). This chapter describes one of many possible analytical pathways to incorporate 'a shift from examining entities (whether they be individuals, groups, organisations, or matter) to attending to what we refer to as 'language and language processes' (McNamee, 2014: 74). The chapter starts by describing how social constructionist ideas on language construction (Bakhtin, 1981/2006; Gergen, 1994; Wittgenstein, 1953) can be unfolded as an approach to analysing in-situ language use and social meaning construction (Alvesson & Kärreman, 2000b; Gergen, 2014; Potter & Wetherell, 1987). A step-by-step description of the applied method is then presented.

Where to Start?

The inquiry presented in this chapter began with theoretical readings. I came across several shared points of interest in social constructionist language philosophy and postmodern discursive theories and found it interesting to develop a method of analysis from this perspective. Thus the following paragraphs will describe how a combination of these ideas was developed and how this evolved into a guiding method for conducting my data analysis. This chapter provides practical examples of the inquiry and how the method was used.

In searching for ways to enable the analysis of the ongoing language-based processes of meaning construction, I became intrigued by Alvesson and Kärreman's (2000b) ideas on discursive pragmatism and by the early writings of Potter and Wetherell (1987), and developed a method for how to combine these methodologies with the basic assumptions posed in social constructionist writings on language as ontology (Cunliffe, 2011). Table 7.1 illustrates how these can be combined in order to study processes of in-situ dialoguing.

Interested in applying a social constructionist approach to the study of the ever-changing stream of local dialogic construction processes, I searched for a method that would enable me to capture some of the in-situ processes of social construction in organisational life (Grant & Hardy, 2003). Wittgenstein's (1953) ideas on language games became the starting point for my search – in particular, the idea that in-situ language use is both constituted by and constituting for the meaning construction process. These processes have been described as an ongoing flow of centripetal and centrifugal forces in conversation (Bakhtin, 1981, 2006). The centripetal forces can be seen as the warp of the tapestries of human interaction – the rules of the language games – and the ongoing co-construction processes as the weft illuminating the constant in-situ reconstruction of context and meaning from within the language game, illustrating the interweaving processes of meaning construction (Bakhtin, 1981, 2006; Wittgenstein, 1953).

In social constructionism, emphasis is placed upon language use as constructions of past/present/future (Shotter, 1996). The aim of the developed

Table 7.1 In-situ Dialoguing

Language as ontology	Social constructionism – through relational interaction, shared meanings are co-constructed
Durability	Emerging/fluid/dynamic
Meanings	Meaning is co-constructed in dialogue
Historicity – time/space	Past-present-future meet in dialogue
Epistemology – form of knowledge	Pragmatic knowing – in-situ
Research interests – organising	The ongoing processes of meaning construction – language as constituted and constituting in social interaction
Research approaches	Conversation/co-constructed inquiry/ongoing dialoguing
Metaphors	Language game/centrifugal/centripetal

method is to zoom in on language use and capture the *past* constructions of formerly developed meaning constructions (centripetal forces) and how these become resources in the *present* conversation as ways of constructing a here-and-now perspective on organisational life. At the same time, this enables a study of how ever-changing combinations of language resources and the polyphonic, interweaving processes of old and new meaning constructions can hint at how these *present* constructions can become part of re-constructing actions and interpretations of the *future* (centrifugal forces).

The method described here is an approach concerned with analysing locally produced talk-in-interaction. It focuses on the idea that language is primarily a performance or in-situ effect in the local context. This idea has been further developed in discursive psychology, resulting in a linguistic reframing of social psychology (Potter & Wetherell, 1987). Concepts such as identity, legitimacy, blaming, disclaimers, rationality, and power are seen as effects that are inter-subjectively constructed with others in conversation. The aim is to study the ongoing accomplishment of social organisation (Wetherell, 1998). This methodological approach suggests how these ideas on language construction can be connected with social constructionist ideas on dialogue. This chapter gives only some of the many in-situ performances and effects of relevance to organisational research that may be interesting to pursue through this form of analysis. It is a way to provide interesting information on the in-situ linguistic resources that organisational members draw on when they construct identity, legitimacy, disclaimers, rationality, power, etc. in organisational settings (Gergen, 2011; Potter & Wetherell, 1987).

This form of analysis offers a way to conduct a study from within the local somewhere of the organisational members. It is important to situate the research in conversations and observations in the local setting and to emphasise both the centripetal and centrifugal forces of language in the analysis. Applying the ideas of the interpretative repertoire (Potter & Wetherell, 1987) in the analysis provides a way to study the embedded language practices in organisations. Analysing how language use both constitutes and constructs the world of the organisational members enables the researcher to zoom in on the ongoing interweaving processes of social construction and social action (Wittgenstein, 1953). By emphasising attention to both the macro-level rules of the language game and the micro-level activity of language construction and functionality, one is able to illuminate how the language game plays out in the local context.

In my analysis I was particularly interested in identity construction in the conversations I had with employees. In line with social constructionist writings and discursive psychology, identity construction is seen as a discursive action that gives meaning in a social context. It is seen as a performance or effect that provides a certain in-situ construction of the social world in the conversation. Identity is, therefore, seen as an ongoing relational construction or performance (Gergen, 2011: 113; Potter & Wetherell, 1987).

Alvesson and Willmott (2002) refer to this as ongoing identity work. Identity construction is therefore tied closely to the situational context of the conversation and becomes a performance or an in-situ effect that can be analysed. Identity construction is closely linked to meaning construction, legitimacy, and power construction, and these can also be analysed as performative in-situ effects. (see Potter & Wetherell, 1987, for further examples, such as blaming, disclaimers, and in-group/out-group constructions).

The research method I will describe is based on the following:

1) Social constructionist ideas on language as ontology and as an epistemology that emphasises the ongoing and temporal nature of social co-construction
2) Studying organising as before-the-fact processes of becoming
3) Recognising that when interacting with organisational members the researcher takes part in co-constructing ongoing dialogues within the organisation
4) Recognising that the research presented is just one temporal way of interpreting the data; different constructions are possible

The Inquiry

When beginning the empirical work with the company ABC, I knew that they had just embarked on implementing a new IT system and, as described earlier, I wanted to find out how this implementation process was socially constructed by employees. I find it important to find a theme of interest for the inquiry quite early in the research process. When looking at social construction processes and language construction, it is an insurmountable task to grasp everything about these processes within an organisation. It is, however, important to co-construct the theme of inquiry with organisational members in a way that makes sense to both parties in the inquiry (see Chapters 4, 5, and 6 for further inspiration).

The inquiry began with an initial conversation with the IT-system project manager. He invited me into the company and gave me access to conversations with nine ABC employees (including himself) close to the IT-system implementation process. Because I was interested in following this process, we agreed that the study was to be longitudinal. This meant that I followed this implementation process at ABC for one year, and during this time I had nineteen conversations (thirteen taped) with the employees; in addition, I participated in an IT-system training session for ABC employees.

Working from a social constructionist philosophy, the conversations were open and co-constructed on the theme of the IT-system implementation process. Adjusted responses (see Chapter 2) were primarily used to get to know the socially constructed world at ABC and in particular the local constructions of the conversation partners, though on some occasions the unadjusted responses were applied; however, the conversations provided room for reflection on the process for both conversation partners (see Chapters 2 and 3 for further exploration of ways to engage in conversations). During the conversations, I allowed the conversation to flow freely in the construction of a multitude of different perspectives. On a reflective note, I found it important to follow the conversation partner in this flow of constructions because I wanted to partake in a co-constructed dialogue with organisational members about their in-situ meaning constructions of what was relevant for them in the local conversational context. It was also important, when I went back for second and third conversations with the employees, to engage in conversation with the idea that each encounter is a new flow of co-constructions for both the organisational member and the inquirer and creates new locally constructed moments of meaning construction. In practice this meant that I was open to following the conversational flow and refrained from making comments like, 'This is different from what you told me last time', and asking questions like, 'How has this developed since last time I was here?' It is important not to introduce or reintroduce certain fixed meaning structures from previous conversations and not to introduce a chronology based upon your previous conversations and your own study into the conversation. Chronology, from this perspective, is also a social construction.

The role of the inquirer as a conversation partner and the conversation/interview as a source of data material has been challenged by several authors. In these writings the idea is postulated that the best empirical data is 'naturally occurring talk' (Potter & Wetherell, 1987; Potter & Hepburn, 2003; Potter, 2004) not based on inquirer-employee conversations. The argument for using 'naturally occurring talk' is that the researcher's subject position and the setting as such will influence conversations with organisational members. However, when language is ontology, this influence will be present in all conversational settings and, seen from a social constructionist perspective, is a natural part of the conversation. As inquirers, we should not place ourselves in brackets, but must rather embark on research from within, remaining aware of our role and our pre-understandings and reflect upon how we co-construct the conversations in which we engage (Shotter, 2016). In practice, it can be a challenge to access 'naturally occurring talk' from an ethical perspective, and if the organisational members know they are being taped, this can influence the construction process. It is, however, important to pay attention to the processes of co-construction between the inquirer and the employee, both when engaging in conversations and when analysing the data.

How to Analyse?

When I had transcribed the thirteen taped conversations and looked at my field notes I found myself in a state of dismay over the massive amount of data in my possession. Where should I start, and how could I analyse it all? As described earlier, informed by my social constructionist readings and greatly inspired by Potter and Wetherell's (1987) book on discursive psychology, I developed the following method for analysing the data. In the following paragraphs, I develop these methodological ideas on how I chose to analyse my data with the hope of inspiring the reader's own process. The steps described as follows must be seen as a way to structure the analytical process, which is very difficult to structure and describe. As Hosking and Pluut (2010) write, 'Our relational constructionist premises invite a view of research processes as ongoing processes of (re)constructing self (perhaps as a researcher), other (perhaps the researched) and relationships' (p. 62). They go on to identify the research process as ongoing dialoguing, emphasising the importance of reflexivity both during the inquiry and when analysing and writing up research. During this process, one must continuously reflect on 'what is construed as "data", how data is analysed and "theorized", the language used and the style of writing' (Cunliffe, 2011: 665).

Step 1

As described earlier, the initial inquiry at ABC was guided by the chosen theme and by co-constructed questions. I was interested in studying the ongoing processes of meaning construction in the in-situ conversations with the employees at ABC. Inspired by social constructionist writings, I was interested in exploring from within:

- How do the different employees make sense of and discursively construct the IT-system implementation process at ABC?

This initial question guided the way the inquiry was co-constructed with the employees with whom I had conversations. During the inquiry I applied an open, intuitive, and ongoing reflexive approach to my experiences at ABC; further reflexive research questions emerged from this initial interest in following the social construction of the IT-system implementation process:

- How can I understand the co-constructed world-making processes by focusing on local relational interactions at ABC?
- How can I focus my analysis on how understandings and knowledge were constantly crafted and re-crafted in relational interactions?
- How is it possible to explore dialogic processes as both constituting and constitutive?
- How can I explore the IT-system implementation process in a past-present-future becoming perspective evolving through meaning, identity, legitimacy, and power constructions in local here-and-now conversations?

In the **first step** I transcribed the conversations and started an iterative process of coding the material. The process of coding included, at times, a lengthy and very frustrating reflexive process. In praxis this meant reading and re-reading the conversations many times, then cutting them into sections according to themes. Having done this, I sorted these clippings into different boxes according to topics of interest. I then selected some themes for further analysis based upon how much data I had gathered on the topics and how interesting I found them to be in relation to my initial research question – the social construction of the IT-system implementation at ABC.

Step 2

In the **second step** of the analysis I set out to construct a theme for the analysis. It is important to note that this theme was different from my initial research question. In my experience, a slow and time-consuming iterative process of reading and re-reading elaborate transcripts, combining these with theoretical readings, and maintaining a reflexive sensitivity towards the process of co-construction in the conversations leads to a sudden realisation of the theme for the analysis. This moment, when the pieces of the puzzle within the vast amount of data seemed to come suddenly to life, led me to the following theme of analysis: the ongoing social construction of success. This theme is further elaborated in this chapter.

It is important to note that this reworking of the initial research question to this new theme of analysis can be seen as a way of reconstructing my own pre-understandings of the research topic and entering into a dialogue with the data. This process is iterative, and new meanings and constructions will continue to occur throughout the entire research process. As Hosking & Pluut (2010: 71) describes, it is an ongoing process of '"turning back" on the construction of the "inquiry"', a process of constant reflexive dialoguing with the conversations, the theories, and one's own experiences.

Step 3

In the **third step** of the analysis I reworked the piles of coded data into an empirical corpus for the study. This meant re-coding the data and thereby selecting important quotations for further analysis. It is important in this process to remain open towards the data and also to allow for further reflection on the meaning of the text excerpts and how they can be interpreted in the data analysis. It is important to stress that this is not a classic content analysis (e.g., a process of searching for exact words in the text), but rather a cyclical process of reading and re-reading while trying to construct patterns of social construction in the data. In this process I found, like Potter and Wetherell (1987), that this ongoing coding and re-coding process is of vital importance when handling a vast amount of conversational material.

Step 4

In the **fourth step** of the analysis, I focused on identifying locally produced and re-produced interpretative repertoires. Potter and Wetherell (1987: 149) define interpretative repertoires as

> recurrently used systems of terms used for characterizing and evaluating actions, events and other phenomena. A repertoire, like the empiricists or contingent repertoires, is constituted through a limited range of terms used in particular stylistic and grammatical constructions. Often a repertoire will be *organis*ed around specific metaphors and figures of speech (tropes).

In this process, I found a wide range of interpretative repertoires, and needed to choose some of them for my analysis. I used the criteria of commonality and importance, both within the local conversations and across conversations, and focused on my theme of analysing their connections to the IT-system implementation process. I also re-listened to the tapes in order to search out the repertoires that seemed to be of importance to my conversation partners by listening to their voices.

Seen from a social constructionist perspective, this part of the analysis was focused on finding centripetal elements in the conversations. Centripetal elements represent processes of shared meaning-making that are constructed and reconstructed in dialogue. The interpretative repertories become a language-based representation of past meaning-making and come to represent the socially constructed reality or taken-for-granted ideas that are present in the here-and-now conversation.

This first part of the analytic process is hard to demonstrate and changes from analyst to analyst and from analysis to analysis; however, it is always important to record one's process and reflections while coding data. This makes it easier to describe how the process came about. Some research concerned with language analysis seems to lack a description of this very labour-intensive part of the analysis. I will agree with Alvesson and Kärreman (2011) in his critique that when a description of these reflexive processes is left out, the presented research almost seems to be pigeonholing the text excerpts into pre-defined topics of analysis. I therefore recommend recording the reflection process in order to validate the research efforts for the reader, the final judge of the work.

During the process of re-reading and re-listening to the conversations I had had with the employees at ABC, I found one of the interpretative repertoires in the material increasingly interesting; as I began analysing this repertoire, it seemed to grow and enable further analysis. I can only describe this process as a puzzle coming together, enabling me to see the data in a new light and to see some of the constructed strings that seemed to constitute the IT-system implementation process for the employees at ABC. This repertoire seemed to embody centripetal forces in the conversations. This part of the process can be seen as a classic analytical type of categorisation; however, from a social constructionist perspective these repertoires are seen as 'the nouns from which we construct versions of collectivities' (Potter & Wetherell, 1987: 37).

Rather than exploring how these repertoires define the individuals' cognitive sense-making processes, they become 'building blocks of our many versions of the social world; however, when we look closely at the blocks we see that they themselves are not solid and defined, but have to be moulded in discourse for use in different accounts' (ibid.). In line with this, Shotter (2016: 2) writes, '[N]ot only have some of us moved away from a concern with the inner workings of individual people's subjectivities or mentalities occurring privately inside their heads, but we have also ceased to search for "ideal forms" (static shapes), existing eternally, hidden behind appearances.'

The following example shows the interpretative repertoire that I found to be of centripetal importance in the data. The presented data material in this chapter is based on Madsen (2007).

Peter, the IT Manager at ABC

Peter (P): 'The bottom line is that Andy (the IT-system implementation project manager) had a perfectly clear idea about how to create a success. You create a success by saying it's a success.'

Inquirer (I): 'Yes, I'd like to hear more about that . . .'

P: 'A wise man once said to me, "I've discovered what it is that Andy can do. He knows how to say something is a success, and when Andy says that it's a success then it turns out to be a success."'

In the same conversation a few minutes later:

P: 'Right, then you shift your focus and if you shift focus and people feel proud because they are proud of being part of a success that creates energy and momentum, and it creates creativity and it is easier to overcome the tough days. Because if you want success, you come in on weekends, you want success, you did it, you met the deadline, you had it up and running as planned. Those sacrifices are easier to bear in a sort of rush of success, than it is in a sort of dodge-failure feeling.'

I: 'So it's a way of defining other people's reality for them?'

P: 'In any case you help suggest an alternative reality to their often . . . stressed and fragile, perhaps somewhat negative reality, where they overstate problems and understate successes. Behind that, when you get more involved, then you sometimes think, "Wait a minute, you're cutting it a bit tight now Andy, aren't you?" But when it comes to reality it's like this: . . . your reality is not the same as mine.'

Andy, the IT-system Implementation Project Manager

Andy: 'There were six months where we practically didn't talk about success. We did that deliberately. We knew it would come out wrong. But when we got things going and we were running according to schedule, etc., we thought that all in all we could announce success. No IT-system implementation projects are implemented without problems. I tell you, there aren't any. It's an enormous change. We're dealing with a bunch of very different people, and there'll always be some that think you're nuts and so on. That can't be avoided.'

Points of Reflection

It is important while reading the previous quotations to bear in mind that the presentation of the data is in itself also a construction. The critical reader should question why exactly these quotations were included here and not the other thousands of quotations that were available to the researcher. How and why are they put together in this particular way? What do these short quotations say without the conversation context? What was the part played by the inquirer in this co-construction process? How was the empirical data generated? The researcher must also reflect upon these critical questions when constructing the data analysis and when writing.

I chose these excerpts for the analysis because the idea of constructing the IT-system implementation process at ABC as a success seemed to serve as a way to talk the process into being and to construct particular versions of the social world at ABC. The social construction of what I have termed the 'success repertoire' is talked into being. In the previous excerpt, Peter, the IT manager, describes how this repertoire came into being with intent from Andy the IT implementation manager, and how Peter has supported this construction because it advances the implementation process among the employees.

The quotation from Andy describes how he finds it necessary to construct this version of the implementation process as a success in order to overcome the problems and resistance that, in his experience, often occur in IT implementation processes. As he says, at the beginning of the implementation process, he felt that constructing the implementation process as a success would be premature and would not be accepted by the employees as a legitimate version of the organisational world they lived in; however, six months into the implementation process he began to construct and co-construct the success repertoire with other organisational members.

After this initial identification of the success repertoire in the data, I re-coded the data and back-tracked the conversations to find out more about the content of the success repertoire. I found from the data that it comprised three sub-repertoires.

1) **The failure of others.** In the data I found that stories about how other organizations had failed to implement the IT system and how ABC employees had managed to implement it successfully became a way for Andy and Peter to construct a compelling version of the repertoire to the employees.
2) **The active construction of success.** It was important to further explore how this success repertoire was constructed primarily by Andy and Peter as a way to influence the employees engaged in the implementation process. Additionally, the success repertoire, as defined by keeping to the budget and time schedule, was presented to the board of directors and to the public in external seminars. The first part of the analysis was aimed at unfolding the repertoires that I had found to further inform the reader of the content of this success or failure repertoire.
3) **Keeping to budget and time constraints.** This sub-repertoire described how success was defined. It meant that, compared to other companies, ABC was successful in keeping to the budget and time schedule of the implementation. I found in my analysis that success was construed as keeping to the budget and the timeframe of the implementation process.

As Chris, an IT consultant, said in one of our conversations:

Chris: 'It definitely hasn't been a disadvantage that we have been able to promote ourselves in this manner. That we actually have made a very successful implementation, that we have . . . kept to the budget and the time deadline that we promised.'

In my conversations with organisational members at ABC, this organised system of terms and tropes describing the implementation process as a success were often accompanied by stories of how other companies had failed in their implementation, namely by exceeding expenses and spending much more time on the implementation than they had planned.

The analysis of the terms and metaphors of the success repertoire was helpful because it revealed some of the centripetal forces of the repertoire and how the term 'success' was socially constructed. If I had wanted to present a classic content study of the success story and tell a centripetal narrative from it, my data analysis would have ended here. From a social constructionist perspective, the success repertoire can metaphorically be seen as the warp of the tapestries, the centripetal forces in the language game. As Shotter (2016: 62) writes, the language game can be described as the 'inheritance', that is, our routine understanding of each other and our social world within a linguistic community. Drawing on Wittgenstein (1953), this 'inheritance', or taken-for-granted understanding, is seen as an important means by which we communicate. However, as Shotter (ibid.) continues, '[A]lthough acknowledging it as "inherited" situates the process involved with the hurly-burly of our everyday lives, it does not clarify the nature of that process further'. It is therefore important to focus the analysis on the onto-epistemological idea 'that we all occupy a fluid, indeterminate, not yet finalized reality' (Shotter, 2016: 62). This means that to be able to study the ongoing processes of making sense in a community, we need the next step of analysis to look further into the ongoing dialogic construction processes in the data. Staying within the metaphor of the tapestries, we now focus on the ongoing dialogic interweaving processes of constructing pictures of our social worlds with others in order to look further into how, in conversations, we simultaneously work towards constructing shared meanings and are thrown into the 'hurly-burly of our everyday lives' (ibid.).

Step 5

In the **fifth step,** we turn towards the data and begin forming suggestions about the in-situ constructed functionalities and performances of the interpretative repertoires identified in **Step 4**. Again, it is important to narrow down the analysis to theme relevance and to link the analysis with the identified interpretative repertoires.

In my analysis, I suggest that the success repertoire at ABC, constructed by telling stories of how other companies failed to implement IT systems, constructs a performance or an in-situ functionality in the conversation, a dichotomy between how ABC had succeeded when so many other organisations had failed. As can be seen in the previous examples, both the IT manager and the IT project manager were very focused on the word 'success', and when and how they could say the implementation was a success. As Peter said, 'If Andy, the IT project manager, says the implementation is a success, it will be a success'; he went on to tell me how they together sought to construct a storyline where the IT-system implementation was a success. This suggests the success repertoire is a relationally constructed storyline constructed by Peter and Andy with the purpose of controlling the IT-system implementation process. They even worked with the media who also reported it a success. These processes can be seen as managerial language constructions aiming to control the centripetal forces of language construction at ABC; this language construction can be traced in my conversations with other employees at ABC.

However, it is also important to note that my analysis showed that the success repertoire, although reconstructed in my conversations with other ABC employees, is varied and used for other performances and in-situ constructions in the conversations. As can be seen from the next excerpt, Carina, a member of the IT-system implementation team, struggles with the effects of the success repertoire on her work.

Carina (C): 'I remember once, we had a few laughs about that, there was this big headline, in Computerworld or something . . . Yeah, "Much gain, no pain". We weren't too keen about that. It was too much. I remember that in the finance department they blew it up and put it on the wall. But of course, we're proud of what we have done. Especially afterwards . . . But obviously we felt that . . . the management was thrilled to bits. It was oh so cheap and . . . the IT staff was ever so competent and so on, and it's also true, but there was a tendency to take a rosy view on things. I know, you shouldn't be a pessimist, but . . . maybe the IT staff, and they're busting their butts, are thinking what do they (the managers) know about how much work we do? Do they appreciate it, or what? Sometimes you doubt they do when you see things like that. But that's probably just how Andy and Peter think. I sometimes wonder a bit about this. But the reaction on the IT team was not always that positive, but of course, we were proud.'

(In the same conversation a few moments later.)

C: 'Exactly, but then the blue-collar workers aren't . . . as easily persuaded. That's probably the difference. They know their rights and . . .'
Inquirer (I): 'They're a bit more defensive, perhaps?'
C: 'Perhaps. Whereas up here [the administration] we . . . just do it. You know, if you have ambitions then you have to . . . fall into line. It sounds so terrible, but we're actually all right.'

As can be seen in the conversation with Carina, one of the local IT implementation consultants, the success repertoire caused problems for her in her dealings with the finance department. The term 'Much gain, no pain', used in *Computerworld* by Andy and Peter to describe the implementation process at ABC, seemed 'too rosy' to the employees. However, as we look for variations in the use of the success repertoire in the quote, one can see how Carina attaches the success repertoire to gaining approval and praise from the management. Then she changes to constructing a critique of the success repertoire by saying, 'it's not as easy as Andy and Peter make it out to be.' A few seconds later, her application of the success repertoire changes again into an in-situ effect of constructing how pleased she is with being recognised for her efforts by the management, saying 'but of course we were proud'.

This changes again when she finalises the conversation by constructing how she and the other members of the administration are much more likely to obey orders from the top than the blue-collar workers in the processing factory. In this way, she constructs an ongoing variety of critique and in-situ identity as someone who obeys orders. By zooming in on the co-constructed conversation with me, the success repertoire is used to construct identity, resistance, and power issues. Zooming in on the polyphonic language game in the in-situ conversation, she uses the success repertoire as the warp of shared meaning construction (the rules of the language game) when constructing how proud she is to be part of the success and, at the same time, applies the success repertoire as a way to construct resistance towards the implementation process and the consequences it had for her and other employees at ABC. The analysis of our co-constructed conversation here becomes a way to illuminate the ongoing interweaving processes of polyphonic meaning construction (Wittgenstein, 1953; Bakhtin, 1981, 2006) in our conversation. The aim of this step in the analysis is to find a way to describe the ongoing language game played out in the conversation.

Step 6

The next and final part of the analysis is to examine the conversations and the found interpretative repertoires and suggest ideas about their 'functionality' in the conversations (see Potter & Wetherell, 1987). As described earlier, in social constructionist research, identity, legitimacy, and power are seen as ongoing constructions or performances in our conversations with others. The following paragraphs describe how and why I analysed and suggested ideas about how the found interpretative repertoires could be connected with the ongoing construction processes of identity, legitimacy, and power in my conversations with employees at ABC.

I found it helpful to start **Step 6** by analysing the ongoing construction of identity in the conversations and how they were connected to the interpretative repertoires. Identity construction (Gergen, 2011) or identity work (Alvesson & Willmott, 2002) is, in this form of analysis, focused on the constructions of organisational members from within the conversational dialogue. It is focused on representing a diversity of voices in the conversation; this diversity extends to the idea that identity is not a core representation of a 'true' self but rather an ongoing accomplishment or performance in the conversation (Gergen, 2011; Potter & Wetherell, 1987; Tate, 2007). This means that in the analysis of a single conversation, variation in the way the self is presented by the organisational member, as seen in the previous example, is to be expected. The accomplishment of identity positions is seen as an ongoing negotiation process in the conversation. This is not to say that anything goes into a conversation. Not all identity positions can be taken in the conversation: based upon prior meetings with the conversation partner one cannot one day construct identity as a 'couch potato' and the next as an 'elite athlete' without going into a negotiation process of reconstructing identity positions. From this perspective, applying language becomes a way of doing or performing identity; this is also valid for constructions of legitimacy, power, and other social psychological phenomena (Butler, 2004; Potter & Wetherell, 1987).

By drawing on the success repertoire, Andy and Peter constructed managerial identity positions in the conversations as authors of creating a successful implementation at ABC. They constructed how they had constructed and co-constructed the success repertoire with the purpose of creating pride among the IT-system implementation consultants. However, this way of constructing the implementation process also legitimised ways of exerting power over the employees at ABC.

Thus, the success repertoire becomes a language resource that could be tapped into to create legitimacy for these actions because it provided resources for communication and legitimated the sacrifices that employees like Carina had to make: working after hours and on weekends to meet the project deadlines. In this sense, the success repertoire becomes a power tool in the organisation.

It is interesting to zoom in on the quotes previously presented to see how Carina struggled with the success repertoire. During the excerpt she taps into the repertoire and constructs how she and the other members of the IT implementation team were proud to be a part of the unique success at ABC, but at the same time, she questioned whether management saw or acknowledged her sacrifices. The success repertoire, thus, created variation in her identity constructions. During our conversation she shifts back and forth between identity positions. By mentioning the attitudes of the blue-collar workers at ABC she taps into a critical stance towards the implementation process, constructing a difference between employees in the administration and blue-collar workers at ABC and how they more openly criticise and resist the changes that the implementation brings to their work. Belonging to the group of administrative employees, she constructs how criticism is subdued among these organisational members who feel pressured to comply with management's orders. At the end of the quote she makes a disclaimer: 'It sounds so terrible, but we're actually all right.' One can only speculate why this disclaimer is used in the conversation: perhaps because she recognises the researcher's relationship to the management and doesn't want to be portrayed as negative about or critical of the implementation process. It is important to stress the situational aspects of the conversations researchers have during inquiries and the importance of including them as part of the reflexive analysis process. Research ethics must also be kept in mind.

Discussion

The preceding is just a small excerpt from the data and analysis presented to illuminate the processes of personal and organisational identity construction and how these can be seen as related to the construction of legitimacy and power at ABC. From a social constructionist perspective, the analysis is an ongoing exploration of how organisational members locally construct meaning in conversations by tapping into the success repertoire, thereby constructing local conversational in-situ effects and performances of identity, legitimacy, and power.

The analysis illuminates both the centripetal and centrifugal forces of language construction. It is, however, important to keep the analysis open-ended and balanced when applying a social constructionist perspective to language construction. The centripetal forces in the conversations, in my experience, have a tendency to invite the analyst into deterministic ideas of discovering a 'general currency of explanation', which becomes a socially constructed truth about 'the way things are' (Potter & Wetherell, 1987: 152), or pigeonholing research results (Alvesson & Kärreman, 2011).

However, from a social constructionist perspective, the ongoing variations in the language games are far more interesting. They make it possible to zoom in on the ongoing processes of language construction and on a here-and-now perspective on organisational life. The fluid and indeterminate processes of organising aim not only to capture the 'social constructions' of an organisation, but also to open up for an analysis of the variation in the language game processes aiming for the following:

- A study of the processes of linguistically expressed meaning and circumstance construction and how these are constructed and developed into 'shared anticipations as to how we should respond to events occurring in those circumstances if we are to act as the others around us will respond to those events' (Shotter, 2016: 62)
- Illuminating how the 'not-finalised reality' continuously develops in the polyphonic dialogic interweaving processes, enabling a study of the processes of organising as past/present and future linguistic processes of how old and new meaning constructions continuously meet and develop

Conclusion

Although research design, data collection, and analysis are often outlined in published research as linear, pre-defined best practices, I have found the process to be highly iterative and interactive with both research ideas and ideas from my conversations. Influenced by research interests and research findings, the analytical process should remain open to things that puzzle, disturb pre-defined research interests, and send the researcher in a totally different research direction.

It is very important to have an open mind when entering into co-constructed inquiries, always being critical of both the experiences they bring and one's own taken-for-granted interpretations of the inquiry and the role of the researcher. Analysis is a constant interpretation and re-interpretation process of both theoretical assumptions and empirical findings that is never finished (see Cunliffe, 2011; Hosking & Pluut, 2010; Sandberg & Alvesson, 2011 for more information on these processes). It is especially important to reflect upon these differing approaches when choosing a method of analysis. The choice of method of analysis used here was just one approach, and researchers must contemplate how their own choices can best be fitted to their inquiry aspirations.

References

Alvesson, M. & Kärreman, D. (2000a) Taking the Linguistic Turn in Organizational Research. Challenges, Responses, Consequences. *The Journal of Applied Behavioural Science*, 36 (2), 136–158.
Alvesson, M. & Kärreman, D. (2000b) Varieties of Discourse: On the Study of Organizations through Discourse Analysis. *Human Relations*, 53 (9), 1125–1149.
Alvesson, M. & Kärreman, D. (2011) Decolonializing Discourse: Critical Reflections on Organizational Discourse Analysis. *Human Relations*, 64 (9), 1121–1146.
Alvesson, M. & Willmott, H. (2002) Identity Regulation as Organizational Control: Producing the Appropriate Individual. *Journal of Management Studies*, 39 (5), 619–644.
Bakhtin, M. M. (1981/2006) *The Dialogic Imagination—Four Essays*. Austin, University of Texas Press.
Butler, J. (2004) *Undoing Gender*. London, Routledge.
Cunliffe, A. L. (2002a) Reflexive Dialogical Practice in Management Learning. *Management Learning*, 33 (1), 35–61.
Cunliffe, A. L. (2002b) Social Poetics as Management Inquiry. A Dialogical Approach. *Journal of Management Inquiry*, 11 (2), 128–146.
Cunliffe, A. L. (2011) Crafting Qualitative Research: Morgan and Smircich 30 Years On. *Organizational Research Methods*, 14 (4), 647–673.
Gergen, K. J. (1994) *Realities and Relationships. Soundings in Social Construction*. Cambridge, MA, Harvard University Press.
Gergen, K. J. (2011) The Self as Social Construction. *Psychological Studies*, 56 (1), 108–116.
Gergen, K. J. (2014) Epilogue. Discourse Study: A Movement in the Making. In: Bozatzis, N. & Dragonas, T. (eds.) *The Discursive Turn in Social Psychology*. Taos World Share Books, PDF version 2014, pp. 205–215.
Grant, D. & Hardy, C. (2003) Introduction: Struggles with Organizational Discourse. *Organization Studies*, 25 (1), 5–13.
Hosking, D. M. & Pluut, B. (2010) (Re)constructing Reflexivity: A Relational Constructionist Approach. *The Qualitative Report*, 15 (1), 59–75.
Madsen, C. Ø. (2007) *The Social Construction of Success—a Discursive Psychological Study of SAP R3 Implementation*. PhD Thesis, Department of Marketing and Statistics, Aarhus School of Business.
McNamee, S. (2014) Research as Relational Practice. In Simon, G. & Chard, A. (eds.), *Systemic Inquiry: Innovations in Reflexive Practice Research*. Farnhill, UK, Everything Is Connected Press, pp. 74–94.
Potter, J. (2004) Discourse Analysis as a Way of Analyzing Naturally Occurring Talk. In Silverman, D. (ed.) *Qualitative Research: Theory, Method & Practice*, 2nd edition. London: Sage, pp. 222–243.
Potter, J. & Hepburn, A. (2003) I'm a Bit Concerned—Early Actions and Psychological Constructions in a Child Protection Helpline. *Research on Language and Social Interaction*, 36 (3), 197–240.
Potter, J. & Wetherell, M. (1987) *Discourse and Social Psychology—Beyond Attitudes and Behavior*. London, Sage.

Sandberg, J. & Alvesson, M. (2011) Ways of Constructing Research Questions: Gap-Spotting or Problematization? *Organization*, 18 (1), 23–44.

Shotter, J. (1996) Now I Can Go On: Wittgenstein and Our Embodied Embeddedness in the 'Hurly-Burly' of Life. *Human Studies*, 19 (4), 385–407.

Shotter, J. (2016) Undisciplining Social Science: Wittgenstein and the Art of Creating Situated Practices of Social Inquiry. *Journal for the Theory of Social Behavior*, 46 (1), 60–83.

Tate, S. A. (2007) Foucault, Bakhtin, Ethnomethodology: Accounting for Hybridity in Talk-in-Interaction. *Forum Qualitative Sozialforschung/Forum: Qualitative Social Research*, 8 (2), 1–12.

Wetherell, M. (1998) Positioning and Interpretative Repertoires: Conversation Analysis and Post-Structuralism in Dialogue. *Discourse and Society*, 9 (3), 387–412.

Wittgenstein, L. (1953) *Philosophical Investigations*. Oxford, Blackwell.

8 Working with Data Is a Polyphonic and Future-Forming Endeavour

Mette Vinther Larsen

Introduction

To set the scene for this final chapter, I'll take a trip down memory lane. A few years ago, I travelled to a beautiful Greek island. I remember myself at a resort with the most amazing weather; the wind is warm and mild, crickets chirp, the sun shines from a clear blue sky, and I have that relaxed and content feeling about how wonderful life is on a Greek island. I am here to attend a conference held just before summer vacation. On the second day of the conference, just after having enjoyed a cup of coffee on the terrace looking over the turquoise rolling water, there is a plenary in one of the big ballrooms.

As the conference participants enter the high-ceilinged ballroom, heavy red velvet curtains surround us, shutting out the light and ocean view and reminding us of why we are in Greece. Were the curtains not drawn, it would have been difficult for us to see the PowerPoint slides that, in just a few minutes, would accompany the first keynote during his presentation. As we find our seats, the big doors behind us are shut to keep out distracting noise from the sea, bumblebees, birds and laughing holiday visitors. After the silence has set in and we all have our notebooks open in front of us on the tables, the keynote speaker begins to share his story of the significance of meta-awareness.

As part of his presentation, the keynote speaker shares a story of how he and a colleague had meditated with a group of monks as the sun was setting in the Himalayas. To give us all a sense of the experience, he has brought a PowerPoint photograph to illustrate the very beautiful sunset. As the keynote speaker unfolds the story, he respects and practices all the accepted norms for how a researcher should present his results: he uses all the right theoretical terms and has empirical data to support his argumentation, and he makes compelling connections between data and theory.

Sitting in the ballroom and listening to his presentation, I begin to think that he makes a qualified and convincing keynote presentation. I feel confident that the experience he had meditating with the monks was a wonderful way to develop meta-awareness. Despite this, I am not drawn into the story.

I cannot create a sense of how it feels to be in the Himalayas, meditating with these monks. I begin to search for clues to help me build up a sense of what the temperature and altitude were like there: what smells, sounds, and senses surrounded them. Looking at the very beautiful, but also very static, picture of the sunset does not help give me a sense of the contextual details I'm searching for.

Perhaps the keynote speaker's purpose is not to create such an atmosphere, but rather to present and develop what he believes are the seven key features of mindfulness. Hence, maybe I should stop trying to recreate the atmosphere in the Himalayas and instead listen to his presentation on the key features. In the midst of thinking about this, something truly magical happens. A butterfly that has somehow gone astray is flickering around the ballroom – maybe it is looking for the light or for a way out. Suddenly, the butterfly flies in front of the light of the projector and its beautiful movement around the room is – for just a few seconds and in an unforeseen way – projected as a shadow dancing against the sun as it sets on the picture, making the light and skies of the picture come to life.

The static picture of the sunset and the lambent movement of the butterfly mesh and, for a brief moment, I get a sense of how it feels to be sitting in the Himalayas meditating with those monks as the sun sets on that particular evening. I can sense the temperature and altitude, and I enjoy the silence surrounding me. And then the moment is gone. The keynote presenter pays no attention to the unexpected flickering butterfly as he continues developing the seven key features of mindfulness. None of my colleagues noticed the enchantment of the butterfly and no one referred to it afterwards over lunch. Had it not been for the drawing of a butterfly with the word 'life!' next to it in my conference notes, I would be tempted to say it had all been a figment of my imagination.

Whether or not the butterfly flew through the room is not the point of the story. The story illustrates the significant future-forming role that researchers play in the stories – written, performative, and oral – that we share concerning what constitutes organisational life. Every time a researcher presents his or her results, he or she invites others to make organisational life be understood and practised in specific – and not other – ways. It only takes the flickering of a butterfly's wings to turn the understanding all around and create a different story.

Language, as mentioned multiple times in the book and argued by Cunliffe (2002a: 130), is ontologically constitutive: 'It is within our embodied responsive dialogue that we articulate and create relationships with our surroundings and in doing so, (re)create ourselves, others, and landscapes of possible actions, that is new forms of life . . .' As researchers write a text, prepare a presentation, etc., we do our utmost to figure out how we in the best way possible can share what we have discovered in our data exploration. What the unforeseen flickering of the butterfly humbly but persistently reminds me, as a researcher, is that data can be explored in innumerable ways. Each time a researcher tells a story, he or she embraces and explores the ever-present multiple possibilities of sharing what he or she has come to know.

This does not mean that there is one right story to tell or that it is our job as researchers to uncover it. On the contrary, 'there is no "getting it right." The analysis is itself a construction' (Gergen, 2014: 52). Neither is it a critique of the way an esteemed colleague gave a keynote presentation on how he understood the significance of meta-awareness, because the presentation he gave was honourable and meaningful. It is merely a gentle reminder that it does not take much – like the unforeseen flickering of a butterfly's wings – to open up completely new ways of talking and enacting organisational life into being. As Gergen (2015: 21), a relational constructionist, argues: 'It is time for social sciences to channel their substantial resources of intelligence and ingenuity into creating more viable ways of living together.'

This chapter is a response to Gergen's argument and is an invitation to jointly explore how it is possible for researchers to integrate the possibilities for creating viable ways of living together in how we tell the stories of what we have come to know. In this chapter, I present five practices that I rely on in my work, while also embracing the possibilities for creating more viable ways of living together in our stories. These practices are:

1) Engaging in reflective pragmatism
2) Embracing radical presence
3) Striving toward before-the-fact inquiries
4) Relying on resonance as a way forward
5) Turning storying into living events

To include the voices of others, I draw attention to other scholars who incorporate and work with these practices. I also revisit several of the chapters in the book to exemplify how we, as authors, have worked towards incorporating the practices as we share stories of organisational life. As in the other chapters in the book, the practices presented are not methods you should follow as a guide. They are invitations to help develop your own practices in dialogue with the co-researched data, managers and employees who are involved, philosophers, theoreticians, and whomever else inspires you and co-authors with you.

Before presenting the five practices, I want to highlight the significance of the relational stance. It is important to acknowledge – even when writing – that we are relational beings (Gergen, 2009). When researchers return to their offices and revisit the data that they have taken part in co-constructing with the purpose of writing up a report, article, or book chapter or of planning a workshop, conference, seminar, dialogue meeting, or similar, they might physically be the only person in the room. However, this does not mean that they are no longer *in relation*. Every thought, feeling, intuition, question, and understanding that emerges is a social, relational, and co-authored construction. As the opening example illustrated, the ability to make stories come to life and resonate with people is a relational process. The keynote speaker and I (with help from the butterfly) engaged in a joint process for us to be able to co-construct a unique there-and-then meaning. As relational beings, people can achieve together what they cannot accomplish in isolation: 'we construct our knowledge about any topic in collaborative interchange with others' (McNamee, 1994: 72). Acknowledging this premise is significant, especially when we sit physically alone in our offices and attempt to figure out how best to present what we have come to know. This means that we are never really alone; others are always present in the process.

Furthermore, a relational constructionism stance draws attention to what happens as we tell a story. As a relational constructionist, I have come to treasure how the stories I present serve as invitations to co-construct meaning with my conversation partners, namely the people reading and listening to the stories. Both an understanding and a co-construction of meaning emerge when we as conversation partners actively engage in co-constructing meaning. In addition, the co-constructed meaning emerges out of how the here and now resonates with how life is being lived within the local 'somewheres' that mesh in the conversation. Working with data is a relational, polyphonic, and future-forming endeavour. This is both the alluring and terrifying aspect of the stories that researchers co-author.

It is alluring because it reminds us that there is never only one story to tell; they are multiple and we jointly co-author them. Organisational life evolves and develops as we change these stories. It is also terrifying because we must pay the utmost respect to the future-forming aspects of our work – and acknowledge that as we tell a story, we offer possibilities for people to create more viable, reflexive, responsive, and ethical ways of living together. It is also terrifying because the stories we present are invitations for other local realities to be discussed and acted into being (Cunliffe, 2002a). Hence, researchers depend on others to participate in co-constructing more viable, reflexive, responsive, and ethical ways of living together. This should not scare us, however, but only enlighten our curiosity, creativity, and desire to share and further develop what we have come to know together with others.

Engaging in Reflective Pragmatism

One manner of conveying how working with data is a relational, polyphonic, and future-forming endeavour is to practice what Gergen (2014, 2015) refers to as reflective pragmatism: 'whatever exists makes no necessary requirements on representation.' A reflective pragmatic stance means to embrace that there is no one way to present or construct data, experiences, etc., but rather there are multiple. To work with data in reflective pragmatic ways involves moving beyond the need to represent a truth, or to determine who is right or whose opinion is better than that of the others. Instead, the purpose is to engage in a reflexive inquiry, whereby various ways to move forward in generative ways are jointly explored (McNamee, 2014).

This process distances researchers from searching for a meaning inherent to a considerable amount of co-researched data and instead reverses the process until the researchers begin to ask themselves what it is – based on what we have come to know as we co-researched – that we want to accomplish with our research. What is the interesting story that can be shared with our conversation partners? Then, researchers dive right into asking each other how they can partake in future-forming ways to create more viable, reflexive, responsive, and ethical ways of living together in the stories that they co-author.

This is a way to practice what Cunliffe (2002b: 38) invites researchers to reflect upon: 'we construct the very accounts we think describe the world. We therefore need to question the ways in which we account for our experiences.' As researchers, we not only co-research, we are also 'agents of social change' (Gergen, 2014). Therefore, we can invite each other to explore with curiosity the voices and ideologies that are privileged and those that are silenced in the stories that we share (McNamee, 1994; Vološinov, 1986). To engage in reflective pragmatism does not mean that anything goes and we are free to tell a story in whatever way we choose. Indeed, 'one is not free to simply construct the world at will. We are ultimately dependent on each other to make our worlds' (McNamee, 2016: 100).

As in the opening example with the butterfly, the keynote presenter could not construct meaning on his own. Meaning had to be co-created and develop between him and the listeners. To support the development of joint meaning, the keynote presenter respected and practised socially and tacitly agreed conventions, norms, and generally taken-for-granted ways of doing a keynote presentation. These norms were shared with many of the conference participants because many of us had been in various but similar situations before and were able to anticipate what to expect of a keynote presentation (Gergen, 2014; 2010; McNamee, 1994; 2014; Shotter, 2006). Every scientific community has developed its own tribal dances, routines, and taken-for-granted ways of speaking and acting that enable the group members to be and to see each other as legitimate and sensible members of 'their tribe'; 'to "do science" is to participate in particular community-based practices' (McNamee & Hosking, 2012: 34). These tribal routines enable the group members to gesture and respond in adjusted ways and nearly instantaneously co-construct meaning.

Just as tribes need shared rituals, each scientific community needs its discursive practices to be able to communicate with each other and act in legitimate ways. These discursive practices have emerged, and are still emerging, based on well-founded, well-argued, and well-positioned arguments between distinguished and qualified scholars. This means that as we co-research and co-author, we often intuitively and reflectively make sense of data in ways that are congruent with existing and previously co-constructed meanings within the tribe. Based on accepted discursive practices within our research communities, we are able to legitimise most experiences and processes (Gergen, 2014). As we practice these tribal dances, we do not always pay attention to how we, by reflex, talk and act a known worldview into being. Indeed, 'we are largely unaware of how persistently we work to maintain the sense of a solid, stable, and continuing worldview' (McNamee, 2014: 79).

There is nothing wrong with practising these tribal dances as long as there is an acknowledgement of the discursive forms that are relied on in order to talk and act one out of many possible local realities into being (McNamee, 2014). It is important to reverse the process and consider the question: 'What does the research ultimately contribute to the world more generally . . . For whom are the outcomes useful?' (Gergen, 2014: 4). Based on how we respond to those questions, researchers can figure out how to invite others into co-authoring organisational life.

Just as a butterfly's flickering wings can lead to completely new ways of making sense of organisational life, the possibilities to engage in co-constructing different meanings and telling other stories are multiple. As practical co-authors of our own and others' experiences, the knowledge and learning of the polyphonic and multiple ways to tell stories about our experiences lie in the palms of our hands. We must only be bold and dare to loosen our firm grip, lift our fingers, and explore what is right before our eyes. Furthermore, we must share the stories that we believe support the creation of more viable, reflexive, responsive, and ethical ways of living together.

We, as authors of this book, can invite you, the reader, into co-constructing meaning. The processes, models, and glimpses into practice that you read about here are the outcomes of our efforts to embrace the future-forming aspects of our work. It is our attempt to present our research in ways that could be useful for scholars wanting to explore the polyphony of relational research practices in their parts of the world. It is our hope that what we present will work as gestures that you will respond to in reflective, pragmatic ways as you and your co-researchers bring them to life through the development of your own meaningful ways of supporting the creation of viable, reflexive, responsive, and ethical approaches to living together.

Reference to Other Work

McNamee (2014) is a researcher who, in her work, continuously aims to move beyond the notion that there is only one story to tell. She embraces the notion of reflective pragmatism and invites researchers to curiously explore how the various ways of co-researching and co-authoring, which exist in local scientific communities, can intersect with and enrich each other. She has illustrated how various academic disciplines are not necessarily mutually exclusive. They all offer ways to co-research and co-author organisational

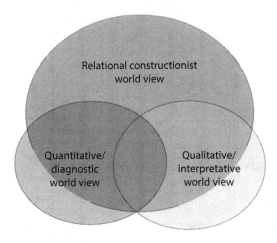

Figure 8.1 Relational Constructionist Worldview
Source: Reworked from McNamee, 2014

life; perhaps more interesting ways of sharing stories of organisational life emerge when we as researchers begin to consider what our conversation partners would be interested in learning more about.

Figure 8.1 illustrates how it is possible for us to let go of the illusion that somehow – if only the right practices were applied – we could uncover the motives, processes, relations, etc. that have led to a certain outcome. There are always multiple possibilities for moving on and working with co-authored data. McNamee (2014) invites us to acknowledge that quantitative/diagnostic and qualitative/interpretative worldviews are only, as Wittgenstein writes, 'language games' that we can choose to participate in or not. These language games, or tribal dances, offer us different and multiple ways of taking part in speaking and acting certain worldviews into being. The games each have their own tribal dances, taken-for-granted norms, and discursive practices, which we are able to use as ways to make sense of co-researched data. This process enables the researcher to explore how to tell a story about what they have come to know in ways that are useful and contribute to the becoming of the local reality in viable ways.

At conferences, seminars, or PhD workshops, I have often heard Gergen advocate for a reflexive pragmatic approach to the way we tell a story about what we have come to know. During a PhD course at Aalborg University (Denmark), Gergen gave a lecture on the founding principles of social constructionism. In fielding a question from a participant, Gergen's response exemplified a nuanced way of practising reflective pragmatism. The PhD student shared a story that, she felt, exemplified quite clearly how a manager in an organisation she was co-researching had used his power to undermine the staff. Based on her presentation, the student asked Gergen directly if what she had just presented was not a question of power. Gergen responded by saying: 'It might be and it might not be. The question to ask yourself is what possibilities in your writing you gain from positioning the story as a question of power. What possibilities does it give you to frame it as such and who will benefit from such a framing?'

This question and response remind me of the multitude of ways that we can story about what we have come to know. As future-formers, we are able to embrace and in reflective, pragmatic ways explore whose voices and actions are silenced and whose are privileged in the stories we share. Furthermore, could we be reflexive about whom the stories we share should and could be generative for (McNamee, 2014; McNamee & Hosking, 2012)? This foundation invites us to be curious and explorative and allows for multiple ways for the story of what we have come to know to emerge. Then, based on what and with whom we want to engage in a relational construction of meaning, we must gesture in ways that invite people to jointly create viable, reflexive, responsive, and ethical ways of living together.

Reference to This Book

This book is also an illustration of how it is possible to practice reflective pragmatism. In the process of discussing how we, the authors, could include stories 'from the field' in ways that are congruent with what we wanted to achieve with this book, and therefore illustrating how the philosophy behind relational constructionism can be transformed into research practices, we have made many choices about which data to include, in what ways, and for what purpose. What this book presents has been co-authored with the sole purpose of inviting the reader, to embrace how you as a co-researcher and co-author can partake in creating more viable, reflexive, responsive, and ethical ways of living together.

For example, as the authors of this book had to figure out how to present both the process model developed in Chapter 6 and the stepwise process for making a dialogic analysis, as presented in Chapter 7, we engaged in dialogues and explored the multiple ways of doing so. Based on what we thought the reader, with whom we wanted to be in conversation, was interested in learning more about, we have chosen to reduce complexity in certain ways and not in others. Thus, our aim has not been to mirror or describe in accurate terms how the co-research was carried out then, and as the research was carried out, we did not follow the specific models or processes presented in the chapters of this book as we co-researched. On the contrary, the concrete practices and processes presented in this book have emerged out of the unique joint processes that we participated in with managers and employees. Stories of organisational life continually evolve and unfold, meaning that the managers and employees we interviewed took part in developing how the co-research processes were carried out at the given time and place. These processes cannot and should not be repeated, and therefore, we have not presented them here. The processes researchers use should live on and inspire others to develop their own when they are 'out in the field'.

Embracing Radical Presence

Embracing radical presence can make room for engaging in reflective pragmatism. Radical presence was presented in Chapter 3, and revolves around continually being sensitive toward what local reality we talk and act into being based on the meaning being co-constructed (McNamee, 2016). It is a curious stance toward how life is being lived, whereby meanings are co-constructed and sensible actions are carried out in diverse ways. This curiosity is paired with a belief that out of a joint exploration of new and different understandings other – and maybe more viable reflexive, responsive, and ethical – ways of living together can emerge (McNamee, 2016).

As I co-research and spend time with managers, employees, and other organisational members, I am constantly faced with people who gesture and respond in adjusted ways that are different from mine. Their generalised others differ from mine and their norms, taken-for-granted assumptions, and reflex ways of talking and acting local realities into being are unlike mine. As conversation partners, we seize upon these differences as a way to enrich conversations and allow for new understandings of everyday or extraordinary organisational challenges to emerge. We embrace that taking a radical stance towards the way we speak and act allows us to co-research and co-author stories of organisational life that we, in that unique moment, believe make room for more meaningful and viable ways to move forward and deal with organisational challenges.

The challenges that come from embracing radical presence will most likely occur when I am removed from the people who talk and act in different taken-for-granted ways than my own. Then, when I converse with people from within my scientific community and I am among significant others again, I am again met with responses and gestures that are adjusted. Here, I am able to anticipate how others will respond and how they will expect me to respond, and accordingly react in shared legitimate and meaningful ways.

Inside our communities of science, we have become so good at gesturing and responding in adjusted ways that we do so instantaneously. Automatically, we help each other reconstruct a solid and coherent understanding of organisational life. This is an understanding where we, with well-rehearsed subtle elegance and a few convincing exchanges about philosophy and practice, make the unknown known and sidestep the ever-present possibility to pause and look at the uniqueness of what we are in the midst of making into a common understanding. We know this dance by heart and help each other perform it with increasing excellence. Changing the steps breaks the established rhythm, makes us feel clumsy, and increases the risk of stepping on one another's toes.

As relational constructionists, we ask organisational members to be reflexive from within the organisational dilemmas that they are enmeshed in as we co-research. The researcher voluntarily enters into meaning-vacuums, by pausing the immediate co-construction of meaning for a moment, and invites each party to question his or her own ways of making sense of organisational life (Cunliffe, 2002b). We are able to be as reflexive as we co-author. By engaging in reflective pragmatism and figuring out how to invite people into co-constructing meaning with the ways that we speak and act organisational life into being, we can embrace radical presence in our writing and be reflexive from within. As relational constructionists, we can explore the different understandings and allow them to enrich each other, develop together, and co-construct new knowledge.

Being reflexive revolves around exploring the unadjusted aspects of the co-researched data and dwelling with what does not immediately make sense to us. Shotter (2016) suggests that researchers work with the sense of dissatisfaction rather than the dreams of perfection. By pausing our immediate, tribalised way of making sense of data, we can render our thinking and experience more complex by exposing dilemmas, contradictions, doubts, and different possibilities (Cunliffe, 2002b). This process allows us to be struck by our data. Instead of rapidly and neatly organising the data according to familiar rhythms and moves, we can slow down the pace and postpone the gestural invitation in order to co-construct meanings of organisational life.

The possibilities we have at our disposal are often unlimited: 1) we can focus on different genres, jargons and lines of reasoning that our co-researchers have used that we do not immediately understand; 2) we can ask the organisational members to take part in co-authoring the stories that we are developing; 3) we can ask esteemed colleagues from beyond our scientific community to share their reflections on the stories that we are co-authoring; 4) we can ask the people whom we are conversing with what they are curious about; and 5) we can express what we discover in ways other than through words.

These actions help us break away from the known steps and wait for embodied responses to the events occurring around us to emerge. To dwell in the not-knowing is to embrace what we might not immediately grasp but need to further explore in order to allow for a new sense of the situation to emerge (Cunliffe, 2002b). To make room for such processes in our co-authoring is a step towards radical presence and an acknowledgement of Gergen's (2014) notion of researchers being social agents of change: 'our inquiries could open up new possible ways of being human and new possible ways of going on together' (McNamee & Hosking, 2012: 43). As our inquiries as co-researchers advance based on differences that mesh and make room for new meanings to emerge, our inquiries as co-authors, which take part in talking and acting viable organisational realities into being, can be characterised by radical presence practices, if only we support each other in being so bold.

Reference to Other Work

Cunliffe (see 2002b, 2004) describes how the concept of 'reflexive conversations' emerged as a budding conceptualisation while she was busy co-researching something else: how managers work and learn in their everyday organisational settings. Cunliffe experienced that when she and the managers were exploring managerial processes, the managers tended to use a number of metaphors, embodied specific tone rhythms and speech genres, and made gestural connections that resonated with her and gave her a vivid sense of the processes they were referring to. Cunliffe (2002b, 2004) felt invited to respond in ways where certain understandings and practices were talked into being as legitimate and reasonable. Furthermore, Cunliffe experienced that as she and the managers conversed, she was not only listening to their stories, but based on their gestures and responses, took an active part in co-constructing poetic conversations about how managers work and learn.

The co-constructive role Cunliffe had in the becoming of the stories during the management inquiries struck her. Thus, she engaged in a reflexive process and began exploring why it did so. She paused her routinized, academic way of making sense of the data and instead began to listen and re-listen to the recorded conversations several times. This process made her rethink what actually took place during the conversations with the managers:

> my conversations with managers were not about accessing their realities but offering ways of constructing a shared sense of the managers' experience. This initiated a number of arresting moments for me as I connected the idea of dialogic interaction with the lived experience of the research conversation . . . My rhetorical strategy became the relationally engaged practice of social poetics – how researchers and organizational participants (managers and others) together interpret and constitute social experience through language.
>
> (Cunliffe, 2002b: 136)

The process that Cunliffe writes about here illustrates the richness of radical presence in two ways. First, it illustrates how she 'arrests' her initial and intuitive ways of understanding what takes place in the conversations and postpones the co-construction of meaning. Instead of organising her data in neat and known ways that reflect her scientific community and enable her to reproduce a story of how management inquiries can be understood as plausible ways of accessing the managers' realities, she paused this immediate co-construction of meaning. Instead, she began to explore the surprising (unadjusted) aspects that did not fit neatly into her existing academic understandings of organisational life. By breaking out of the familiar patterns, she dwelled on aspects of the data that she might not have thought about previously, or even paid attention to during the inquiry. This exercise made her reflex and her reflection-based thinking more complex, and evoked her curiosity. Cunliffe made room for doubts and different understandings to mesh incrementally with snippets of her existing knowledge. The purpose was to explore if other and maybe more meaningful ways of exploring her data could lead to other possible – and maybe more viable – ways of making sense of organisational life.

Second, Cunliffe embraces how the conversations with managers can be understood as a forum for her and the managers to jointly be radically present and explore the incidents, metaphors, speech genres, silences, etc. that occurred during their joint poetic conversations and that struck them. Cunliffe (2002b) describes how she began to videotape some of the conversations with the managers. Subsequently, she and the managers viewed the videos together and paused the recordings when their way of co-constructing meaning caught either Cunliffe or the managers' attention. This is a fine illustration of how '[f]ieldwork and writing [can] blur into one another . . .' (Helin, 2016) and make room for new practices and understandings to emerge.

Cunliffe embraced this new approach because she became curious about what understanding and knowledge she and the managers would be able to co-author if they jointly explored the co-constructive aspects of the inquiries. Another purpose for Cunliffe was to further complexify the existing local understanding of the conversations she had reached. She wanted to further explore how people jointly and in embodied ways co-author different understandings into being by being responsive toward each other and by talking and acting in certain ways. Practicing this kind of radical presence is a bold move and one that is only possible if all of the involved parties support such a move. Luckily, many knowledgeable managers and employees are willing to break with existing tribal routines and explore new and unknown territory with the purpose of co-constructing more viable, reflexive, responsive, and ethical ways of living together.

Reference to This Book

In Chapter 4 we presented various practices that Jørgen and I applied as we explored jointly with the participating leaders the interplay between strategising and organising in smaller Danish fashion companies. I will briefly dwell on one of these practices because it exemplifies how radical presence was embraced and incorporated in the way the research project unfolded. The purpose of the practice was to make room for different perspectives to mesh and enrich one another and to allow for new practices and understandings to be talked into being and accordingly shape the knowledge that was being co-constructed.

As Jørgen and I were approximately halfway into the two-year study, we left one of the joint seminars with a feeling that the participating leaders were very competent in discussing and giving each other feedback on practical aspects of their daily management. On the other hand, however, they only peripherally engaged in discussions about the more interpersonal and sometimes challenging aspects of their managing. Sometimes, primarily through indirect and passing remarks, they mentioned difficulties with employees, but they did not engage in joint explorations about these in order to dwell upon them. This seminar was not the first time that Jørgen and I had considered the leaders' difficulties with exploring more challenging aspects on their own. However, this time it seemed different to us and on the way home from the seminar we discussed it.

We talked about why we were struck by this data. We knew we were in a room with leaders who gestured and responded in other adjusted ways compared to us. Hence, we – based on our taken-for-granted assumptions and generalised other – felt it 'natural' to dwell upon and engage in joint explorations about interpersonal managerial challenges, which did not necessitate the same 'naturalness' from the leaders. For us, this meant that we had to be radically present as we explored why it struck us that they distanced themselves from discussing the interpersonal aspects of management. On the one hand, it was significant for us to integrate what struck us as a part of the continual process of co-authoring and co-researching. We sensed that engaging in conversations about how the more interpersonal challenges could be handled would enable the leaders to engage in conversations with each other where new and unknown ways to handle such dilemmas could emerge. On the other hand, we were cautious because we did not want to impose our taken-for-granted assumptions on the leaders.

We decided to pause our immediate co-construction of meaning and not make an immediate decision on how to deal with the dissatisfaction we felt. We wanted to question our own ways of making sense of organisational life before we decided how to respond to it (Cunliffe, 2002b). After a week, we listened to the recording of the joint seminar. Subsequently, we discussed how to respond to what struck us in ways that would enable the differences in taken-for-granted knowledge to mesh and create room for new knowledge to be co-authored between the leaders and ourselves. We wished to remain sensitive and radically present toward the local reality; we would invite the leaders to talk and act into being as we began to respond with a gesture.

While we pondered the conversations among the leaders and our dissatisfaction, a method used by Ripamonti et al. (2016) to support reflexivity among leaders came to mind. We began to discuss if and how we could use the method to respond to what had struck us. This led to the development of a scheme (Figure 8.2) for the input we would use in the coming seminar. We sent the scheme to the leaders, accompanied by the text presented in Chapter 4:

[Before the next seminar], we want you to think of two managerial episodes that are significant to you. They need to revolve around a situation where you, your employees, or your colleagues found it difficult to reach an agreement or solve a situation. These episodes are still present in your memory. Maybe they have not been solved, or you are not pleased with the outcome. There are two columns on the paper [we have emailed to you]; in the first column, describe this challenge so that everyone can understand it. The second column is a bit more difficult: it has to be used to reflect upon what this says about yourself, your management, and thoughts about your firm.

Describe a challenge and/or a significant question you are pondering.	Reflect upon what this situation makes you think about yourself as a leader, the challenges you are facing, and your company.

Figure 8.2 Reflective Exercise

The purpose of sending this scheme to the managers was to complexify both our and their thinking about leading by inviting them to co-author how the interpersonal and managerial challenges should be understood. A radical presence was supported here, as we jointly invited our different local taken-for-granted assumptions to mesh and make room for new understandings of what kinds of relational challenges the managers experienced and how exploring these could make room for new understandings to emerge. Before we sent out the input for the coming seminar (the completed schemes that we had received from the leaders), we added a third column, reproduced in Figure 8.3:

Describe a challenge and/or a significant question you are pondering.	Reflect upon what this situation makes you think about yourself as a leader, the challenges you are facing, and your company.	When reading about this managerial challenge, the following comes to my mind . . .

Figure 8.3 Reflexive Exercise

The purpose was to further complexify our thinking and work in radically present ways. A meeting discussing the various ways to reflexively make sense of the interpersonal managerial challenges would embrace the ontological aspects of language. It was a way to enrich the conversations between ourselves and the leaders, and to allow for new understandings of everyday or extraordinary organisational challenges to emerge. This example illustrates how researchers can allow for a joint exploration of incidents that strike them in order to use radical presence as a way of co-researching and co-authoring viable reflexive, responsive, and ethical ways of living together.

Striving toward Before-the-Fact Inquiries

As a co-researcher within a relational constructionist stance, I have come to know organisational life as being fluctuating and constantly in motion. Within a few months, the challenges that preoccupied managers and employees' minds and hearts have become obsolete; they have resolved themselves or have been replaced with other equally relevant, time- and energy-consuming issues and different organisational challenges. Through my process of co-researching, I meet managers and employees with the purpose of solving concrete and current challenges in the here and now. The people I encounter are in the midst of initiating a reorganising process, developing a new strategy, coming up with new ways of cooperating with people in the environment, etc., and often these adjustments must happen quickly and efficiently.

I visit organisations and co-research with managers and employees to learn more about how organisational life unfolds within the unique 'somewheres' that I have taken part in co-constructing. This is knowledge that I subsequently spend a considerable amount of time trying to make other sense of while figuring out how I, in reflective, pragmatic ways, can share it with research communities. The differing and yet enmeshed purposes that researchers and managers/employees have as they co-construct here-and-now meaning can be quite interesting to ponder upon. It is interesting to consider how to understand and practice co-research and co-authoring as a way to story organisational life.

Organisational life is constantly evolving and we, as researchers, want to participate in its co-construction in viable, reflexive, responsive, and ethical ways within the unique here-and-now moments that we participate in. However, since these moments are multiple, once occurring, and are spoken and acted differently into being by the people experiencing them, then we might need to rethink how we want to tell the story and how we understand storying. Sometimes we tend to divide between co-researching and co-authoring and argue that storying of organisational life primarily is a part of our co-authoring. What if we paused this tribal dance – even just for a moment – to make room for a different way to make sense of storying.

Indeed, what understanding would emerge if we stretched our thinking a bit and understood co-researching and co-authoring as integral parts of the same practice, namely storying? When I partake in co-constructing more viable ways of talking and acting organisational life into being, I not only co-research and generate data, I simultaneously invite managers and employees to take part in co-constructing stories of organisational life through the stories that we jointly generate. These stories are local, unique, and co-authored from within. These stories 'leave prints' as the co-constructed meaning slides into and shapes the ways in which managers and employees move forward and co-author organisational life.

The stories that the managers or employees and I co-author as we co-research become generative and future-forming and are attempts to talk and act more viable, reflexive, responsive, and ethical ways of living together into being: stories that not only retrospectively tell us what happened, but stories that are also prospective as they allow us to talk and act a given future closer to the present. Shotter (2016: 1) suggests that we embrace a 'before-the-fact' kind of thinking as we story: 'we need before-the-fact . . . inquiries that can "set out" inner "landscapes of possibilities", to think with and to provide guidance as we try in our more scientifically organized efforts to achieve socially desired outcomes in particular socially shared situations.'

These stories in radically present ways embrace the prospective, future-forming, and generative aspect of language. 'Before-the-fact' thinking enables us to view co-research and co-authoring as integrated elements of each other, where imagination and social poetic forms of communicating are prioritised to make room for new understandings and meanings to emerge (Shotter, 2016). To understand our stories as before-the-fact inquiries invites us to see our work as a long line of enmeshed co-researching and co-authoring processes where the people involved jointly, reflexively, and by being radically present toward each other figure out how to speak and act out a desirable future closer to the present.

Gergen (2014) asks researchers to consider whether or not they are unfolding something which does not yet exist, but which could be created. To embrace the interweaving between co-researching and co-authoring and understand ourselves as future formers can open up a completely new world. Language is ontologically constitutive and as we co-research, we are simultaneously in the midst of storying and bringing a more desirable future closer to the present. As Gergen (2014: 10) writes: 'the best way to predict the future is to create it.' The stories I invite managers and employees to co-construct are a part of generating a local and desirable future that we attempt to speak and act closer to the present. The stories they tell will incrementally allow for new understandings and practices to emerge within the local 'somewhere' in which I am momentarily invited to participate (Gergen, 2014). It becomes possible to proactively embrace the possibility of making room for before-the-fact inquiries in co-research and co-authoring practices: 'what if we closed our eyes and began to imagine the worlds of our hopes? What if we replaced the persistent rush to establish "what is the case" and began to ask "what kind of world could we build?" ' (Gergen, 2014: 8).

Similar to the keynote presenter introduced in the beginning of this chapter, we are completely dependent on our co-researchers and co-authors to be able to co-construct meaning. As Shotter (2016) writes, before-the-fact inquiry is 'a kind of thinking that oscillates back-and-forth between our exploratory movements within a circumstance and our sense of our progress so far in achieving within it an outcome acceptable to the others around us . . . a kind of thinking in which we only find out what to do in the course of doing it' (Shotter, 2016: 5). We are relational beings and we are morally responsible for co-constructing each other in ethical ways. We can use before-the-fact inquiries to support each other in generating desirable prospective memories, which enable us to bring more viable reflexive, responsive, and ethical ways of living together closer to the present.

Reference to Other Work

The significance of before-the-fact inquiries is a central part of how Ness and colleagues (see Ness et al., 2014a, 2014b; Sælør et al., 2015) work with mental health care. The recovery of substance users, people suffering from mental health issues, is understood as a relational process where the community is also responsible (Ness et al., 2014b). Service providers, family members, and service users are all active partners who work together in synergetic ways. All professionals involved listen to each other and take each other seriously as they jointly develop the collaborative health practices that the service users receive. Central to the development of these practices are the service user's thoughts, hopes, and dreams. Service providers cannot 'recover people directly' (Ness et al., 2014a). However, their experiences and perspectives should be integrated into the services offered to the service users. Ness et al. (2014a) present the processes of metaphorically and physically walking alongside the service user and taking a point of departure in their life situation, as they negotiate and jointly explore how to create generative processes and contexts for the recovery process.

The studies that Ness and colleagues have conducted highlight the fact that hope is an integrated part of recovery among mental health and substance users (Sælør et al., 2015). Hope is relational and depends on the service user's own efforts, but also the support, around the clock availability, and dependency on family members and service providers who play a central part in the recovery of the service users. The service users explain, through first-person accounts, how the ability to solve practical challenges such as economic chaos and housing issues was significant for them to regain their hopes and dreams of other futures (Sælør et al., 2015). Ness and colleagues argue that the use of dialogic reflection and the maintenance of the human relationship between service users and providers are vital for the practices and processes developed to support recovery.

Their studies illustrate that co-researching and co-authoring are interwoven, since the ways in which Ness and colleagues engage in the processes mean that they also explore an active embracing of the future-forming aspect of the way that researchers not only engage in practice from within, but also share stories of these processes afterwards. As Ness and colleagues engage in developing processes around mental health and underline the community and relational aspects, they not only participate in solving concrete challenges in the unique *here-and-now* moment, the 'everyday life details ... practice ... responsivity' (Shotter, in Cunliffe, 2002b: 11). They also actively embrace the ever-present possibilities to participate in building the futures they hope for.

The knowledge that Ness and colleagues have generated incrementally over the years and the processes that struck them about how recovery is practised feed into their ways of talking and acting as they co-research and co-author together with service users, providers, family members, politicians, etc. Furthermore, they are meshed with practices, knowledge, and taken-for-granted ways of acting and talking among the other central meaning makers. The differences among these local perspectives and taken-for-granted ways of talking and acting realities into being also enrich each other. In addition, based on a shared desire to develop generative recovery practices that lead to more viable reflexive, responsive, and ethical ways of living together, new possibilities emerge that shape peoples' before-the-fact inquiries of the ways in which recovery should and could be practised.

Furthermore, the way that they write journal articles and share their experiences at conferences is not guided by a desire to 'establish "what is the case"' (Gergen, 2014: 8). On the contrary, they write, speak, and act in ways that are shaped by a desire to explore ' "what kind of world could we build?"' (Gergen, 2014: 8).

Reference to This Book

The desire to engage in co-research where before-the-fact inquiries and the future-forming aspect of organisational life are an integrated part of how co-research is conducted is also embraced in the inquiry we present in Chapter 4 (although we here focus on Chapter 4, the practices we present in Chapters 5 and 6 are also shaped by the same guiding assumptions). In Chapter 4, managers from different organisations are brought together quarterly to jointly explore the managerial, organisational, strategic, and everyday challenges that they are currently dealing with. This practice provides space for the managers and researchers to support each other in momentarily pausing their initial reflex ways of understanding and dealing with an organisational challenge. Furthermore, such seminars provide social poetic ways of exploring the multiple and polyphonic ways of moving forward, as the participants inquire into the challenges and share their reflections with one another. This creates a space where the managers, in relation to a concrete organisational challenge, can explore how to help each other become more reflexive about the possible ways they can act and talk their way out of the organisational challenges in which that they have caught themselves.

The purpose of the seminars, however, is also to invite the managers, during the active research process, to become reflective about and take a more radically present stance toward the way that they manage their organisations. Often, the managers of the organisations primarily discuss organisational challenges with their co-manager or someone else who lives in the same local 'somewhere' as they do. Since they all come from the same local 'somewhere', their positions resemble each other, and often gesture and respond in adjusted ways. The seminars offer a space where, over a period of one or two years, the organisational leaders can discuss organisational challenges with people who live in other local 'somewheres', with gestures and responses based on a different generalised other, allowing unadjusted responses to emerge.

As a part of the process, they are time and time again put in situations where they come to realise that there are multiple different, but equally meaningful, ways of making sense of and dealing with an organisational challenge. This process may be anxiety provoking and frustrating at first, but incrementally, the unadjusted responses to their gestures become a taken-for-granted way for them to communicate. They begin to look forward to presenting organisational challenges to each other and receiving unadjusted responses that allow for social poetic and explorative ways to discuss their organisational challenges. They begin to long for moments where they can jointly explore what might not yet be, but which could become. As the research process unfolds, the managers incrementally become more radically present in their conversations with each other and with us as researchers. They come to appreciate the richness of being met with unadjusted responses in the overall management of their organisations. These before-the-fact inquiries enable them to imagine the worlds of their hopes.

Sometimes, after a research process – as the one referred to here – has come to an end, leaders make take the initiative to continue to meet quarterly to discuss their organisational challenges with each other. The processes that we as researchers have facilitated, where the managers continually have been met with unadjusted responses to make room for social poetics and reflexivity in relation to their management, have left a mark.

The knowledge we as researchers have of how organisational life is the by-product of a shared construction of meaning and the initiation of sensible actions has shaped how we engage in the joint co-research and co-authoring processes with the managers. Incrementally, these new forms of talking and acting local realities into being have shaped the leaders' taken-for-granted ways of making sense of and dealing with organisational challenges. The inquiries the managers pursue have before-the-fact characteristics, just as the radical present stance toward the way the managers communicate have opened up a plurality which supports and respects how local life is being lived within the unique 'somewheres'. These factors, meanwhile, embrace the ever-present possibility of talking and acting a more viable reflexive, responsive, and ethical ways of living together into being.

Relying on Resonance as a Way Forward

The practices that I present in this chapter surrounding possible ways to work with data are most likely not new at a philosophical level. Nevertheless, practising them at a more concrete level can sometimes be challenging because engaging in reflective pragmatism, embracing radical presence, and striving towards before-the-fact inquiries often involve moving beyond our well-known reflex and reflective ways of talking and acting local realities into being. Relying on resonance can aid in daring to pause the tribal dance and make the first awkward moves towards reflexivity. Resonance evokes images, memories, and emotions and makes new connections among the well known and the completely unknown in order to reach a more viable understanding of the processes being explored (Meier & Wegener, 2016).

To rely on resonance is a process shaped by curiosity. It takes time and curiosity to co-construct new understandings and meanings – founded in differences and in what does not instantaneously make sense. It is a process guided by a constant reliance on doing more than just reproducing what one already knows and takes for granted within one's own research communities. The process must respect conversation partners' local ways of talking and acting an organisational reality into being and reframe researchers' ways of thinking to make room for the many voices and unadjusted responses. It is also a process wherein agreement or an ordering of the polyphony is not sought. On the contrary, multiplicity is embraced, which makes one's thinking more complex. Meanwhile, it is important to engage in as many real and imagined conversations with researchers, poets, musicians, children, friends, etc. that one can possibly find – and dare to go where there is no solid ground under one's feet.

Resonance is twofold. First, the new connections between the known and the unknown have to resonate with the researcher, enabling him or her to reach a more viable understanding of the processes being explored. If the understanding does not resonate with the researcher, it will be challenging to make it resonate with others (Cunliffe, 2002a; Meier & Wegener, 2016). Thus, the initial aspects of relying on resonance revolve around understanding writing as 'an invitation to "get lost"' (Helin, 2016: 3) in the data and dwell within the moments that struck the researcher – not only in the process of co-researching, but also in the process of co-authoring. Helin (2015, 2016) refers to this process as 'dialogical writing', where the researcher curiously explores what does not immediately make sense and tries out various forms of expressing what is still not known, but is on the way to becoming known. It is a process of being in dialogue with the co-researched data and of using deliberate thinking and radical presence to ensure the researcher does not simply reproduce existing discursive practices, but rather, in dialogical ways, allows for new meaning to emerge (Cunliffe, 2002b; Helin, 2016; Shotter, 2016). The purpose in this dialogical approach is not to establish the case, but rather to make room for new meanings to emerge: 'The searching itself is the story' (Meier & Wegener, 2016: 4).

Shotter (2016) describes this as a process of 'wandering around' within the situation, testing possible ways in which to express in words what has struck you, while sensing how data and the striking moments 'talk back' and allow you to know whether the words used are fitting or not. Cunliffe (2002b) refers to a similar process by describing how searching for new understandings can feel like looking through a glass of 'muddy water', whereby you sense that there is something, but you are not yet able to see what it is. Doubtfulness emerges and it is only by being sensitive to the situation as a whole that conversation partners can come to grasp the root of the situation and determine how to act (Shotter, 2016). Resonance is coming to an understanding by experimenting and trying out various ways to make sense of what conversation partners have experienced: 'in terms of such "tryings" and "pointing out" – "perhaps it can be described like this rather than like that" or "done like this rather than like that" – . . . we . . . begin to arrive at those practices of inquiry in which our activities are, or can be, coordinated in with those of others' (Shotter, 2016: 10).

Suddenly, while in the shower, out jogging, reading a fairy tale to one's children, or engaging in some other activity, an idea, image, connection, rhythm, new move, or metaphor emerges: something that resonates with the researcher and allows him or her to see and understand things in a new light. Cunliffe (2002b: 43) describes how she experienced resonance in the following way: 'I felt this way of talking [part of her data that had struck her] was somehow important but didn't know why, I had neither the language nor the explicit knowledge to articulate and construct any sense. It took me many months of reading and talking to colleagues before I began to put bits and pieces together.' For resonance to proceed and allow for new understandings to emerge, one must be patient and curious and enjoy exploring aspects of the process. It takes time to learn new moves and let them shape the tribal dances. Once resonance is reached, it can initiate movement (affective practices) and enable new ways of speaking and acting (Cunliffe, 2002a; Meier & Wegener, 2016).

The second way in which resonance works is that once new understandings have embedded themselves within a researcher, he or she must invite the people with whom she wants the understanding to resonate with to help co-research and co-author the new understandings in ways that also resonate with them. If stories of organisational realities do not resonate with people, they will not be able to co-construct new connections between the known and unknown. And they will not be able to reach a more viable understanding of the processes being explored (Cunliffe, 2002b). In the process of making room for resonance to emerge between reader and text, one can leave room for the reader to fill out the empty spaces based on their own imagination (Meier & Wegener, 2016). As mentioned previously, storying of organisational life is like engaging in a conversation with people, knowing that your conversation partner has many experiences, ideas, hopes, and dreams. To respect and embrace this, the text should be an invitation for the reader to participate in co-authoring the story in ways that support the co-construction of more viable reflexive, responsive, and ethical ways of living together.

Reference to Other Work

Helin (2015) tells stories about the process that she went through in making sense of and figuring out how to present a huge and rich amount of qualitative data from Brunnsala Coffee, a family-owned business that she cooperated with during a research project. One of the significant challenges she faced was figuring out ways to present data that resonated with the processes, complexities, and general messiness of human life that she had experienced as she had co-researched in the business. Helin (2013, 2015) writes that the only aspect guiding her as she struggled with figuring out how to tell a story about the processes in which she had taken part was the notion of withness-thinking.

Helin tried out various ways of organising the data to make her stories resonate with what she had experienced. She started by sorting her data material according to the logic of chronology and content, but she realised that the processual aspect was lost in the decontextualized fragments of conversations, meetings, and dinner conversations she was left with. This led to a second attempt wherein Helin (2015) revisited the fieldwork material in order to explore how the dialogical elements unfolded in the dialogues. Although excerpts illustrating various aspects of the dialogues could be found, Helin felt that the excerpts were decontextualized and did not allow the reader to understand the 'big picture' of how one conversation was related to a polyphony of others. Helin (2015) writes how the first two attempts to organise her data suffered from 'theoreticism', in which the living events she had taken part in were turned into closed structures.

Helin continued her quest and realised that Bakhtin's work which presents a 'polyphonic novel' could be helpful. In a polyphonic novel, multiple voices are allowed to co-exist and the reader is invited to co-author the story as it unfolds (Helin, 2015: 174). Embracing unfinalized writing, coupled with an active reader and a writer with a radically present stance, appeared to resonate with how Helin made sense of the polyphonically and lively data that she had co-constructed. It also opened up ways to present and take part in writing a given organisational reality into being (Helin, 2015). This way of co-authoring data resonated with Helin and allowed her to move forward in ways where she was able to story from within the organisational life she had participated in, which was the intention she had when she initiated the process.

Helin (2015) suggests how the writing in itself can be understood as a creative process of exploring. Helin was inspired by Bakhtin's polyphonic novel idea, but she never intended to write a novel herself. However, exploring this genre enabled Helin to relate to the co-constructed field material in different ways and opened space for different perspectives on what to include and how. In Helin's (2015: 183) own words: 'if I were to summarize, in just one sentence, what I found most fulfilling in learning about the polyphonic novel, it would be how the genre made me reconnect with the engaged and spontaneous mode I had felt during the fieldwork, and how that helped me appreciate the process of writing.'

The process Helin went through illustrates how relying on resonance and accepting the sometimes very protracted process of wandering about in muddy water is an integral part of discovering how to story about the processes, lives, and interwoven complexities experienced when co-researching. Learning how to put the unknown, sensed, and experienced into meaningful words that, hopefully, will resonate with people afterwards is a process of exploring various possibilities of storytelling, understanding data, and making connections between theory and practice. It is a process of leaving solid ground, stepping out into unknown territory, and sensing the way story of processes and practices talks back to you. Furthermore, resonance includes exploring in reflective ways whether the responses that you receive from the material allow the meaning, sense, and experience that you hoped for to emerge.

Reference to This Book

In Chapter 3, I present the term 'memories about the future' and illustrate how exploring desirable future memories can broaden the possible space for action that people believe they have in the present. Looking back at how the term incrementally emerged as I revisited some of the conversations with managers I had participated in over a one-and-a-half-year period, and how it made its way toward becoming a theoretical term, illustrated the need to rely on resonance. It was a process that took time. I remember feeling struck in the middle of a conversation – re-listening to conversation recordings and not being sure what took place. In the recordings, several of the managers expressed firm beliefs about how certain, often problematic, situations would unfold in the nearby future. They even non-verbally expressed embodied feelings of how uncomfortable they were going to feel as they, in the future, had to carry out certain actions and deal with certain responses from the other people involved in the problems. I had, at the time, no idea what these emotions meant, but I knew they meant something.

I remember how I – while riding my bike home from work or out jogging – thought back on these conversations. There were sentences that had been uttered that stayed with me and replayed over and over inside my head. I could not, based on my reflex responses, figure out what the managers meant. How could they know what would happen in a future that had not yet happened?

I did not mind not knowing what these stories revolved around; I was curious and wanted to work in more radically present ways and use deliberate thinking to pause my instantaneous urge to make sense of the stories based on what was already understood as meaningful within my scientific community. I could follow the social norms and conventions that, within my local 'somewhere', were understood as legitimate ways to work with qualitative data, or, as Helin writes (2015), could find a way to present these stories in ways that resonated with what had taken place in the conversations between the managers and myself and equip myself with a language that matched my experience with the managers.

This initiated a longer process of wandering through the data transcripts, highlighting certain aspects and getting lost in the stories, trying to inquire into what they could become. At that time, I did not have the words I needed to engage in conversations and explorations with my colleagues about the conversations I had had. Some colleagues were frustrated with me for engaging in conversations with managers and not knowing what I was doing. I realised it was necessary to have the experiences resonate with myself before I could make them resonate with others.

During that period, I was re-reading Lewis Carroll's *Alice's Adventures in Wonderland* and *Through the Looking Glass* and was in the middle of reading how the Queen of Hearts puts a bandage on her finger before she pricks herself on her brooch. In Wonderland, memory works both backward and forward, and the Queen of Hearts remembers how she will prick herself in the near future. All of a sudden, the multiple stories and sentences that had struck me, and which I had not been able to make sense of, made sense. The managers were putting a bandage on their fingers before they pricked themselves. Their memory of the future told them that they would prick themselves shortly. They could even feel the pain from the needle. As a result, they prepared for it in the present. Moreover, by preparing for it in the present, they talked and acted the future memory of pricking themselves into being as they moved forward, even though they wanted to avoid pricking themselves.

This image of how the Queen of Hearts puts on the bandage resonated with and spoke to me, and although I knew that the image would likely not resonate with anyone else, it enabled me to move forward. I presented the idea of future memories and the need to develop desirable future memories to a smaller group of the managers who had shared their stories with me, and they caught on to the idea immediately. The idea of remembering the future resonated with the challenges they often found themselves in, and their responses helped me move forward. As one of the managers said during my presentation of the concept: 'I see what you mean – there is a difference between packing my suitcase for a hiking trip or for a chartered holiday. It will take me different places, and I might as well pack for the vacation I want to go on.'

Energised and excited by knowing the term had resonated with the managers, I began putting it into theoretical terms and sent a short paper to a conference, where I shared some of the stories that the managers had told about their future memories. Alas, the excitement did not last long. The short paper was not accepted. The track chairs did not understand what I was trying to express, and as an esteemed colleague wrote to me after reading the short paper regarding the feedback from the track chairs: 'you need to position your work better within accepted ways of writing about these things.' It sent me right back into the 'muddy waters' and initiated a third round of wandering around. Relying on resonance, however, helped me as I began testing out different ways of making the experiences, and after several readings of Mead's philosophy of time and exploring how a concept like 'prospective memory' is understood and researched by brain scientists, the concept of a future memory came closer to a legitimate way of engaging in management inquiries (see e.g., Larsen & Willert, 2017). It was a term that could be presented in ways where, like Gergen (2015: 57) suggests, it is linked to relevant dialogues in the field, is rigorous in its design, and is written in coherent and understandable ways.

Turning Storytelling into Living Events

In this final practice, I return to one of the opening arguments of the chapter: how all construction of meaning depends on people's responsive engagement with each other and the environment. No action done or word said alone contains meaning: 'words and actions do not carry meaning; it is in the responsivity among persons that meaning is crafted' (McNamee, 2016: 93). Each spoken and written word is an invitation to co-construct meaning and the responses generated allow for meaning to emerge (McNamee, 2016). This is also true for how we story of organisational life – both in our written and spoken words.

As I invite a conversation partner into storying organisational life, I am unable to know how he or she will respond. While this is a challenge, it is also the magical aspect of words, because you never know what organisational life you are capable of jointly talking and acting into being through gestures and responses: 'a word is dead when it is said, some say – I say it just begins to live that day' (Dickinson, 1961). These intriguing aspects of words and the relational foundation for generating meaning can slide into and shape the purpose of our stories. I can use the texts I write and presentations I give to invite my conversation partners to become dialogical and co-authoring partners of the stories they are a part of (Helin, 2015).

Helin (2015) invites researchers to think of how we, in the texts that we write, can invite the reader into co-constructively participating in the process of bringing the stories to life. As researchers tell stories, how can we proactively open up space for co-authoring between reader and text? How can we 'approach writing as a mode of exploration in itself' (p: 179)? Not just as a resonant exploration for researcher, as co-authors, that paves a way for new understandings to emerge, but also as an exploration for readers that allows them to be struck by the material and invites them to rely on resonance and make viable connections between what they already know and do not yet know.

Raising questions to your conversation partner as you converse can be done in very inviting and clever ways. However, the stance I invite you to consider is more radical. It is an active embracing of how each and every co-construction of meaning is unique and completely depends on how the people involved in the conversation talk and act a local reality into being. This also means that we understand every text as a gesture – an invitation to co-construct meaning – that requires an adjusted response if meaning is to emerge. The consequential aspect of this is that each time a story is read or told, new and unique meanings will be co-constructed that not only bring the story to life but also co-author it in new ways. As Helin (2015: 176) writes: 'we should stay away from having "the last word" about who the character is and what the character can become.' The plot of the story is no longer something we, as storytellers, can order or arrange; instead, it will emerge as our conversation partners engage in dialogue with the stories that we share (Helin, 2015).

As we story, we participate in the co-construction of the plot, and the stories that we share have emerged out of previous relational co-constructions of meaning that were meaningful then and there. The stories represent how, based on discursive practices and what is considered as legitimate within certain research communities, we have co-constructed a coherent and meaningful story of the processes we have co-researched. At the same time, however, words are alive and evolve, luckily! Therefore, we have the possibility to take a radical stance as we story and invite the next possible meaning to emerge between the text and the reader (Helin, 2015). Instead of trying to reach a certain predetermined endpoint, we take a 'not-knowing' stance as we story (Helin, 2015; McNamee & Hosking, 2012).

Meier and Wegener (2016) suggest that as we tell a story, we make room for the reader to sense and feel how it is like to 'be there'. In a similar line of thought, Gergen (2014) invites us to write in ways that our conversation partners are invited to 'experience with' the people and processes of which we create stories. At the beginning of the chapter, the story of meditating with the monks came to life as the butterfly flickered by the projector and evoked a sensation in me, wherein for a brief moment I felt as though I were sitting in the Himalayan mountains mediating with the monks as the sun set across that particular evening. I could feel the temperature and altitude and enjoyed the surrounding silence. In this way, I experienced the event with them.

What this reminds me of is that we need a 'telling, feeling style of writing' (Shotter, 2016: 16) that gives our conversation partners a before-the-fact feeling of how it feels to be in a specific moment and face a situation in which the circumstances are still partially indeterminate (Shotter, 2016).

In turn, this invites us to practice a kind of prospective writing or a 'listening writing' (Helin, 2015), which embodies curiosity, unpredictability, and readiness toward the next possible word. This type of writing offers possibilities and not only conclusions (Helin, 2015; McNamee & Hosking, 2012).

Researchers should work toward writing in open-ended ways that invite the reader into the process of unfolding various generative possibilities of how things and phenomena might or could be understood or practised (Cunliffe, 2002a; McNamee & Hosking, 2012). Researchers can incorporate elements of social poetics and use metaphors as we story and invite readers into a joint co-construction of meaning. These conversations can create possibilities, support imagining, embrace multiplicity, give colour to a situation, and leave many things open to the imagination. Cunliffe (2002a) writes,

> [M]eaning is never fully present but 'a kind of constant flickering of presence and absence together' . . . in speaking metaphorically and using words from one context to make sense of another, we are not defining and specifying facts but startling the listener by juxtaposing images of what is and what is not. We are creating space for an imaginative, and often embodied understanding . . . multiple related meanings being created in the stream of responsive conversation.
>
> (p. 138)

Thus, the stories researchers tell can also be understood as the unfinalized dialogues, and not monologues, that they are. By practising this way of writing, researchers are able to 'explore how the vibrant use of language – metaphor, stories, irony, poetic imagining, gestural statements, and resonant ways of speaking – may construct shared experiences and meaning' (Cunliffe, 2002a: 143). This way of writing does not aim to be the final mediator of meaning, but rather to create space for conversation partners to fill in the blanks and gaps (Helin, 2015). When researchers are able to work from within the dialogical understanding itself as they story, then they can allow themselves to focus on exploring possibilities of what *might be* rather than presenting what *is* (Cunliffe, 2002a).

The purpose of acknowledging how storying makes words and the co-construction of meaning come to life is to use stories to draw attention to how all of us, incrementally and based on our everyday gesturing and responding, talk and act local realities into being. This also means that our ways of storying can be invitations for our conversation partners as well as ourselves to see, understand, and make sense of processes and phenomena in many different ways. This process invites researchers to humbly and reflexively embrace how everyone co-authors the stories that we live in and surround ourselves with – we all play a part in co-constructing more viable reflexive, responsive, and ethical ways of living together.

Reference to Other Work

The urge to not have the final word and invite the reader to becoming an active co-author of a written text was a significant part of how I wrote my PhD thesis (see Larsen, 2014). The thesis revolved around how the managers of a Danish service company worked on anchoring value-based management in their everyday practice. As a part of the co-research process, I held research conversations with eight managers from different levels within the company over a one-and-a-half-year period. During those research conversations, I quickly learned that the eight managers strategized and worked with the values in eight very different, but equally meaningful, ways. I also quickly acknowledged that the stories I could share about the different ways to strategize were only one out of multiple polyphonic stories. I initially found it frustrating, because I felt as though I had to figure out the one 'right way' to tell the story based on how life was being lived and the values that were spoken into being in the different local organisational realities. This was impossible, however, because while I sat in my office and wrote about that local organisational reality, namely what was being taken for granted, how life was being talked and acted into being there, that very same life was unfolding just a few miles from me in ways I had no idea about.

I found these realisations important to respect and proactively work with. Thus, in the process of deciding how I could share the stories of how the eight managers strategized and worked with the values in very different ways, I longed to write unfinalized and open-ended stories that made room for the conversation partner to feel what it was like to *be* there (Gergen, 2015). These stories could invite the reader into co-authoring the stories of who the managers were, and how they attempted to anchor the values in their everyday practices (Helin, 2015). Instead of presenting the plot of each of the stories, the plot would, instead, emerge between the reader and the stories. This presentation would make room for multiple different plots to be co-constructed. My task was to write the stories in ways that created possibilities, supported imagination, embraced multiplicity, and left much open to the imagination. I wanted to invite the reader to participate in filling in the gaps and blanks of who the managers were and how they strategized. Based on the experience of the conversation partner and what was taken for granted within his or her local 'somewhere', a kind of social poetic dialogue between him or her and the text would emerge, which would lead to an understanding of the managers and their work that would resonate with the conversation partner (Cunliffe, 2002a; McNamee, 2000; Meier & Wegener, 2016).

As I tried various different ways of presenting the stories about how the eight managers strategized, I tried to apply what Shotter (2016: 16) referred to as a 'telling, feeling style of writing' that would give the reader a before-the-fact feeling of what it felt like to be in the moment. The main assumption that guided me was that I wanted to 'stay away from having "the last word" about who the character is and what the character can become' (Helin, 2015: 176). It took me months and many experiments before I succeeded in presenting the stories in ways that not only resonated with how it had felt to partake in organisational life, but also how this participation shifted into different stories depending on who read them. I remember sitting in a meeting with my research group, where I had asked my colleagues to read the stories, asking them to tell me their impressions of who the managers were and how they worked with the values. As my colleagues shared their stories, the managers in the service company and the anchoring of the value-based management strategic initiative came to life in very diverse ways. My colleagues had continued the co-authoring in different, but equally meaningful, ways and they began to discuss the appearance of the managers and who had understood the process and the managers in 'the right way'. As I witnessed these dialogues and the ways in which my colleagues and I had allowed for different plots and understandings to emerge in distinct ways as the text was read, I felt confident that I had written the stories so that they turned into living events.

Reference to This Book

The purpose of writing this book has been to turn the inquiries and processes into living events. The words are of little use if they only stay as words on pages in this book. The inquiries and processes presented here are snapshots that offer glimpses into the ways that we work with relational research practices. As the title of the book suggests, however, this is an invitation. The plot and the way for you to move forward do not lie in what we have presented in the book. Rather, both plot and the way forward emerge as you read the stories that we present and allow them to interweave with your experiences and with what you take for granted, while engaging, in radically present ways, in a reflexive exploration of what kind of reality you want to participate in, and, accordingly, speak and act into being as you co-research and co-author.

As McNamee (2000: 151) writes, 'there is nothing to discover or explain, but rather linguistic turns to be jointly made.' With these concluding and reassuring words I wish you all the best with your processes of co-researching and co-authoring. I hope that along the way you will engage in reflective pragmatism, embrace radical presence, strive towards before-the-fact inquiries, rely on resonance, and turn writing into living events as you invite conversation partners into co-constructing more viable reflexive, responsive, and ethical ways of living together.

References

Cunliffe, A. L. (2002a) Reflexive Dialogical Practice in Management Learning. *Management Learning*, 33 (1), 35–61.

Cunliffe, A. L. (2002b) Social Poetics as Management Inquiry—a Dialogical Approach. *Journal of Management Inquiry*, 11 (2), 128–146.
Cunliffe, A. L. (2004) On Becoming a Critically Reflexive Practitioner. *Journal of Management Education*, 28, 407–427.
Dickinson, E. (1961) *Emily Dickinson's Poems*. Boston: TH Johnson.
Gergen, K. J. (2009) *Relational Being: Beyond the Individual and Community*. Oxford, Oxford University Press.
Gergen, K. J. (2010) Co-Constitution, Causality and Confluence Organizing in a World Without Entities. Draft for Hernes, T. & Maitlis, S. (eds.) *Process, Sensemaking, and Organizing*. Oxford, Oxford University Press.
Gergen, K. J. (2014) Pursuing Excellence in Qualitative Inquiry. *Qualitative Psychology*, 1 (1), 49–60.
Gergen, K. J. (2015) From Mirroring to World-Making: Research as Future Forming. *Journal for the Theory of Social Behaviour*, 45 (3), 1–24.
Helin, J. (2013) Dialogic Listening: Toward an Embodied Understanding of How to 'go on' During Fieldwork. *Qualitative Research in Organizations and Management: An International Journal*, 8 (3), 224–241.
Helin, J. (2015) Writing Process After Reading Bakhtin: From Theorized Plots to Unfinalisable 'living' Events. *Journal of Management Inquiry*, 24, 174–185.
Helin, J. (2016) Dialogical Writing: Co-Inquiring Between the Written and the Spoken Word. *Culture and Organization*. [Online] Available from: http://dx.doi.org/10.1080/14759551.2016.1197923 [Accessed August 2016].
Larsen, M. V. (2014) *Strategising Through Organising: The Significance of Everyday Relational Sensemaking*. Chagrin Falls, OH, Taos Institute Publications.
Larsen, M. V. & Willert, S. (2017) Using Management Inquiry to Co-Construct Other Memories About the Future. *Journal of Management Inquiry*. [Online] Available from: https://doi.org/10.1177/1056492617696889 [Accessed August 2017].
McNamee, S. (1994) Research as Relationally Situated Activity: Ethical Implications. *Journal of Feminist Family Therapy*, 6 (3), 69–83.
McNamee, S. (2000) The Social Poetics of Relationally Engaged Research. In: Deissler, K. & McNamee, S. (eds.) *Phil und Sophie auf der couch: Die Sozialepoesietherapeutischergesprache* [Philosophy in therapy: The social poetics of therapeutic conversations] Heidelberg, Germany: Carl-Auer_SystemeVerlag, pp. 146–156.
McNamee, S. (2014). Research as Relational Practice. In: Simon, G. & Chard, A. (eds.) *Systemic Inquiry: Innovations in Reflexive Practice Research*. Farnhill, UK, Everything Is Connected Press, pp. 74–94.
McNamee, S. (2016) The Ethics of Relational Process. In: Cocoran, T. & Cromby, J. (eds.) *Joint Action—Essays in Honour of John Shotter*. Oxon, UK, Routledge
McNamee, S. & Hosking, D. (2012) *Research and Social Change—a Relational Constructionist Approach*. New York, Routledge.
Meier, N. & Wegener, C. (2016) Writing with Resonance. *Journal of Management Inquiry*. [Online] Available from: DOI: 10.1177/1056492616673911 [Accessed August 2016].
Ness, O., Borg, M., Semb, R. & Karlsson, B. (2014a) Walking Alongside: Collaborative Practices in Mental Health and Substance Use Care. *International Journal of Mental Health Systems*, 8 (55), 1–8.
Ness, O., Karlsson, B., Borg, M., Biong, S., Sundet, R., McCormack, B., & Kim, H. S. (2014b) Towards a model for collaborative practice in community mental

health care. *Scandinavian Psychologist*, 1, e6. [Online] Available from: https://doi.org/10.15714/scandpsychol.1.e6 [Accessed August 2016].

Ripamonti, S., Galuppo, L., Gorli, M., Scaratti, G. & Cunliffe, A. (2016) Pushing Action Research Toward Reflexive Practice. *Journal of Management Inquiry*, 25 (1), 55–68.

Sælør, K. T., Ness, O., & Semb, R. (2015) Taking the Plunge: Service Users' Experiences of Hope Within the Mental Health and Substance Use services. *Scandinavian Psychologist*, 2, e9. [Online] Available from: https://doi.org/10.15714/scandpsychol.2.e9, [Accessed August 2016].

Shotter, J. (2006) Understanding Process From Within: An Argument for 'Withness'-Thinking. *Organization Studies*, 4 (27), 585–604.

Shotter, J. (2016) Undisciplining Social Science: Wittgenstein and the Art of Creating Situated Practices of Social Inquiry. *Journal for the Theory of Social Behaviour*, 46, 60–83.

Vološinov, V. (1986) *Marxism and the Philosophy of Language*. Cambridge, MA, Harvard University Press.

Contributors

Charlotte Øland Madsen, PhD, is associate professor in the Department of Business and Management at Aalborg University, Denmark. She teaches within the fields of organizing, sensemaking, and organizational learning for bachelor's and master's students in Business, Organization, and Strategy. Charlotte acts as a teacher and supervisor to managers at the Master in Public Governance programme at AAU and to MA students. She is currently engaged with research projects on relational leading, dialogic learning processes, and relational constructionist methodology. For further information on Charlotte's publications please visit: https://orcid.org/0000-0001-5350-047X

Mette Vinther Larsen, PhD, is associate professor in the Department of Business and Management, Aalborg University, Denmark. Mette's research areas revolve around strategizing, organizing, communication, and leading. Mette is especially interested in how these phenomena are researched and practiced informally every day by competent organization members and how organizational life is co-constructed in incremental ways. At Aalborg University, Mette lectures and supervises on different master's programmes for public and private part-time and full-time students. Furthermore, she lectures at the bachelor's programme in International Business Economics. For further information about Mette's publications, please visit: https://orcid.org/0000-0002-4966-8090

Lone Hersted, PhD, is assistant professor in the Department of Learning and Philosophy at Aalborg University, Denmark. Her teaching and research are concerned with leadership, organizational learning, coaching, innovative and creative change processes, dialogue training, conflict dissolution, and collaborative team development. At Aalborg University, Lone is coordinator and lecturer of the Master in Organizational Coaching and Learning programme. Lone has also worked as a consultant since 2003 and, in addition to her academic work, contributes to organizational learning processes through coaching, workshops, and lectures. For further information on Lone's publications please visit: https://orcid.org/0000-0003-0934-1170

Jørgen Gulddahl Rasmussen, PhD, is professor of organization in the Department of Business and Management and faculty of social sciences at Aalborg University, Demark. Jørgen lectures and supervises within bachelor's and master's programmes in Business Administration and Economy and has worked more than a decade within the Master of Public Administration, Master of Public Governance, and Master of Business Administration programmes. In addition, Jørgen has been the main supervisor and bi-supervisor for PhD students at the Department of Business Studies and the Department of Learning. His main teaching subjects include strategy, organization, and management, and his research projects focus on strategic and leadership development and sensemaking in small- and medium-sized firms. Jørgen has from 2004–2017 been the leader of the FIRM (firms, innovation, relations, management) Research Group. For further information on Jørgen's publications please visit: https://orcid.org/0000-0003-4502-3903

Index

action guiding anticipations 22, 39, 63
action guiding assumptions 22–23, 31, 34–35, 43, 51, 56
action learning 1, 64, 66, 69, 70–71, 76–78, 80–81, 83–84
action research 39, 63, 84–87, 90, 111, 114–117, 127, 139, 141, 190
adjusted responses 9, 20–22, 24, 27–29, 36–37, 40–43, 47, 49, 58, 61, 68, 145
arresting moment 47, 170

becoming 2–5, 8, 10, 18, 48, 52, 56, 66–67, 84, 136, 145, 147, 166, 170, 179

centrifugal 110, 143, 144, 157
co-constructing 2–5, 8, 18–21, 28–31, 37, 40–45, 50–51, 56, 58, 65, 70, 101, 108, 110, 114, 121, 145, 162–165, 169, 170–176, 186–188
coding 147–149
collaboration 1, 5, 25, 27, 67, 69, 71–72, 88, 112, 117, 140
complexifying 61
conflux 19, 62
construction of meaning 2, 20, 38, 41, 42, 45–48, 58, 163, 169–172, 178, 184–186
constructivism 3, 4

dangerous dance 120
data material 146, 150, 181
dialogical writing 179, 189
discourse 3, 12–13, 42, 113, 119, 140, 150, 158–159
discursive psychology 144, 147
disorienting dilemma 124–130, 135

embodied 9–10, 14, 22, 31, 34, 43, 45, 63, 118, 121, 159, 161, 169, 170–171, 182, 186, 189
epistemology 5, 8, 10–11, 110, 142–143

flux 4–5, 66, 111
future-forming 6, 86, 160
future-forming 1, 7, 86, 96, 112, 161–165, 175–177

generative moments 69

here-and-now 19–24, 29, 36, 47, 52, 56, 61, 77, 79, 89, 94, 102, 111, 144, 147, 149, 157, 174, 177

inter-act 19, 22–23, 27, 29, 31, 36, 44, 50, 51–54, 60
interpretative repertoires 149, 153, 155, 159
iterative 147–148, 157

joint construction 17

language as ontology 18, 143, 145
language game 3, 113, 117–119, 129–130, 143–144, 152, 155, 157, 166
legitimacy 144–145, 155–156
listening with 33
local somewhere 46, 144

managing 8, 14, 62, 65, 69, 71, 76, 116, 141, 172
meshed 19, 23, 28, 32, 45, 52, 56, 62, 177
meshwork 18–19, 22, 27, 29, 32–35, 44, 48, 50–53, 59, 67–68, 73–74, 80–83

Index

metaphors 8, 47–48, 54–56, 143, 149, 152, 170–171, 186
multiplicity 8, 46, 92, 109, 135, 139, 179, 186–187

narrative 27, 118
non-organisational anchoring 18, 35–36, 49, 60, 68
not-knowing 27–28, 38, 60, 114, 169, 185

ongoing dialoguing 10, 113, 143, 147
ontology 8, 10, 11, 45, 54, 66, 69, 110, 146
organisational life 3–4, 9–10, 15–19, 23–25, 40–45, 143–144, 157, 161–169, 171–175, 177–178, 180–181, 184, 188
otherness 111, 125–126, 136–137

paradigm 2, 85, 119, 140
participatory 8, 86, 90, 107, 111, 114, 117–118, 123, 128, 136, 140
polyphonic novel 181–182
polyphony 39, 63, 66, 70, 73, 78, 81, 91–92, 97–98, 103, 112, 165, 179, 181
power 8–9, 113, 123, 144–147, 154–156, 166–167
practical knowledge 11, 68, 81
pragmatism 2, 4, 9, 143

radically present 25, 46, 51, 54, 61, 135, 172, 175, 178, 181–182, 188
radical presence 13, 39, 62, 115, 135, 139, 140, 162, 168–169, 170–174, 179, 188
reflecting team 9, 85, 91–94
reflective pragmatism 7, 162–169, 179, 188
relational being 13, 38, 62, 67, 83, 115, 140, 162–163, 176, 189

relational constructionism 5, 10–11, 40, 54, 65, 69, 113, 163, 167
relational stance 162
research conversation 5, 15–19, 20–21, 26, 28, 31–36, 40–42, 45–57, 60–62, 170, 187
resonance 119, 162, 179, 180–185, 188–189
resourceful conversation partner 15, 19, 23, 26, 29, 37, 40, 44, 48, 58, 60
role play 127, 128, 130

scenario 82, 97, 102–103, 109, 117, 120–127, 129–134
social change 13, 39, 62, 84–86, 115, 118, 140, 164, 189
social constructionism 2, 3, 4, 5, 8–9, 12, 14, 116, 141–143
social poetics 12–13, 38–39, 47, 62, 158, 170, 178, 186, 189
social world 2, 7, 9, 120, 135, 138, 142, 144, 150–153
stereotyping 134
systemic 13, 85, 91, 127, 129, 140, 158, 189

taken-for-granted 4, 8–10, 18, 29, 35, 40, 48, 54, 58, 70, 91, 98, 109, 113, 128, 130, 135, 137, 149, 152, 157, 164, 166, 168, 172–173, 177–178
theatre 118, 121, 125, 134, 139
transformative 1, 85, 115, 118, 124, 135, 140

unadjusted responses 37–38, 40–44, 47–48, 50, 53–56, 58, 60–61, 68, 74, 178–179
unfinalized 181, 186–187

wayfarer 54
wayfaring 16, 86, 90–91, 115
'withness' thinking 39, 110–111, 136, 141